MOTIF:

It makes no sense, this music, and ~~...~~ ~~...~~ no
seem to have mastered it, who have willed their voices and hands to gift us the
precious things held in hearts and hips. Even then, there's no answer.

Within this beautiful book are thousands of words that offer poetry and laughter, peace and respite, Piano Red and Patty Loveless. There are burgundy shoes here, and feet that tattoo the earth. There is Roy, the wino who worked for Bud Whedbee doing maintenance jobs. There is bourbon and ginger, and melody and harmony in between the lines. All adorn the mystery, with no notion to unravel.

– PETER COOPER
music critic, *The Tennessean*

Writing By Ear reminds us of music's power to form and transform, to ascend to the heavens and descend into despair, to create bridges and carry us across them, to bring together and strengthen those who struggle for social justice, and to comfort those who are alone.

MOTIF editor Marianne Worthington has woven these stories, songs and poems with music's silken threads, creating a symphony that rocks, sways and syncopates in rhythm to the heartbeats of humankind and follows the melodies and harmonies flowing through our veins.

The writers' voices reflect the rich forms and styles of their deliciously diverse home places. From lullabies to rants, lonesome fiddle tunes to sassy saxophone improvisation, past the blues through jazz and hip-hop, *Writing By Ear* takes us on a journey on the wings of words sure to connect us with the songs of our souls.

– SUE MASSEK
songwriter, Reel World String Band

For Elgin—

Motif v 1
WRITING BY EAR

an anthology of writings about music

I'm proud to know ye!
Silas Hamm
28 March 2009

∞

See you back
at MHLF.
Jordan Loving

edited by
MARIANNE WORTHINGTON

[signature]

**MOTES
BOOKS**

MOTIF[v1]: Writing By Ear

An Anthology of Writings About Music

edited by
Marianne Worthington

Vol. 1 in the MOTIF anthology series

© 2009
All Rights Reserved.

ISBN 978-1-934894-08-8
LITERARY ANTHOLOGY

Book design
ERIK TUTTLE & EK LARKEN

Cover design & photo
ERIK TUTTLE

LOUISVILLE, KENTUCKY

WWW.MOTESBOOKS.COM

DEDICATION

For my mother, Haroldine Painter Worthington,
and for my father in memoriam, Thomas Andrew Worthington,
who loved stories sung to the high lonesome sound.

MW

∾

PROGRAM

∞

ROOTS

∞

PASTORALES

∾

BACK BEAT

∾

THE DECEPTIVE CADENCE

∞

NOTES

∞

LYRICS

∞

NOCTURNES

∽

TALKING BLUES

∽

TRITONES

∞

CHANTS

∾

∾

FOREWORD

To Our *Motif* Anthology Series

This collection inaugurates MotesBooks' *Motif* anthology series. In *Volume 1: Writing By Ear* we focus on a favorite avocation and obsession – music. As the series progresses, each volume will center on a different motif, and we can only hope that we will always receive as many perspectives and insights as these first submissions have elicited. Themes in the *Motif* series are open to any and all angles of interpretation by writers who want to play with us inside language and meaning and a diversity of spirit that this project intends to inspire. Writers around the world submitted work;in doing so they made this first outing more satisfying than we could have imagined. Readers, you are attending a unique literary concert. Good for you for getting your ticket.

Some have asked how I came to create the *Motif* anthology concept. Short answer:I have always been intrigued with thematic connections,fascinated that ideas can be approached from endless perspectives, interested in bringing thinkers together. *Motif* has the capacity to satisfy these possibilities.

So, why designate *music* the motif of the moment? That was an easy and natural a fit for this first outing because music is familiar territory carved out of all the places and ways that music and living intersect. Anyone who has a relationship with music knows at least one (and probably several) such intersections. The very fine editor of this first *Motif* volume, Marianne Worthington, has had similar experiences, making her the perfect conductor for this labor of love. My gut rightly intimated that music would be a resonant universal motif for writers and readers alike. After all, human interaction with music – because of the myriad ways music touches personal and social existence – is one of the most fundamental relationships we build in a lifetime.

A most personal musical crossroads takes me back to being a preschooler sitting beneath my Mamaw's piano keyboard with my ear pressed into the resounding wood near her knees, *feeling* more than hearing the music she played. I do believe that the visceral essence of all music merged with my physical and emotional entities right then and there. Music was more than sound, it was touch. Music was outside, and it was inside too. There seemed no disconnect between me and music, for the flow forth and back was unimpeded by air, space, time. In this posture I felt, listened, melded with the music my Mamaw played (hymns or sheet music). She let me push her feet randomly down on whichever pedals I wanted to, never complaining that I disturbed her musicianship, probably because she understood that I was learning something about instrumental workings and the quality of sound. Being wise, she recognized it, too, as a way to pass her love for music along to me, her namesake. She always was smart.

I can still, half a century later, feel that wood quivering. Still delight in my brand new knowledge that music moved from her heart and mind and fingertips to the keys, the hammers, the strings and wood, right through my skin, muscle, blood, bone. And as a result, I'm convinced that her music and many other musics found a channel through which they have merged into me, forever to reside. The singular memory of that singing wood against the side of my face thrills me to this very day. Keeps Mamaw with me, too, in a private way – a peculiar connection based on a recurring event that I'm positive no other on earth had with her. That same spinet, now in my mother's house, is destined to be in mine one day.

When I was seven years old my daddy taught me seven chords on a pawn shop guitar. Seven chords and how to keep time, which was just about everything he knew about playing music back then. In a way, that's every basic thing anyone needs. All roads lead out of there. We had moved from Kentucky to California, having left behind Uncle Mark, an old man (no relation of ours) who had taught those seven chords to Daddy, and all the other fellows they usually jammed with. So far away from all the familiar of a lifetime, Daddy sorely needed somebody just to sit and play music with. Music was lifeblood to him, after all, so he looked around and, spying me at an age not yet jaded and certainly eager, decided that I'd be as good a place as any to start. It worked out for us both. Fortunately, I was a quick learner – born to it, it seemed. I wrote my first song as soon as I had mastered three chords, immediately joining generations of folk musicians tied to the oral tradition of playing, singing and songwriting "by ear."

In the ensuing 45 years that I have written songs and played music of all genres, I've come to realize that my dad was either especially intuitive or entirely lucky that I was clearly meant to play those six strings. I took what he gave me and ran with it – watching hands, studying lyricists, searching out nuances, listening hungrily to radio and records, stealing licks from every player I encountered, developing a style of my own. Music for me, too, is lifeblood; I have my dad to thank for opening that instrument case for me. He gave me a huge gift with those first seven chords. By the time I was a teenager, Dad and I were members of a little rock & roll band – we called it The Generation Gap.

Mother played her part in my musical development, as well. I stood beside her in our little country church (back in Kentucky after only one year away, which was all any of us could endure at the time), sharing a hymnal and learning to sing harmony (for hymns were the best and, later, just about the only part of church that I could truly embrace, everything else there being so

16

problematic for a questioning, outspoken and logical child). Mother also made sure I took the obligatory piano lessons, which I endured for two-and-a-half years. I gave them up after having learned the Boogie Woogie by ear (feeling that there was finally a good reason to play the piano!). I clearly recall delaying the start of my lesson one autumn afternoon so that I could demonstrate for my teacher this exciting accomplishment. "Miss Louise, look at what I learned this week!" I was so young and, therefore, naively shocked when she appeared, in spite of her ever-present civility, generally unimpressed. She seemed to want, instead, to discuss how practicing my lesson might be a preferred approach to learning piano. Shortly thereafter, believing that, though I adored her, Miss Louise and I didn't have enough in common for me to waste my time or Mother's three dollars a week continuing, I was able to cut a deal with my parents: I was allowed to terminate piano lessons if I agreed to play clarinet in the tiny school band that was just being formed. That lasted another year or two, and then both the clarinet and the band itself drifted into the past. But with piano and school band, I learned to read music (and this came in handy for activities such as Quad-State Chorus). Mother was right to push me in the direction of formal study as long as she could.

Music has always surrounded me – live, recorded, broadcast. When music is present, I can't not listen. Early on, it was country and pop, rock and folk. It was always, always blues, too. Then came my fascination with jazz, musical theatre, the classical composers, followed by an admiration for world music. Countless musical experiences shaped me in my youth and shape me still, leading me to offer an aural motif within a literary construction – just the kind of thing a one-time English teacher, songwriter, book publisher (I'm guilty on all counts) will do. The result is the volume you are encountering in the immediacy of this fine moment. Oh, and some of the rest of this story is that my mother's family owned newspapers, so printer's ink is in my veins. My dad's people were teachers, so the need to educate is part of it too. Is it any wonder that music+publishing+study have all come together in my work? That's just about as satisfying as it gets for an artist-nerd like me.

We're glad you are here at this crossroads with us, and we hope all who read this book will appreciate the excellence, energy and intellect that many good folks have dedicated to it. Moreover, we hope to continue to satisfy the interest and curiosity of readers and writers who favor our thematic concept as we move to Volume 2 in the series next year. The motif for that one? *Chance.*

Until next we meet, you take good care.

EK LARKEN
Publisher – MOTESBOOKS

∞

INTRODUCTION

My Grandmother Worthington owned a 1926 Hamilton upright piano she had hauled like a burden when she moved from her farm in Russellville, Tennessee, to a house in Knoxville. It sat unplayed, a massive boulder that hogged the whole wall in her front room. When I was six years old, she sent it off to be completely refurbished and then gave it to me. I began taking piano lessons and didn't stop until I graduated high school. I played in school and church, accompanied choirs and tap dancers and soloists and instrumentalists at music competitions. My piano teachers (Merle Houser, Earl Jones and Benton Miller, may they all rest in peace) pushed me to understand not just the notes on the page but also the complex relationships of the composer's intentions and the historical and cultural contexts of the compositions with my responsibilities as a thoughtful but unripened musician. Later, while a student at Carson-Newman College, I studied organ with Mary Charlotte Ball who never let me play a note of a Bach chorale until I had first looked up and copied down the text of the hymn on which the chorale was based. Her pedagogy forced me to think first about the words so that I could make informed choices about registering the organ and playing the notes. Little did I know that these experiences were paving my way for putting together this anthology of writings about music.

Similarly, my Aunt Josephine worked for a time as a librarian's assistant. When the library discarded books, she brought some of the rejects to me. I received hard-backed but weathered copies of *Danny and the Dinosaur* and *Mike Mulligan and His Steam Shovel* (named Mary Anne – just for me! I thought). My favorites were long narrow editions of *The Tall Book of Mother Goose* and *The Tall Book of Nursery Tales*, lavishly illustrated by the famed Russian-born artist Feodor Rojankovsky. I read these over and over, relishing the rhythms of lullabies and cautionary tales written in verse, matching words with Rojankovsky's compelling (even oddly disturbing) watercolor paintings. Not all the books Aunt Jo gave me were age-appropriate, however.

I still have the copy of a music appreciation textbook she dropped off sometime during my childhood. Published in 1948 and written by one Howard D. McKinney, Professor of Music at Rutgers University, the book is titled *Music and Man: A General Outline of a Course in Music Appreciation Based on Cultural Backgrounds*. Despite its exclusive title (many of the working musicians I knew as a child were women) this throw-away, outdated book gave me a start in thinking about how music connects to other art forms. Every chapter begins either with a poem, historical photograph, ancient engraving, political poster, or mural.

Music and Man opens with a painting by Peppino Mangravite called "The Song of the Poet." The poet is barefoot, strumming a guitar, with his head thrown back in mid-song. He is sitting on a ridge above a valley, surrounded by mountains; below him is a farmer with horse-drawn plow and a little settlement of houses. As a young reader, I thought that Peppino Mangravite surely must have lived near me, in the foothills of the Great Smoky Mountains, must have known the legends about all the barefoot kids carrying guitars who had walked out of the Tennessee mountains onto the stage of the Grand Ole Opry: Roy Acuff, Chet Atkins, Dolly Parton, Carl Smith. (Only while preparing this anthology did I discover that Mangravite had indeed grown up in the mountains – the volcanic mountains on the island of Lipari off the coast of Sicily, some 5,200 miles from the green hills and valleys of east Tennessee.) The author of *Music and Man* posed this question to the reader about Mangravite's painting: "What is the poet singing about?"

I kept thinking about that question while editing this anthology: As writers, what *are* we singing about? What are our common connections to words and music?

I learned some of the answers to those questions while reading the nearly 450 submissions we received for this anthology. The 115 poets, fiction writers, essayists, journalists, and lyricists chosen to "sing" in this collection have similar but unique musical experiences. Many of us took music lessons (some under duress with disastrous results); our ancestors, on the other hand, tended to play their instruments by ear; as musicians we craved fame but would settle for seeing, or even dreaming about, our musical heroes; we were shaped by certain songs; we found music in nature as well as in television shows and radio broadcasts, in diners and drive-ins and bars, bus stations and barns, in kitchens, living rooms, bedrooms and on porches.

Motif: Writing By Ear contains lyrical narratives about the music of our mothers and fathers and how they struggled with, rejected, or embraced the music of their children. The writers in this collection have honored their musical mentors: Don Gibson, Les Paul, Bruce Springsteen, Patty Loveless, Bon Jovi and Johannes Brahms; Hank Williams, Norah Jones, Mississippi John Hurt, Stephen Foster, John Coltrane, the Rolling Stones, Piano Red, Yo Yo Ma and Nina Simone; Johnny and June Carter Cash, Mary Travers, Miles Davis, The Kinks, Johann Sebastian Bach, Tupac Shakur, Buddy Rich, Billie Holliday. The diverse cultural and religious backgrounds of the writers are bridged by music. Melodies define us as individuals yet bring us together as common observers.

What I hope the inaugural volume of *Motif* illustrates is how imaginative language is the instrument that describes and celebrates the music that accompanies our lived experiences. Our ordinary routines, while shared, are as unique as our own voice prints; timbre and quality and tone mix with words and connotations to form a harmonious recitative. Our story-songs are playful, dreadful, informative and influential. Our choir is warmed up and ready to sing, and I hope readers will find their own tunes here in these pages.

MARIANNE WORTHINGTON
Editor – MOTIF Vol. 1

∞

ACKNOWLEDGEMENTS

Several people and organizations helped make this anthology possible in various ways through generous deeds:

Erik Tuttle, for design assistance; Kathi Whitley, for securing permissions to reprint song lyrics; The Gap House Writers and Swarpers, for friendship and advice; RB Morris, for honoring our hometown in word and song; Stephen Carden and Anne Shelby for assistance with the Literary Estate of Belinda Ann Mason; the support of many friends, writers, and musicians at the annual Appalachian Writers Workshop, Hindman Settlement School, Knott County, Kentucky, and the annual Mountain Heritage Literary Festival, Lincoln Memorial University; The Barren River Writers Group; Haroldine Worthington, Jane Worthington, Keith Semmel, and Katelyn Semmel for unconditional love.

Work on this book was partially funded by a generous grant from the Kentucky Arts Council. Marianne Worthington was awarded an Al Smith Fellowship in recognition of artistic excellence for professional artists in Kentucky through the Kentucky Arts Council, the state arts agency, which is supported by state tax dollars and federal funding from the National Endowment for the Arts.

Grateful thanks to the editors, publishers, musicians and authors who granted us permission to reprint the following:

"a background in music" by Evie Shockley appeared in *Pluck! The Journal of Affrilachian Arts & Culture*, Vol. 4, 2008. Used by permission of the author. "Appalachian Refugee" by Scott Miller will appear on the forthcoming CD *For Crying Out Loud*. ©Cheap Ain't Cheap Free is Cheap Pub. Used by permission. All Rights Reserved. "Blues Talking" by Frank Jamison appeared in *Spillway*, Vol. 13, 2007. Used by permission of the author. "Burgundy Shoes" by Patty Griffin appeared on the CD *Children Running Through*. ©2007 Almo Music Corp. and One Big Love Music. All Rights Administered by Almo Music Corp. (ASCAP). Used by permission. All Rights Reserved. "Excerpt from Merle's Story" by Belinda Ann Mason is from an unfinished novel, Belinda Mason Papers, 1997MS348, Special Collections and Digital Programs, University of Kentucky Libraries, provided to *Motif* by Anne Shelby. Used by permission of Stephen Carden, executor of the Literary Estate of Belinda Mason. "Hootenanny Heaven" by Greta McDonough appeared in the *Messenger-Inquirer*, 17 Sept 2008. Used by permission of the author. "In Memory of My Heart" by Buddy and Julie Miller most recently appeared on the CD *Love Snuck Up*, 2004. ©Bughouse/Music of Windswept (ASCAP). Used by permission. All Rights Reserved. "Ladino Concert at Spoleto" by Davi Walders appeared in *Midstream Magazine*, July/August, 2005. Used by permission of the author. "The Name of the Place" by Linda Parsons Marion appeared in *Mother Land*, Iris Press, 2008. Used by permission of the author. "Nocturne: Rogersville, Tennessee, 1947" by Jeff Daniel Marion first appeared in *In Place: A Collection of Appalachian Writers*, Center for Appalachian Studies and Services, 1988, ed. by Ronald K. Giles. Used by permission of the author. "Ravel Sonata for Violin and Piano Second Movement" by Gertrude Halstead appeared in *space between*, Allbook Books, 2008. Used by permission of the publisher. "Rhonda Hears Dolly Parton Sing 'The Silver Dagger'" by Noel Smith appeared in *The Well String*, MotesBooks, 2008. Used by permission of the author. "Roy" by RB Morris appeared on the CD *Take That Ride*. ©1997 Oh Boy Records. Used by permission of the author. "Symphony" by Brenda K. White appeared in *Duets: Art and Poetry Together*, Whitesquirrel Press, 2008, ed. by Gayle Waddell and Jamison Brumm. Used by permission of the author. "Up On Sexton's Creek" by Silas House, Kate Larken & Jason Howard, ©2008, Little Betty Music/Kiss Me Quick (ASCAP). Used by permission. "Women's Voices" by Georgia Green Stamper appeared in *You Can Go Anywhere From the Crossroads of the World*, Wind Publications, 2008. Used by permission of the author. "Yea, the Old Devil Is Real, and, Worse, He's Hereabouts" by Stephen M. Holt appeared in *Elegy for September*, March Street Press, 2008. Used by permission of the author.

MW

ROOTS

"I know what I am inside. I'm an honest to God storyteller
and I use my guitar to help me along my way."

– Brownie McGhee

Feet on the Ground, Reaching for the Stars

When she was twenty-four, my mother married in Elkton, Maryland, a brackish wind off the Susquehanna tweaking her violet sari as she stood on the front step of City Hall signing the license against my father's proffered back, her signature slanted where the pen bumped over his spine. No church, no priest. No family present. In marrying an Indian citizen, in bearing a mixed baby, she broke her religion. Broke from the long line of close-knit Irish Sullivans. Broke the extant miscegenation law in Maryland's constitution, struck down six years earlier but still in the pages and memorized by law students for another twenty years.

On the 29th of January, 1971, my father had flown into JFK with his forehead pressed against the slick window of the plane. Forty-four dollars, a work visa, a photocopy of his medical degree, stuffed in the right front pocket of his grey polyester pants. He had one tiny suitcase. As the plane turned south, he saw the green arm of the Statue of Liberty, a speck in the harbor, felt the same crash of wonder my great-grandmother, Catherine Galvin, felt when she saw that forearm in 1897 from the deck of a coffin ship bound for Ellis Island from Dingle Bay. She had noted its thickness, a peasant woman's arm capable of bearing harvests, children, sorrow. It was the bulk of the arm, the hard beauty of the woman's face, that made Catherine Galvin believe in America. She did not believe in streets paved with gold. She did not believe in an endless supply of butter. She did not believe that anything in life could be easy or free. Nor did my father. He stared at the foreign skyline and whistled a bit of Beethoven's 7th for courage, his cheeks sucking in and out like slim bagpipes.

My mother always hummed while she ironed my father's work shirts. The smell of the iron steaming, smoothing cuffs stitched by Indian tailors. No American store-bought shirt ever fit my father. They were all too big. My mother hummed high reedy versions of "Silver Dagger," "Molly Malone," "Paddy's Lament," coasting the iron over my father's slender Calcutta sleeves. She sang the few words she remembered, startling, here and there in her humming. When she was truly happy, she sang, "O Sacred Head Now Wounded," her favorite hymn, a grim and gruesome Lent dirge. She knew all the words to that one.

She got my father into Simon and Garfunkel and he taught himself the chords to "The Boxer," singing it as only an immigrant could, like the words were made for him. He learned to play guitar by ear, as all Indian musicians learn music, sitting cross-legged on the floor. He would play, head hung over the guitar, and strum, sad, soft, sweet-voiced. He never said the words reminded him of himself, but he didn't have to. My mother and I sat next to him and listened and cried. For him, for our family, for the ache of lonely, endless, landless, wandering.

When I left my home and my family, I was no more than a boy
In the company of strangers
In the quiet of a railway station, running scared . . .

I was not allowed to listen to popular music. Old Irish ballads, Nina Simone, Lata Mangeshkar, Cat Stevens, my grandfather's Bing Crosby and Mario Lanza and James Galway and Tony Bennett records, the *Awara* soundtrack, *Jesus Christ Superstar* (my parents loved Judas' voice), jazz, and anything classical, eastern or western—all passed parental approval. But no Top 40. Nothing that had to do with mainstream America and what my mother called, "shallow materialism." She taught ninth grade in the Long Island public system and had seen her students roaming the hallways with dollar bill earrings and off-the shoulder "Material Girl" sweatshirts revealing black lacy bras. She felt protective of me. She got my father to agree easily because he didn't like music with a heavy beat. "Noise, noise," he'd say, twirling past rock music on his way to a classical station. He liked wordless music, music not tied to one language or another. My mother said: "Read, listen to a record, or sit in silence with your own thoughts. Why would you want to mush your mind? No Boob Tube, No Idiot Box, No Top 40," and left it at that. They both found the electronics, the banging, the bold sexual innuendos of the 80s, strange and somehow inhuman.

If I missed the school bus, my father drove me. He played the Mool Mantra, the holy sung Sikh prayer, in his tape deck, beating the rhythm, lightly, against his own chest. He played it loud, like a teenager with rock and roll. The words flowed around us. I loved the Mool Mantra, the ache of reach in the singer's voice, the sacred heights. But when we passed the first yellow crossing sign, a woman with a purse and child, I pushed back against the softness of the seat. I dreaded the moment of release, in front of school, all those people milling. Catholics and Christians and Jews. The car door opening, me stepping outside, the Mool Mantra blasting out with me, unknown, alien, not holy to them. I was strangled with the same kind of fear I felt when my mother said, "Don't put metal in the microwave or it will explode." I would remain vigilant. I would slip out fast and slam the door quickly to protect the Mool Mantra, my Daddy, myself.

26

I was eleven and I felt un-American. There was no one else like me at school, no one half Indian, half Irish, no one a mix of Hindu, Sikh, Sufi, and Catholic. No one who read John Donne at recess. I was ignorant. I did not understand what most of my peers talked about: *The Facts of Life*, the "Thriller" video, Ring Dings.

My best friend Allyson's older brother, Marc, always played Queen, the Beastie Boys, Billy Joel, and the Police when I slept over at their house. He was fifteen to our eleven and loved pop culture with a scientific passion and discriminating palate. He was the kind of boy who read the newspaper every morning, memorized music trivia and the batting average of all the Mets, even the benchwarmers. He sneered at the Top 40 but seemed to understand my need for it. He set about molding me into a fan of what he called The Right Music, making me mix tapes, calling me into his room to show off a poster he had picked up at a concert, correcting me when I messed up the words to "Paul Revere/The New Style." I approached it all like math, something to be earnestly studied.

Everyone in Allyson's family knew I wasn't allowed to watch TV or listen to the radio; they considered me a sweet and deprived innocent, a space creature, somewhere between Alf and their great-grandmother who spoke only Yiddish. They included me in their family as one of their own. I fasted with them for Yom Kippur, learned to make kugel, walked the dog, watered the plants, wandered the Walt Whitman Mall and tried on all kinds of outfits my parents would never let me have. Sleep-over mornings, I'd wake up at 6 a.m. to watch at least three hours of MTV before anyone in the house even stirred.

It was 1985. MTV had existed for four years. It bloomed with strange and beautiful cartoons, talking dogs, dancing ferns, and busty women with twisted senses of humor. The whole channel seemed to be making constant jokes and references to things I didn't understand. And the music. Such music. I sat very still on the white expanse of the Latmans' leather couch, and felt it rushing all through me. When the Latmans woke up, they'd wander downstairs and laugh to see me mesmerized by the TV, curled around the family dog, Taffy Toenails. Allyson would say my name over and over but I wouldn't hear; she always complained that between the TV and her brother, I never spent any time with her.

All the Latmans agreed that my mother's tactic was backfiring. I was more consumed by TV and pop music than someone who had grown up with it. What everyone else took for granted or had a sensible, casual relationship with, was for me a deep-seated obsession. They said I was like the kids in *Footloose*. I had no idea what they were talking about since I'd never seen *Footloose*. But I knew for sure there was something illicit and pleasurable about popular culture, and I wanted more of it.

I'd heard about a man on the radio, Casey Kasem, who was Lebanese. I learned of him because of a Jewish classmate whose father would not let her listen to him for that very reason. I was thrilled. I figured if Casey Kasem was as American as apple pie and the Top Forty Countdown, then maybe I could be, too.

I decided that the most American thing I could do was listen to Casey Kasem's Top Forty Countdown. I fixated on the idea. Telling my father that Freddie Mercury had been born Farrokh Bulsara, a Parsi, had gotten me the Queen single "I Want to Break Free." I told my parents that Kasem was Lebanese and pronounced his name correctly. "He's an Arab," I said, "A Druze from Lebanon. You know he wouldn't play anything bad. Let me listen." They were not convinced.

Then, in October of 1985, Marc Latman introduced me to Z-100, 100.3 FM. He gave me a bumper sticker for the station and said, "If you tune in on Saturday from 6 to 10 a.m., you'll hear the Top 40." He told me that Z-100 had once been a Jersey station but when they moved their antennae to the top of the Empire State Building, Long Island was able to pick up the signal. He said the first song they'd played in '83 was Survivor's "Eye of the Tiger." I sat at the edge of his bed and he blasted the song louder and louder till the posters on his wall thrummed. I felt I'd never be the same. It made my hair stand on end and I couldn't stop rocking back and forth. It was the first time I truly understood pop music with my emotions and instincts, the first time I showed my enjoyment of it to someone else, without shame.

Z-100 had been broadcasting the American Top Forty for two years and I had yet to hear it. Now I was determined. My parents, grandfather, and I stayed home most weekends, raked, mowed, or shoveled, worked in the garden, read, cleaned, food shopped, as a family. I knew I would never be able to listen to the Top 40 live, so I devised an alternate plan. Our stereo was in the living room—an Aiwa that had what my father proudly called, "Good stereophonics." We had recently gotten a tape deck to stack underneath the tuner and turntable. My father let me use it but I had to be very very careful to not harm it in any way. I read the manual by flashlight, in bed, under the covers, and found out I could make tapes from the radio. But how to do it without being discovered?

Late one night, I experimented with the volume off. To my delight, it worked: I could turn the volume down, but the tape would record at normal sound level. It seemed a miracle. The only problem was that the fancy red lights on the front of the stereo blinked and surged to the bass and tempo of each song. After days of furtive testing, I discovered that if I raised the blinds to half mast, the morning sun coming through the east-facing windows struck the glass door of the stereo hutch and the lights could barely be seen.

A second issue—I only had three ninety minute tapes. So I'd have to create a distraction and switch tapes throughout the countdown and be quick about it so as not to miss any music. It was a lot of effort and it was risky. But Casey Kasem and the American Top Forty were worth it.

I made my first successful tapes on Saturday, November 16, 1985. On Sunday, November 17, I stole the dictation machine that my father used for patient charts. It came with a little headphone set, a soft black foam pad stretched over each ear piece. Monday, my sixth grade class was taking a field trip to the Long Island Pine Barrens, about an hour and a half east of Vanderbilt Elementary School. I knew I'd be sitting alone on the bus because Allyson wasn't going on the trip. It would be the perfect time to experience the Top 40. The Dictaphone—powered by six D-cell batteries—weighed about eight pounds and, long and wide as a textbook, fit perfectly inside my white canvas gym bag stamped with black hearts.

It turned out that the headphone set was mono so it only played in one ear. I was happy and undaunted. I sat on the bus and let Casey Kasem's American Top Forty pour into my right ear and fill my hungry soul. I loved that the Top 40 counted down backwards; I loved the suspense. I learned all kinds of things and believed everything I heard: that I could fix my acne with Oxy 10; that Bain de Soleil was for the Saint-Tropez tan; that Ford's new Taurus was revolutionary. I snaked my hand into the gym bag and memorized the Dictaphone by feel. There was the large speaker, speckled with holes. Underneath that the front-loading cassette bay, and beneath that, a row of buttons that required a strong push. Pause, Stop, Fast Forward, Rewind, Play. From right to left. Record was an orange plastic ledge perched above Play; I had to be careful not to press them at the same time.

I listened from Forty to Twenty on the way to the Pine Barrens, wrapped up in "Raspberry Beret," "Oh Sheila," "Shout," alone in my seat on the bus. Usually I was uncomfortable sitting alone, but with Casey Kasem for company I didn't even notice. I rewound "We Don't Need Another Hero" at least seven times, discovering I could watch the number counter and stop the tape in just the right spot to hear it again.

I watched the trees at the side of the Long Island Expressway stream by, November-bleak, leafless, under the grey seaside sky. I was bursting out of my skin; those beats, the fearless thump, the raw emotion, the frivolous, sexually-charged lightness of Top 40. It was pure. It spoke to me. It was hedonism and, with that blessing pouring into my right ear, I was alive and I was American. I felt I was learning something about myself, my generation, my country. I could hardly bear to stop listening when we arrived at the Pine Barrens, Long Island's last remaining wilderness.

As we trooped through the woods, our steps muffled by the thick carpet of orange needles, everything around me seemed more beautiful, more precious. The nature ranger said we were walking through the remnants of a pitch-pine forest that had once covered a quarter million acres of Long Island, back when Shinnecock, Corchaugs, and Montauks had called this place home. I thought I could see their sad, wronged ghosts flitting through the trees. We dipped our hands in the Peconic River and watched it run clear through our fingers. I felt strangely close to my classmates, though I did not talk to them, nor they to me. Something about the Top 40, that shared water, those tall swaying trees, brought us together in my mind.

On the bus ride back to school, I listened to the second and third tapes: Numbers nineteen through one. Jan Hammer's "Miami Vice" theme song, Stevie Wonder's "Part-Time Lover." I nearly died waiting for Number One. There always seemed to be a commercial at the most suspenseful moment; I liked being teased. Somewhere during "Smooth Operator," two boys leaned over my seat to shout to each other and noticed the rapturous look on my face and the headphones poorly concealed by my hair.

The Walkman had only been around about a year. A few kids had one but those who did were banned from bringing them to school. Everyone crowded around my seat. "What are you doing? Is that a Walkman? Are you crazy? You'll get caught!"

I said I was listening to the American Top Forty Countdown. I said it awkwardly and with a kind of pride that must have seemed strange and overly reverent. "I taped it," I explained then held the headphones away from my ears so they could hear it. They said I was insane for breaking the rules. I was confused and opened my canvas bag to show them it was a Dictaphone machine, not a Walkman. To me, breaking school rules was not as scandalous as breaking the rules of my household. I had broken so many rules to tape the Top Forty that it didn't occur to me to worry about the principal of Vanderbilt Elementary. He was nowhere near as strong or scary as my mother. Everyone kept crowding, looking at me with a kind of newfound respect that I only vaguely noticed because I had already stuck my hand back in my bag, released the Pause button, and gotten swept into Sade's smooth, low seduction.

From the front of the bus, Mr. Garvey hollered, "What's going on back there?" Everyone dispersed quickly, so he didn't investigate.

That week, "We Built This City," by Starship was number one. It was pure poetry; it tore me apart. It was all so good: my ringing right ear, the Lebanese DJ, the German synthesizer player, the revamped band from Woodstock "Shooting all the way to Number One." This was a piece of America I hadn't known and hadn't realized was just as complex as Irish dirges and the Mool Mantra. I was part of it, too, and I loved it for being something I could lose myself in, like everyone. And while I knew my parents were right to keep me from drinking too deeply of it, and while I felt guilty deceiving them, I needed the Top 40 for my own individual well-being.

"You must have learned a lot today," my mother said, as she mashed potatoes at the kitchen counter, "Your face is shining."

My father said, "She likes the forest."

They were always right, my parents. As we moved around the kitchen together, setting the table, getting in each other's way, my mother hummed, my father whistled, and I turned my left ear towards them to catch the tune and sing along.

∾

A Short Life of Trouble

The room swelled with voices and strings,
singing with Sunday morning intensity,
two guitars rolling level underneath
a steady rhythm like a car engine idling.
Each voice in this quartet warm and close
to me as the scent of their coffee brewing
or summer air blowing through the open door—
my mother, her uncle, his sisters,
faces lit in harmony on "The Drunken Driver,"
"Little Girl and the Dreadful Snake,"
"A Short Life of Trouble."

My mother picked out a G chord and sang,
  Come listen young fellows, so young and so fine,
  Seek not your fortune in the dark dreary mine.
Now she is the last of them, a pure singer
gone quiet now as the dust her players have become.
It's dark as a dungeon way down in the mine,
but I would dig into the depths of the earth
to hear those voices ringing out one more time.

a background in music

music city u.s.a. it was, nothing doing without a song,
       and not just twangy tunes that rhyme southern drawls
with guitar strings, though it's true i knew charlie pride
       before charlie parker, but music, music, music, broadway
numbers (*one!* . . .) broadcast over speakers in the park,
       pointer sisters fingering ohio players on the school bus,
the elementary chorus performing a patriotic medley
       for the bicentennial, the high school madrigals wringing
the *carol of the bells* out of our overworked throats each
       december, wvol simulblasting *car wash* or *little red corvette*
out the windows of every deep ride rolling in the black
       neighborhoods, melodies to carry over the clap*slap*snap
of our hands clocking time (*miss mar-y mack mack mack*)
       or to keep us out of trouble with the jump rope, pep squad
cheers to perfect, spontaneous spirituals in the church
       parking lot, and, yes, some country, the mandrells, the oak
ridge boys, tuning in to *hee-haw*'s banjo humor and gloom,
       the music was *howdy* and *whassup, hell naw!* and *aw yeah!*,
merry, happy, baby-baby, and *god loves you if no one else does*:
       to ourselves, to applause, in talent shows, in choirs, on cue
and (mostly) on-key, we sang everything there was to say.

∾

Hootenanny Heaven

When I was a child my music fell into two camps. The first music I remember hearing were Sunday morning hymns, once I got sprung from the nursery at church. Around the age of three, they suffered the little children to enter the sanctuary for the eleven o'clock service. There we fidgeted and twisted and rummaged through our grandmothers' purses for an hour or more until the last notes of the invitation hymn faded away.

The hymns didn't so much float over us, even though they were accompanied by one of the finest pipe organs in town. Rather, they seemed to move among us and through us, at just about knee level, until the whole congregation was swaying slightly and calling, oh sinners, come home. The men of the church would mumble the words in a half hum-sing, while the women clasped their hymnals close to their bosoms where the book would bob and loll like the head of a sleeping child.

No one really needed to look at the words.

Our fountains were filled with blood up there on that rock of ages. We took the faith of our fathers and went to work bringing in the sheaves, the whole time wondering if, when the roll is called up yonder, each of us could say, I am redeemed, just as I am.

I worried about this a lot.

And then there was banjo music. My father was mad for it. So, for a brief period in the early 1960s, every Saturday night we gathered around the television to watch *Hootenanny* on ABC. *Hootenanny* was the original "unplugged" experience—unplugged because, of course, these musical acts were always acoustic.

At the height of the folk era, *Hootenanny* was recorded each Saturday on a different college campus. There, in the round, the Limeliters, the Kingston Trio, and the Chad Mitchell trio took turns playing—almost nonstop—and singing songs, often traditional folk music, in close harmony.

And every group featured . . . a long-necked banjo. As far as my father was concerned there was no such thing as a banjo with a neck too long. If a man had to climb a step ladder to tune the thing, well, that was all right by him. I am currently in the market for just such a long-necked folk banjo because my father's daughter *needs* one.

Daddy is a fair-minded man and he embraced the small banjos, too. He especially loved Eddy Peabody, who played a little four-stringed banjo called a plectrum banjo. We had one. If Eddy Peabody could play banjo with fingers the exact size and shape of Vienna sausages, well, then, so could I. So, while my eight-year old friends were taking piano lessons and giving recitals, I was sitting in my living room thumping out "Little Brown Jug" and "Frankie and Johnnie," which I took to be a love ballad.

I believe I once entertained my grandmother's friends—to their horror—with a lively rendition of "There is a Tavern in the Town," a song that I still maintain is simply *made* for the plectrum banjo.

My parents rarely played records. I remember a couple of novelty songs—and a Fred Waring rendition of "Battle Hymn of the Republic" that was less music than a stirring call to arms that moved me beyond all reason. I didn't understand a word of it, but I knew something big was going on and I suspect I thought that once the song ended I might just ascend through the ceiling and right into the ether.

And the ether wouldn't give me back.

I don't remember my parents listening to the radio much, either, so I can't join my friends who grew up in the rural south when they talk of the Louvin Brothers and the Carter Family, or even Bill Monroe, who first played mandolin on Jerusalem Ridge barely thirty miles from where I live. This is music I am learning to appreciate, but it is slow going.

Give me a hymn, though—even one sung in Latin—and I will sit with my eyes closed and sway a bit as it passes by me. Show me musicians gathered in a circle, their knees almost touching as they tune and fret with their instruments. Let them sing a Norwegian or Irish or English folk song. Or a love ballad, a really sad one. I will know it as an old friend, and settle into it, feeling it more than hearing it. My breathing will slow and I am somewhere else. Away.

Perhaps not all of our lullabies were sung by our mothers.

∞

Christmas Mishegas
Mount Saint Francis

Though I am Reform
and not superstitious
moonlight at noon
and a silver cross cast on Lake Saint Francis
make me promise not to quarrel
about the garish tree back at my office,
not to think about the Inquisition
or Bloody Sunday amid the pines of Rumbala.

Sure, unstrung pines are pagan,
rooting for me, too,
deep and slow in the loam. At Chanukah,
Mama wound up "Rock of Ages"
on our silver menorah.
Words breaking swords were the rage
when we kids kneeled throwing dreydels.
We had our martyrs and tinsel.

Now the bells at Mount Saint Francis enfold
the freezing air
and cars pour out of the
parking lot.
"It came upon the midnight clear."
Or didn't.

Honey-throated Rosalie
was not allowed to hum carols
at Oceanside School Number Five.
Her parents were Conservative.
Her daddy owned a stuffed toy factory.
She sat mute while the rest of us howled.
Others could carol, but not utter "Jesus Christ,"
so there were blanks in the air.

I had full permission.
My mother said, "Honey, it's just music.
You sing!"
Yiddishe Negative Capability.
Blend, *shayne madela*,
blend!

Mary

When you were young
and lanky, graceful
bones visible, your wide
mouth and bright hair
made a vivid frame
for your voice.
On either side of you
dark-suited men
played guitars and sang,
their fingers dancing.

Your instrument
was that body.
A woman, you carried
the melody or high harmony
the descant, or low
weave of thirds and fifths
and beauty too.
You had to be beacon
virgin, siren
little girl and vamp.
It comes to us at birth
this mantle –
No way to step onstage
without reference to it.

So you worked it,
shaking your hair
like a flag in the wind.
You were an actress after all.
No use to wear the mantle
like some ratty carpet remnant
when you could perfect
that dazzling twirl

38

managers, photographers
and audiences swooned for.
It wasn't just the erotic
heat you bore like any
torch singer, but the shiny
energy advertising tomorrow
that rides a young woman's flesh.

In fact, you were already
a mother, your daughter
kept out of view. A grand-
mother now – fat, clear
lines gone – you've survived
back surgeries, leukemia, bone
marrow transplant. Peter
and Paul, gray, thick and bald
betray nothing. But you!
Some folks can't hear you
now because of what they
see, since your look was your
sound was your message round
and round the spindle
of image and desire.

Yes, your voice is lower, brassier
but Peter's and Paul's have
grown raspy, too, yet no website
bears their distorted pictures
like ones of you I found captioned
"Repulsive" and "Jabba the Hutt."
And you the same woman who helped
rally the "I Have a Dream" march,
who with mother and daughter
went to jail for protesting apartheid,
who gave your voice to changing
the times, to turning a nation.

These days you come onstage
with a cane and wavy sparse
after-chemo hair, bearing another
torch for us, the light of believing
anyway and laughing, the wise
slow steps of carrying it on.

Barber on the Saxophone

Over the radio comes the sound
Of Barber's Adagio transcribed
For a saxophone quartet.
Why, the critic ponders
Tamper with perfected form?
Because it recalls another time,
When doing it yourself was not a fashion
But merely the only way to live,
Of plunking out on parlor pianos
Or strumming of ukuleles
Bringing the sound of Verdi to the prairie
In the days before Edison claimed the territory
Of music for professionals
And closed the frontier in our ears.
Now these liquid metallic notes go leaping,
Kicking over the traces with a hint of jazz swagger,
Reclaiming the lost community property
Of making music by and for ourselves,
Stamping it with the indelible imperfection
Of making do as a virtue and necessity,
And passing it on to be made and remade over the generations
Like the scraps of outworn clothing reemerging
In the utility and beauty of a quilt,
Remembered and honored in transformation.
Music with the sound of the sweet green taste
Of pepper jelly made for the joy of the making
And the sharing. Because
The soul learns what the hands themselves perform.

Excerpt from Merle's Story

This is me. I still can't believe I'm 16. I'm average in all ways. Medium hair, eyes and height. My face does okay when I'm not restless and keep my hands off the zits. Mattie threatened to have my teeth straightened, but now I'm glad she didn't. There's something prissy about perfect teeth. When I really need to see or want to hide behind something, I wear glasses.

In school I'll be a junior. I'm double-jointed in the thumbs. In the woods, I used to think I could be stepping on ground no foot had touched. I eat out of the pan when I'm cooking.

I was born in Mattie's bed, caught by an earth-hippie midwife and named for Merle Haggard and Mattie's first boyfriend, Allen Day. More than anything I love music and my sister. Broccoli has not passed my lips and I've never counted on my Dad *[Eddie]*. I cry more than I'd ever let another soul know.

I think about myself because I can't help it and I think about girls the rest of the time. I'm not shy but a female voice that says hello on the phone costs me the power of speech.

My one official date and a single kiss more than friendly happened at different times.

For a season, the smartest girl in school was my best friend. Country music by way of the *Music City News*, brought us together. There's potential for a song. "Music brought us together, then it tore her apart."

I saw her reading the *News* in study hall, found out it was on purpose and whatever we said that day drew us to the same table for a semester. At school we talked music and because of her I bought records whose very covers made me mad. "New Country," she called it—Steve Earle, who looked like he'd never bathed and the "Sweethearts of the Rodeo," who got their name from Gram Parsons and their clothes (looked like to me) at the Goodwill. The tapes I customed for Kelly were a labor of love. George and Merle, of course, Tammy and Loretta, and when I felt bolder, Patsy, and both sets of brothers, Louvin and Stanley.

At night, by phone, we were closer. She told me how she cried every morning when she was twelve because her legs were skinny. I told her about Eddie and how even when he was around, he wasn't.

I hadn't turned into a sex fiend yet, but I was old enough to appreciate the difference between us and that juiced up our talk considerably.

What happened to me and Kelly Baker is at the top of a list of what I hate to remember.

Kelly talked me into playing music at the school fall festival. I'm enough like Eddie so that it didn't take much talking. At least part of the attraction was her promise to come home with me and work up songs the week before. I don't believe in ESP, but a wave of something like dread washed me that first evening on the bus while I tried not to notice Kelly's freckled shoulders riding next to me. Then I had thought it was shame. I remembered the night before when I fussed at Mattie about our orange carpet. Then in my room, I hid model cars and took down the picture of Jesus I'd made from buttons once in Bible School.

Kelly stretched long-ways on the bed while I tuned up and strapped on the harp holder I used to play harmonica and pick guitar at the same time. We settled on "I Saw the Light" for its harp break, "Blue Eyes Crying in the Rain," a classic, even though it's modern, we thought people would recognize because it's Willie Nelson, and "Will You Visit Me on Sundays?" a Charlie Louvin number which might be the greatest country song of all.

Kelly was my first audience, unless you count family, and I don't, and there was no doubt that I had her. After the first run through I pretended nonchalance and went to the trinket box on my dresser. She sat up and I laid the string tie with turquoise slide that had once been Eddie's in her hand.

"What you think?" I said, casually.

She answered by standing and dropping it over my head, six inches from my face. She raised the slide.

"I think it's great."

From across the room my cardboard stand-up cutout of George Jones grinned.

The festival was a nightmare. Because of Kelly I forgot what I knew about teenagers and country. From backstage I watched the majorettes twirl fire and football players dressed like women dance with football players pretending to be men.

I walked on to silence and from the back row I saw my western shirt and turquoise tie and wanted to dissolve. By the end of "Blue Eyes" too many people were singing too loud and others, I swear, were faking sobs. The guitar and harmonica rig that had seemed so right in my room was obviously a gross deformity. Big Betty Watts started up the aisle as I broke into "I Saw the Light." Onstage she shook her namesake breasts and sang along in exaggerated growls.

While the walls shook with laughter I exited stage right.

In study hall the next day, I didn't mention my disgrace but told Kelly instead a rare blood disease would probably take my life before Spring break. She swallowed sobs and outside the gym, gave me the only sexy kiss I've ever had. In the wake of what's come down I've wished that lie back more than once.

Kelly believed it and somehow other people heard. When the rumor started to fade, the ulcers I'd been growing for years sent me just in time to the hospital and somebody called Mattie at the newspaper to find out if I was dying.

"That's crazy," Mattie told the caller.

And the whole world found out what a pathetic fraud I was.

And now, like some karma gone haywire, it's true. God should have realized I was just trying to save face. Or fooling around. Or something.

Our Own Music
for Noel Smith

She grew up in Manhattan's Little Italy,
where Sullivan meets Bleecker,
and after Wellesley, she left for Kentucky
even before the War on Poverty
made it the thing to do.

I was sixteen and raging at the mountains
holding me prisoner, when she—needing trees
and open spaces—passed unnoticed
by my house on Highway 421.

A social worker for Frontier Nursing,
she forged streams, crossed swinging bridges,
heard the banjo pulse,
the wail of the fiddle,
the echoes of the hills.

I flew to New York,
worked a summer with poor kids
named Hernandez and Moretti.

Flying out of Idlewild, I gazed down
at the lights, knew I'd return
to live and work,
to spend Saturday nights
on Bleecker Street.

She told of a mountain family,
the music of their lives
and I'm still hearing
the chant of the subway.

∞

Canta, Y No Llores

Mostly, I remember the songs. How they tasted of *tabacco* and *café* as they rolled off my tongue. My Argentinean six-string sported scars from guitar 101 as we tackled whatever melody caught our fancy: "Morning Train," *"Soy,"* "At Seventeen," *"Cuando Sali De Cuba,"* "Killing Me Softly," *"Te Adoro,"* "Torn Between Two Lovers"; so many songs. English or Spanish, I didn't care; I lived for the magic I conjured on those nylon strings, the looks on the faces of those who stopped what they were doing just to hear me sing.

My teacher, Esperanzita, always accused me of choosing songs that were too adult, too intense for a girl my age.

"Mira, Cary," she said one night as I sat deciding between "If I Can't Have You" and "Endless Love," *"aquí tengo algo para ti, mi hijita,* 'dis one is perfect for a girl your age, *"My Favorite Things," de el Sound of Music."*

Never one to do as I was told, I decided on *"Espera,"* an ardent Cuban ballad, instead. When I played it for her the following week, I conjured up so much twelve year-old passion that I scared Esperanzita into calling my mother in order to discuss the origins of my intensity. Later that year, and quite out of spite, I chose to play *"Espera"* at the 1981 Youth Fair Exposition—a virtual cornucopia of young talent, schooled by scores of other "Esperanzitas" around town who were anxious to show off their wares.

I remember how soft my new yellow dress was; the faint smell of my mother's Nina Ricci perfume as she kissed me for luck; the run in my stocking that I discovered at the hollow of my ankle just before playing; the too bright lights, in the too small, too loud auditorium where I sang and won the top prize. But of all that I remember, the one thing that still comes to me with perfect clarity is the sound of clapping: clapping that took me by surprise in its sincerity and admiration; clapping that filled the air and enveloped me; clapping that made me forever hostage to the fleeting sound of applause.

After my victory, my parents went sort of nuts and became obsessed with sending a recording of my singing to the family in Cuba. My mother went all out for the occasion, setting up a state of the art recording studio in my parent's mirrored bedroom: my white plastic Panasonic tape-recorder perched on top of my father's wooden dresser, fully equipped with three blue-labeled, 60 minute Kmart-brand tapes (the kind that came packaged in long plastic sleeves, secured by stapled cardboard that read 3/$1.99), and a dinette set chair perched in front of the "equipment" waiting just for me.

Those were tortured recording sessions. I sat there miserably stiff, bombarded by "constructive criticism" from both my parents, heavy with the burden of making them proud. As I sang my heart out, I tried my best to block out the sound of their nagging and the slow simmer of my anger.

"*Coño*, Caridad," Papi said, "it's *verdaD* not *verdA*. Can't you pay attention? Can't you do it right?"

Do it right? I always wondered, right for whom? For my parents, so preoccupied with appearances that they completely failed to notice the misery in my eyes? For cousin *Pepito y la familia en Cuba*, whom I had never spoken to, and merely seen once or twice in fuzzy black-and-white photographs that only confirmed the enormous distance between us? For my Cuban heritage, handed down, but an existence that would never truly be mine? It turned out that doing it right was for everyone, everyone, but me.

I was no longer playing for the sake of the longing lurking beneath those sublime boleros or for the pride I felt when I mastered a song on those slippery strings, crescent mooned calluses rising on my fingertips. It was no longer about me, the young girl searching for a sense of herself in her past without drowning in a sea of nostalgia and heartache and loss.

A part of me came undone that day and I swore I'd never succumb to my parent's public relations schemes again. While I didn't put away my guitar, I did stop playing *canciónes en Español*, choosing to try my hand at "Hotel California" and "Stairway to Heaven" instead. And years later, vowing that my days of *guaguancos* and *cha cha chas* were behind me, I would refuse to even listen to the copy of the tape my mother kept for herself.

I wish I had that tape now. I'm not sure what happened to it, but if I ever do get my hands on any of those blue tapes, I'll take a seat, have a glass of wine and listen. Listen and take note of myself doing it right.

I see myself then, innocence intact, shiny and new, still uncompromised. I think of picking up my veteran six-string and taking another stab at reviving those songs. It's hard though. Part of me is scared that the melodies I once tackled with such naive ardor will find me older, different, tempered by time, but then I remember that she and I aren't all that different. After all, we're both still here, waiting for applause.

∞

Somewhere There's

Music. How high the...

aged man's hand curls around the fret.
When he removes it, the hand is still hooked,
knuckle-knobbed, long fingers stretching nine

decades for chords. Smiles at the wood neck
thinly mouthing *bee, bop, bah*
a language only the guitar comprehends. Pulls a quick pick
that makes four backup musicians nod and grin.

The band—all strings save piano—
whip into their lush spindly sound,
bass looks like he's playing telephone wires
so thick and deep are the upright's notes.

On acoustic, young heir apparent furiously needlepoints steel,
vibrating fast as wind shaking wheat;
rhythm, a steady and pleasing electric tinnyness;
and the guy on piano dips into ivories as if
those black and white keys were manicure bowls.

Old man asks the acoustic kid, *What key?*
Hearing aids—*damn things*—in each ear.
Fusses with effects switches on nearby box and in his own axe.
At eight years old, he had tried electrifying it, affixing a record and wire.
Back there in Waukesha, we could've said,
Wait until you meet Leo Fender for that.

The more they play, the more a blue light effuses from small table lamps,
listeners calm and settled as half-empty wine glasses, some
gently swaying or tapping to "Indiana" and "Blue Skies."
Old man recalling, how after Bing refused to join a gig—

he had met Mary Ford instead. *Much better*, he sighs.
And you love me like I love you!

People leave, an aural mantle slowing each. A woman tells the old man's son,
When he played 'Over the Rainbow', I floated across the room.
A man starts, *Your father is … oh well, you know.*
The grateful exit shuffle. Every Monday night. At a club called Iridium.
A brilliant metal placed behind diamonds for effect.

A-4

I dance with Daddy
in that old café on 421.
His fingers select A-4,
and dizzy spin of vinyl,
Hank's *Hey Good Looking*,
reverberates on painted cinderblock.

He orders four hotdogs, with,
then lip-synching Hank,
how's about cookin'
something up with me,
extends his hand, reels
me around the room.
I careen in smoky circles.

Checkered tiles echo
a blur of wingtips.
His shirt starched white,
ebony hair curls
over one eye,
like Elvis.

"Feel the rhythm,"
he urges; at forty his feet
twirl faster, lighter
than mine at thirteen.
Smells pulse like gut strings
ringing through a doghouse bass,
chili, onions frying,
bootleg bourbon and Juicy Fruit,
Old Spice and Irish Spring.
Red lights
blink in the neon sign.

∞

Friends in Loud Places:
The Inspiration of YO! MTV Raps

Being a latchkey kid had decided advantages. Each day, I had a golden, parentless hour between 3 and 4 p.m. in which I could do whatever I wanted. This was the hour in which I made my personal discovery. This was the first grade. Every afternoon I hopped off the county bus that passed our street, ran up the road to our house, unlocked the door and switched on the television set. Carefully, I tuned the dial to channel thirty-two. It was *YO! MTV Raps* time.

Cable came to our neck of eastern Kentucky in the late 1980s. I have fleeting memories of Nickelodeon exporting Canadian cartoons, people with large hair and leisure suits putting on puppet shows on weirdly lit soundstages. Kentucky Education Television, our local PBS station, ran a promotion featuring small children gripping large pencils. "Write!" the commercial urged. And I had already started to, by then. Pencil in hand, we were taught a series of symbols, to inform, warn, inspire. I gripped my own oversized pencil and tried to acclimate myself in those symbols, to make sense of it to myself.

Music channels were an attractive part of the new cable package. This was at a time when TNN was still The Nashville Network. My grandmother, chair-ridden by a massive stroke, would holler if any threats to change the channel from TNN were made. She required her daily dose of the Statler Brothers or Randy Travis. When Marty Stewart, hair pomped out and shirt sleeves rolled up, boot-scooted across the screen singing about "way down in old Kentucky where the bluegrass grows", she patted my arm and said, "He's singing about Kentucky. Where we are." When I made up a dance to "There's a Tear in my Beer," my grandmother began to demand it whenever company came. Suffice it to say my music education boiled down to this diet of *Hee Haw* reruns, Boseefus and the Grand Ole Opry. It was my culture, or something I would someday understand to be my culture. Accordingly, I tuned it out.

My world was a rural one, my home a fresh wound cut into the hills for an FHA neighborhood. We were surrounded by tobacco fields, our county one of the last outposts for growth before the mountains grew too large. The wildlife didn't know what to do with itself. Foxes skulked at the periphery of the trailer parks and pod houses. The subdivision was called Foxlawn. If I had any idea that the rest of the world was not exactly like mine—that cattle didn't amble around the roads running out of town, and paths weren't dotted with monolithic gray barns and rotting churches—it was incredibly vague.

Against this backdrop was *YO!* I was into it, or as into it as a six year old could be. The setting for *YO! MTV Raps* was a basement rec room which just happened to contain a DJ, two turntables and an infinite number of tracks. Hosted by Ed Lover and Dr. Dre (not the West Coast MC whose breakthrough record, "The Chronic", I would soon sneakily buy, but a definitive Video Jockey), the show fluctuated between live musical acts, videos and its own brand of witty repartee. Particularly thrilling was Ed Lover's "Ed Lover dance," which consisted of a lot of hip-swaying and feel-good hollering to DJ Kool's "Let Me Clear My Throat."

YO! set a precedent for me. Along with those PBS ads, hymns, the first time I ever picked up *To Kill a Mockingbird*, and the low murmur of relatives repeating stories, that show changed the way I thought about, felt about and processed language. Simply put, hip hop was the most striking example of meter, rhyme, count and pattern I had heard since the nursery rhyme. I was amazed at how, if done correctly, the verses would weave together to create a thing of massive meaning: the number of words, the pronunciation, the fit of one line into the next, fused in meaning, circular.

I fell in love with it. As a friend later succinctly said, wise hip hop had the same quality as the old lady in church who, caught up in the spirit, tilts her head back, opens her throat and begins to sing. Like the best kind of poem, it had the same quality and sound of something or someone doing what they are organically wired to do, the same principle ruling any beautiful and natural phenomenon. Particularly awe-inspiring were the freestyle sessions, during which groups like A Tribe Called Quest and De La Soul—Without books! Or papers! Nothing to look off of!—would rhyme eloquently and wittily, to each other, against each other, with each other. Few others try, so diligently, to commit the world to memory. This was the first time I ever saw someone perform a recitation, something they care for so deeply that they could sing it to someone else in their own voice.

Many of the things I watched would come to be considered culturally definitive, so much so that I found myself buying the album on disc or vinyl years later. I saw the Wu Tang Clan, Eric B and Rakim and Heavy D, often ignoring the videos and drawing comics while listening.

Because it was MTV, more than occasionally a scantily clad woman appeared. The language was, for 1990, thought risqué, though broadcasting nothing more scandalous than the occasional "hell" and "damn" before 9:00 p.m. Nonetheless, a quiet witch hunt ensued among the most upright of town mothers. These were the ones who organized cotillion dances and made needlepoint belts for their children, spelling out their names surrounded by golf or tennis paraphernalia, for their children. An elementary school teacher took time out of math class to inform us that she would "just die" before letting her sons, who indeed wore such belts, watch such filth. Any parent that would was, evidently, questionable at best.

This is not to say that popularized hip hop made no impact whatsoever in the community. The playground contained seas of little boys in expensive cowboy boots and rattails (think the mullet with a thin, graceful strand, or "tail," down the back of the neck, in lieu of the entire hair waterfall) as well as the occasional lucky bastard in parachute pants. Most six year olds had a body weight capable of achieving the Hammer dance to perfection. Many would show off such moves, before being made to stop by the teacher, in breaks between gym class line dancing. "Dude, watch this," yelled a ponytailed boy in a large silver belt buckle and a Kentucky Headhunters T-shirt as he noisily clacked the heels of his boots against the gym floor. "I'm MC Hammer!" Obviously, I wasn't the only one spending an hour after school every day doing the Ed Lover dance, keeping an anxious eye out for the next Digital Underground video.

Often, the paradoxes of the situation were too heavy for interpretation. It extends beyond stereotypes about the South, or small towns: there really are the pursed lips of mothers whose internal alarms are touched off by anything less pious than *The 700 Club*. There really was the weird transfer kid from Lexington whose copy of "The Source" was ganked and thrown in the garbage. There really were the boys who hung out in the parking lot, pounding Master P while confederate flag stickers graced their bumpers. It was a place and time where what something nasally called "rap" by the teachers—something which was not necessarily hip hop and usually godawful, like "Tootsie Roll"—would be played directly after the ceremonious spinning of "I've Got Friends in Low Places" or "Family Tradition." If it was a fit, it still seemed an uncomfortable one. There was no embrace of hip hop, just a smart absorption, becoming headier and more influential with time. I struggled to understand and, meanwhile, kept buying CDs to stash under my bed, kept clipping articles on The Roots and Mos Def out of *Rolling Stone*.

It was when I attended a statewide arts immersion program at sixteen that I met other kids who embraced hip hop as I did and had discovered it through the same channels. During an unfortunate period in which I performed slam poetry, my primary influences were the Beastie Boys and Atmosphere. Fortunately for the art of slam poetry, this was a phase.

I increasingly found myself admitting what I liked, and listening to it more openly. Meanwhile, a small revolution was taking place. I was not the only one who had listened to hip hop in the sticks; there was the unveiling of the rural lyricist. There was Nappy Roots, one of the first big hip hop acts from Kentucky to achieve mainstream success. Witty and articulate, they hold a claim on the land as solid and justified as that of any country act. Impossible to ignore was

Bubba Sparxx, an ex-football player from rural Georgia whose first video single, "Ugly," featured barnyard wrestling, wild hogs and influential Virginia artists Missy Elliot and Timbaland battling atop John Deere tractors. The Sparxx video is a contrast in exaggerated interpretations: the "rural southern" images fall somewhere between *Deliverance* and a Shelby Lee Adams photograph, and create a compelling hybrid with something like a Lil Wayne video. Though I will admit it is cool to see expert breakdancing take place in a hog pen (and it *does*). That it was on MTV at all was a striking development. It was evidence that the music had been received at its own, isolated satellites, far from the original source. It had been absorbed in the rural outposts and bounced back, joined the larger dialogue. We were a part of the world, as we always had been.

In college I found graduate students in poetry workshops willing to name Tupac or Biggie Smalls alongside Whitman and Ezra Pound as influences. In a bar in Copenhagen, I found myself able to recite the entirety of "Ice Ice Baby." Much to the delight of my European friends, I was also able to describe and demonstrate the arm/leg herky-jerky that any former or current Ice fan would be able to recognize as Vanilla's own. Obviously, my mind's crevice doesn't always hold "quality."

I still believe in that place where one holds original language, a prized reserve of words heard in early days, the ones which possess us and carry us to the end of our days. At this point I probably know more hip hop lyrics than Bible verses. I probably consciously know more of the contents of "Ready to Die" than William Carlos Williams or Rilke. I cannot, however, deny the fact that, as a child, MTV was closer at hand than a Yeats volume. I will also never deny that quality insight and good, solid writing can come from the influence of either source. I developed my first ear—my desire to hear the insides of the words, the words moving beneath the words, what the work of language yields—by listening to hip hop. I find myself listening to Merwin and Wright these days with the same ear.

I've reached some sort of adulthood, and *YO! MTV Raps* has long since gone off the air. My preoccupation with words led to an English degree, which led to an editorial job during which I sit down to pages of language which resemble roadkill. Partially disapproving schoolmarm and partially defender, I kill a red ink pen a week making corrections. Sometimes I feel a bit too possessive about language. I don't appreciate seeing it bent out of shape. I don't like it bled, twisted, smeared across on a page with a boot heel and deemed awesome. I'm rigid with my adjustments. On days when I'm feeling a little wily I put on some Boseefus but, mostly, I very quietly play Tupac while I work. "I get around," he insists. I correct, substitute, suggest. I pay heed. I wait.

∞

PASTORALES

"The sun poured in like butterscotch and stuck to all my senses"

– Joni Mitchell

A Legato for Grandfather

In *A Legato for Elizabeth* by an artist
whose name I cannot decipher,
a small gray man plays a cello
for the little girl standing before him,
a hat decorated with wildflowers in hand.
Daughter bought the print
at a flea market, gave it to me,
the girl my namesake, or I hers.
I study the child's eyes,
ambivalent the word that comes to me.
Perhaps she is drawn to the music.
Its strains fill the room,
burgeon beyond the room,
speak to her and the old man
in a wordless language.
Perhaps the hat suggests a different story,
her urge to walk in the meadow,
ride the spotted pony.
The old man, her grandfather,
plays for her but also for himself,
for the years of story that unite,
but distance them.
In homburg and jacket, a watch fob
across his chest, he reminds me
of my grandfather,
who never played a cello,
but hummed a monotone.
Though he rarely talked,
the twinkle in his eye
played a vibrato of love,
a pizzicato of joy.
When I take my hat in hand
and venture into the wildflower meadow,
I hear him humming.

∞

The Music to What I See

I want to be the music.
Hymns on the dulcimer and ole banjo
carried to the seam
of cool woods and night,
filled what didn't know it was empty.
My mother on the fiddle, Uncle Roy on guitar,
the harmonica sieved Paw's breath.

The porch was their stage.
A shoestring pull's
chorus of movement
dispelled the bare bulb's harshness
into peripheral lightning bugs,
those visible clicks of switching on and off.
One container of rhythm
poured into another of crickets and frogs.

I blended with the night edging in.
Confined in the finite yard of childhood,
I could think forever.
Beyond the backboards of Mitchell and the Roan,
the world ended I supposed,
and I might fall into abyssal mine shafts
or they might fill with rusty water and flood
over the dams of those east and west mountains.
Then, the words I made up for songs
and all the music of the world there in Bandana
would be gone.

I have always listened
no matter how small a snail's quiet clung
to a maple's brown underleaf.
I have heard the jazz of baby apples pawing wind,
the piano trill of milkweed pods disorganizing,
and classical violin of the cat tracing the rail.

Perhaps I would have been a ballerina
had there been classes,
but, Reba, in our stretch of Bandana road,
what we could afford was paper and pen.
Veils of an orange sunset
trailed our words read aloud
to the agreeable audience of a daisy field.

Once, we listened to an open can of soda.
Carbon dioxide leaped out like the angels of fleas
to bless the unlit back steps
while measuring their depth of darkness -
a poem I cannot write.

Music I've known all my life:
salamander feet blunt as sassafras leaves
and blue morning glories, wide brimmed,
existing for us to enjoy sight.
I can never get over gold and green together
or the beauty of your face,
a repetitive sudden revelation.

As my own child ran alongside me like ragtime,
I listened and filled.
I waited until now
to let words go like minnows
or the kite strings of prayer
because I don't only want poems.
I want my life to be the music.

∞

Hymns Heard in the
Church of the Front Porch Rocker

First, the chorus of crickets
from the cedar trees,
call and response of the flying crows
and the hawk they chase,
sour notes of the blue jays
in the walnut tree,
trills of the turkeys in a nearby holler,
basso of a low-flying plane,
sweet second soprano of the mourning doves,
robins tuning up to go south on tour,
the recessional howl of Maggie,
the extra-long-eared basset hound
down the road, and shouts
of "Amen, now let's go eat"
from our three dogs.

Outdoor Theater

One morning last week I awakened to sunshine. Quickly with coffee and toast I headed for my "Front porch theater," that little concrete slab facing my green space. Tiny beetles like ushers patrolled the floor as if expecting a crowd. In my favorite place in front and center, I was comfortably seated when the players begin arriving. The acrobatic spiders must have performed earlier. I saw their tight ropes strung from pillar to pillar overhead and their gossamer safety nets spread on boxwood tops. A chipmunk, fur so neat and sleek, danced through the boxwood forest. He was too timid to risk a glance at the audience. A flight of songbirds rose up into a red-leaved shrub the better to see their cue. On stage right two yellow butterflies left their zinnia pad to execute an intricate ballet. Suddenly, on stage left, a VIP robin entered, his head held high, chest out. I could imagine a gold watch and chain carefully threaded along the waist of his immaculate red vest. He sang a loud authoritative sentence. A clump of dwarf day lilies growing beside the stage seemed ready for a congratulatory presentation.

Giving one last loud word over his shoulder, robin stomped off with his lock-kneed gait. Chipmunk eased off quietly through the branchy backdrop while songbirds assumed their flight pattern on the grass. Butterflies made a few extra pirouettes waiting for all the cast to be ready. I wanted to call "Encore, encore," but dared not spoil the moment.

Translating Anger

This is where we are in history—to think the forest will remain where we have pushed it.
—Matthew 18:2

Mama was in the checkout line at Publix, talking with her favorite cashier. "I don't know what we'll do if this drought keeps on. The garden just shriveled up this year because our well's been too low for us to water things as much as they need." The lady in line behind Mama leaned into the conversation. "Oh, I don't have to worry about droughts. I get all my groceries here." Mama swears that was one of the most frightening comments she's ever heard. "What does she think?" Mama asked me. "Does she believe grocery stores manufacture their produce in warehouses out back?"

I think the truth is even more frightening than what this lady said. I think she never bothers her brain at all to figure where things come from. Not long ago I ran across this same state of environmental disconnect while talking with a local realtor. I told him I was concerned about the damaging silting of our streams which could and probably would occur if he developed a subdivision upstream from us. "Oh, you don't need to worry—even if we get rezoning approval, it'll be a year or more before we start paving and building." Oh, good, then there's no cause for me to fret because I had planned to stop drinking clean water after this year, anyway.

But of course I do worry and then I get frustrated and then I get angry and then I find myself teetering right on the fine edge of ranting. I am not by nature a ranter. My mind rejects righteous indignation the same way my body rejects underwater swimming: I rise to the surface, no matter what. When I was grammar school age, I took swimming lessons every summer. To reach a certain level of advancement I had to swim the length of the pool underwater. I couldn't do it. My body bobbed to the surface as if God had pegged it together with cork rather than muscle and bone. Down to the depths I'd dive once more, trying to think heavy thoughts, but I'd boing right back up every time.

Attitude-wise, I'm a floater, too. Many's the time life has slammed me with good and sufficient reason to lie down with Poe on his black bed of Nevermore, times when I've vowed to let depression have its dark way with me. And I've truly tried to stay in those moody depths, but always a little snatch of a Cokesbury hymn wriggles into my mind like a puppy to a lap and I'm lost to optimism again. Those nineteenth-century Methodist hymn writers knew what they were about when they matched lyrics of being washed in blood with an up-tempo marching tune I can't get out of my head and don't even want to. Are my sins as scarlet? Of course they are. But I'm washed in the blood of the Lamb in common meter, crescendo-ing lustily through two satisfying measures. How can any state of affairs seem bleak after that?

When I told a group of friends how angry I was over all the thoughtless things people said to me after I was bitten by a rattlesnake, I admitted that "I just couldn't stay there in that much anger, though." My friend Dick Hague nodded. "It's tachyphylaxis. That's technically a rapidly decreasing response to a drug after repeated applications of the drug—but I think any reactant thrown at us over and over can send us into psychological tachyphylaxis. After a certain number of hurtful comments, we just can't muster the same peaks of anger repeatedly, so our psyches move us in the direction of decreasing response, in order to save us from ourselves. Otherwise, we'd go postal."

I love Dick's analogy, and I love even more that he gave me the next step in my thinking-things-through process, but I also believe in a different, more sideways route away from anger, a road less traveled except by Pollyannas like me. Instead of letting my engine cool down, I take the mid-road turn from anger to optimism. Optimism may be anger's more exact opposite, rather than joy. Rage halts us in our progress, freezes us in a destructive moment. Optimism flings open a window, turns to us, grins, and says, "Hey, it's a gorgeous day. Let's go outside." When Emily Dickinson told us "'Hope' is the thing with feathers/ That perches in the soul," her genius with words shone brightest through her choice of the verb "perches." To perch is to sit on the edge of movement, to be ready to fly. Someone who is perching is poised halfway between staying and leaving. Despite a barrage of hurtful post-snakebite comments, I could not stay forever in my state of righteous rage; I'm a floater, not a sinker. After a long spell of anger I found myself one tachyphylaxic day perching, ready for a reason to sing.

Singing has provided my way out of black moods throughout my life. Singing, and hard work. Or the two combined. Camille Saint-Saens, composer of music lush in the way only the French do lushness, once told a friend, "I like good company, but I like hard work better." I think I'd like working near Saint-Saens. He'd be singing to himself, too, stopping and starting over, trying to remember the words to the fourth line of the third verse of that old French carol. His dogs would stop and look at him with disgust, just as my dogs Fred and Max do with me: "Get it right, would you? You're messing up the rhythm of our nosing around in the woods."

Fred and Max let me know which songs to sing. There are words and tunes and rhythms fit for walking through the woods and others not so. Every occasion has its soundtrack. Kneading bread calls for a steady, hard-driving beat:

"and it's ONE, TWO, THREE, WHAT ARE WE FIGHTIN' FOR...." You can punch that dough to elasticity in two or three repeats of the chorus. Jogging and fast walking, however, require a lively song that rounds back on itself: "I'll be somewhere working, I'll be somewhere working, I'll be somewhere working for my Lo-o-o-rd... I'll be somewhere working...." The last two hours of a solitary ten-hour car trip can be saved from hellish-ness simply by crooning all the verses in their right order of "Come Thou Fount of Every Blessing," followed up by "Puff, the Magic Dragon." And, of course, babies are eased into dreaming with any song that's soft and lilting and repetitive. My daughter, Snow, always gave up the good fight after only a few verses of "We Shall Overcome."

Snow, lifetime veteran of folk festivals, swears she can tell what time it is by what's being played or sung at a late-night jam. Before the midnight hour, fiddlers huddle their chairs in a tight circle of touching knees and working up a lather on "Whiskey For Breakfast" while the singers talk and drink. From midnight until one, fiddlers and singers settle down to "Barbry Allen," "The L&N Don't Stop Here," and "She Walks These Hills." One in the morning until two or two-thirty is the gospel hour, beginning with "Angel Band" and ending with close harmony on "Amazing Grace." Any folkies still functioning after two a.m. attempt to belt out Beatle tunes, "Rocky Raccoon" being the hands-down favorite, but they can always only recall one and a half verses.

Of course, the point is that no one at a music jam cares one hoot what time it is. I'll give up sleeping in favor of singing anytime. A newcomer to one of these music weekends once asked, "When do you sleep?" "We don't," was the quick answer. "We just lie in bed for a couple of hours and vibrate." When you can spend the night singing, sleep is redundant. Both serve equally well to knit up that raveled sleeve of care.

So I sing, and my rage goes away and my blood pressure hums along steady and the tangles in my current writing project smooth out into the needed words which are now so obvious I can't believe I struggled to find them. Singing engenders wholeness. I'm not the first to believe this. Plato in his *Republic* proposed training children with musical skills during their earliest years of education. Their minds would thereby, Plato argued, be primed for study of mathematics and the sciences. Music orders our brains for productivity.

I have a hard time convincing most people of this. I often have a hard time even getting people to let me finish singing when I'm away from places like folk festivals where everyone is walking around singing. You try it sometime—walk down the hall at work quietly singing "In the Garden" and see if you aren't interrupted before "and he walks with me, and he...." I can't decide if singing outside of church and summer camp somehow embarrasses people in much the same way as if I showed up for work in a flowered nighty, or if it's that most people (read: most *Americans*) just never sing. People who do not sing, place little value on singing.

I'm finding the same truth holds when it comes to valuing processes within nature. My fellow Americans think nothing of interrupting me when I'm singing because they view my singing as a frivolous time-filler rather than the hum of my creative motor. I know the truth: singing is an indicator that I'm working. But we of the twenty-first century are becoming blind to indicators. My fifteen-foot crepe myrtles are indicators that their roots have room enough to spread out, to touch toenails with the massive dogwood a little ways down field. Those flat-topped crepe myrtles in the bank parking lot with their feet in cement shoes are choking to death.

The problem is it's hard to work up anxiety over alteration we can't see. In all fast-growing areas of our formerly rural south, I daily watch developers pave over old cow pastures and cotton fields, always beginning their development with the layout and paving of streets, curbs, and sidewalks. If trees were there to begin with, a few are left standing, but skirted now with pavement. Each new house's yard is planted with one crepe myrtle, one elm and two boxwoods near the front door. These atolls of green in a concrete sea make subdivisions and strip malls appear healthy, but it's a ruse. Landscaped trees and shrubs are alive, but weak because their root systems are capped with an impermeable layer of cement. They are condemned to breathe shallowly, drink sparingly. Their life span will be half what it would be in normal growing conditions. I don't know about anyone else, but I prefer not to live in a weak world.

I have the audacity to make that statement even as I spend hours of my free time every week trying my best to break the back of one of the strongest root systems I know — Japanese privet. Privet is an alien, invasive newcomer to the rural south. It propagates through a shallow horizontal network of roots which scoots out in all directions from the mother plant, sending new privet shrubs popping skyward like mammoth green fairy rings. Privet prefers wet feet but it can hang on to life just about anywhere, especially where you most do *not* want it. It alters native habitat like Woody Allen at a family reunion. I hate it with a pure, focused hate. I tell friends that if I go to hell when I die, if there is a hell, hell will be a thick forest of privet, and me with no pick ax. A pick ax and a shovel are my tools of choice in my work to rid our farm of privet: First I cut the privet down to a short trunk, trench around the trunk and chop loose all roots I can see and reach. Then I straddle the trunk, wrap my arms around and rock it back and forth until the tap root breaks. I call it hugging privet to death.

Over the last five years, I've cleared a twenty foot row of formerly privet-choked crepe myrtle this way. These crepe myrtles are magnificent towering beauties taller than Mama's peak-roofed farmhouse. During the years Daddy

65

was dying of cancer, Mama couldn't tend to everything on our demanding acreage. She gave up the privet fight in favor of improving the quality of my daddy's dying. When I came back to the farm, the crepe myrtles were almost completely hidden in a Sleeping Beauty forest of privet. I took up the battle. This is my winter project. During those months when the grass doesn't need weekly cutting and no petunias or daylilies or violets are popping up in the crepe myrtle row, I set forth a few times a week to rid another square foot of invading privet. And since I've been engaged in this war, I've discovered privet's secret: once I have wrenched out a stretch of privet, disconnecting root joins as I go, the next stretch of privet digs up more easily. When I weaken its connections, the whole system weakens. It can't put up as much of a fight.

This has also led me to discover a secret about myself: I feel bad about breaking the back of my enemy. I want even privet that I hate to stay strong, to be an equal contender. Once while I was living in Tidewater Virginia, I flew home from teaching out of state seated beside a young man who had grown up in the plains of the Midwest. He had never seen the ocean. As our plane circled in to the Norfolk airport, swooping low over the Atlantic, he literally pressed his nose to the window, barely able to stay still with his excitement. Without turning from the sight below him, he said to me, "I love the idea that right down there is something man cannot control." I've never forgotten what he said. I, too, love the idea that I can't even come close to controlling nature. Even if I drive out all privet from my acreage, I will be left with open areas where honeysuckle can flourish, or bamboo or some other opportunist plant I don't yet know about.

Only extreme arrogance allows us humans to believe forests will remain where we have pushed them. Out of the wildness there will come a protest, in some form or other. Nature is a singer with perfect pitch. Any disharmony pains the earth like a sour note. Natural gas emissions are a sour note, and our thinning ozone layer is earth's wince of displeasure. Blankets of impermeable pavement are tone-deaf singers, and stunted shrubs are earth's closed ears. Acres of clear-cut tree canopies are forgotten lyrics, and urban heat islands are earth's fit of frustration. Ambient light is a monotone blat, and earth's stars turn away like a disgruntled audience.

When my family came to live at Grace Farm, our woods held nights as black as any ocean depths you may have known. The nights were such deep sea dark we slept in endlessness defined by stars. But then the subdivisions came and staked their space with street lamps whose hazy light spilled into our luscious darkness, heralding the dimming of our stars.

Then why do I keep plugging along, lone individual against a sea of developers? Because we fight for what we love. I love the small bit of wildness which flourishes on my forty acres. Each day as I root out invader species of plants, as I reintroduce native flowers and trees, as I clean the creeks for the sake of darters and salamanders, I am working to build back what has been lost. And isn't building another way of fighting? Building is possibly the best way of fighting. Even my use of the word "building" to imply encouragement of loss of human control rather than the application of human coverings to earth's surfaces, is my way of fighting linear thinking. We do have a choice in how we live on our world. We can choose to share top billing, to sing a duet rather than a solo. Every time I get to wondering what earthly difference I can make, I think about privet. I may sometimes believe I have broken the back of privet's root system, but somewhere on another boggy acre of my land, a new stand of privet is rising, strong and vital. In a way, that heartens me.

A few weeks ago I spent several late-night hours with a group of friends, musicians all. These are people who probably don't go to the bathroom without bringing their fiddles along in case there's someone else in there wanting to jam. Or maybe wanting to dance, in my case. On the first note of the first waltz they played I pulled Jim Webb up by the hand to waltz with me. "Sorry I'm not a better waltzer," he mumbled. *Oh, you're fine, basically.* "But there must be more to it than just walking around in a square in time to the music." There is. The more intricate steps and the deeper feel for how to move with the music come with time and practice and a lot of wrong steps. It has taken me twenty years to learn to waltz. It may take me twenty years more to learn to keep in step gracefully with the music of my land. But what else is a lifetime for?

∾

The Other Shoe

Walnut leaves sweep
golden rain over the windshield.
On the radio, Astrud Gilberto sings live
in New York *circa* 1964.

A hummingbird levitates
before landing in the Osage orange tree.
I don't understand
the language, but the meaning is clear.

This moment, a haiku,
of sense and sensuality.

A few twilights later
a lingering firefly sends
last signals to its love.
I sit in the Jeep watching,
waiting for fall to drop its other shoe.

Faith in Red

Some red you can trust. Not lipstick
or corvette or anything fast kind of red

more like granddaddy's tractor, fresh yams
out the oven, a speck of blood in a country egg

a yella girl's freckle, home made BBQ sauce
or a long faded but still striped barbershop pole

in some place like Sweet Water, Alabama
or Americus, Georgia. Velvet cake

and Easter Sunday church hat red. The inside
of Mississippi John Hurt's lips red. Ecclesiastical

red like that choir of flames on the horizon,
when October's death gives birth to autumn.

Listening to Rudolph Serkin Play Brahms
For Jone Messmer

It's the horn at the beginning
that surprises us:
the call to hunt the fox in ourselves.

And what is Serkin leaping toward
in his arpeggios? Over what fences?
Into what wooded realm?

Once, I remember thinking his fingers
seemed too short, that each stub
was a tree stump reaching out
to grow back what was lost,
then in a quick trill they sprouted
into a whole forest
leafing out lush
with chords and melody.

But trees have nothing to do with fingers,
nor with pianos – except the obvious –

they are just a part of what we enter
when the primeval calls
from the far regions of fox,

and the need for music lifts up
our hands, poises them before
the makers of sound: piano, drum
or unholdable voice –
        we reach for them,
for the place where music hides.

∾

Disturbance

Loud twang of country song
Deflects the peace
I have come seeking in the sunshine,
Silences the music in my soul
That births my written words,
So that each line I pen
Seems cadenced for guitar,
And tells of love gone oh so wrong.

The song's monotonous refrain,
Reverberating twang, collides
With harmony, precludes
Tranquility. I long
For Bach or Strauss or Mozart
To dispel this dissonance.

But parks belong to all
And sunshine is still free.

What She Wants

Not the things I offered: not tuition for her autistic son's school or paying to have her closets redone, much less hiring a housekeeper. She wanted me to take up the flute again so we could play duets as we did when we were children. Though her illness had nothing to do with her mind, my sister, the professional flutist, seemed to have forgotten the lip I split on a steering wheel, the fact I hadn't played in thirty years. I wanted to give something I could point to like a coat of paint on her peeling stairwell, new dishwasher, a blank check which said, "I'm making up for your severed breasts, the brutal surgeries which nearly took your life." Finally, I, supposedly the *smart* sister, gave her what she wanted.

Last Thursday, with a rented Gemeinhardt, I began lessons, the teacher choosing a Brahms duet, delegating the melody to me. When I saw the accidentals, two octave range, and grace notes, my heart fluttered and fell in my chest because I knew I could not do it. She counted 1-2-3-4, and we were off. I didn't miss a note, the teacher's fluid interpretation of the harmony line carrying and pulling me through and back to my childhood, my sister and I perched on flimsy folding chairs in our father's studio where we'd retreated from the volatile house, our mother's wrath, one music stand between us, huddling together, switching parts from one piece to the next, moving on and moving on, mimicking that harmony found only in our music books' scores.

After that duet, I wanted to fall to the floor in a fit of weeping for the teacher's gift, retrieving that teamwork, helping me give my sister the one thing she wants.

When my sister and I played, we dodged our mother's fierce arm, the slaps on the back of the head. Our union, all repair and protection, even if we missed notes or a beat: the willingness to play the music straight through, hearts opening full bore, our practice of faith. My sister, always capable of strong commitment and who I now realize is smarter than I am, never left her flute, never forgot that when two make music together, they are immune, untouchable.

∞

The Mayan Flute Player

Stars drizzle the sky.
The ocean inhales and exhales.

Walking along a moonlit jungle path,
I follow your flute notes home,
eager as a child of Hamlin.

In the morning you sit on a rock.
The white dog beside you
wags his tail, quietly barking
a melodious duet.

"He always comes here,"
you say. As if it was
the most natural thing.

Standing beside you, I do not want
to be mute. The sounds in my chest rise,
but not as far as my throat.

My body sways. My feet tattoo the earth.
This dancing heart will have to do.

Small Lyric: Summer Rain

lets loose, dances a fandango on the roof, improvises patter and rap, a tap-dancing chorus line, double time, a rattle-trap careening down a two lane road; its suddenness startling, the way it pours out of silence a cacophony of drums and hooves, comes out of the sodden leaden sky that has sagged and belled over our heads, all day, as if someone cracked a giant egg overhead. And how I love it, the crash and dash, the wild abandon, no holding back way it unfastens, a Victorian lady unlacing her stays, and it's Annie-bar-the-door. It beats a green tattoo, it jazzes in syncopated time. It makes you think the sun won't come back out, that those summer days, green leaves waving, blue sky chalked with puffy clouds, were a mirage, a dream, the kind that slips away when you wake up, lingers at the edges, an almost-remembered thought. Meanwhile, the rain keeps transmitting its telegrams, goes on and on and on.

Liquid Music Notes

Morning dew dripped liquid music
　　Notes onto the grass
Until the blades blinked and stretched
　　Out toward the sky and began to
Sway with the breeze,
　　The timing naturally perfect.
Its rhythm gently stirred birds to sing songs that
　　Echoed in the trees until they were their own
Chorus, awakening the honeysuckle who offered a
　　Scent from Heaven, a flower's music.

BACK BEAT

∽

"A guitar's all right, John, but you'll never earn your living by it."

– John Lennon's Aunt Mimi

Air Devil's Inn on a Saturday Night

Air Devil's Inn is most alive on a summer night when the humidity is high, and the heat makes your clothes feel a little closer to your skin, a little heavier on your body. Air Devil's Inn, or ADI to the regulars, is the first bar I found when I moved to Louisville. My friend Ben introduced me to the bar with this endorsement: "I can get drunk on ten dollars and still have money for two games of pinball."

Claiming to be the oldest bar in Louisville, ADI is located across the road from Louisville's first airport, Bowman Field. The bar was a hangout for pilots on layover, and it is their namesake. Flyers would cross the road for a couple of hours on the ground and grab a stiff bourbon or an Old Milwaukee. Those air devils are no longer regulars since a newer airport was built thirty years ago on the other side of town. The regulars changed from pilots to bikers, making the Inn a little bit of a rougher place, at least by reputation. While there are a couple of Harleys in the lot on any given night, the regulars now are a wide cross section of white people—roots rock enthusiasts, divorcees on the make, and blue-collar workers getting off of second shift.

The outside of Air Devil's has a mural painted on the wood siding. Faded and peeling in some places, the wall painting features a variety of World War II era planes and bombers in mid-flight and mid-attack. The parking spaces are as faded as the paint. Someone has stolen or taken down the handicapped parking-space sign.

Inside the wooden door, on a weekend night, awaits a bouncer to collect a cover. The person working the door is never on the bar's payroll, but most likely a member of the band playing that night, a friend of the band, or even an ADI regular. The only requirement for working the door is the ability to drink, smoke, and count money at the same time. Most nights it's Paul.

On this particular night, Paul works the door wearing a version of his uniform: cigarette, offensive t-shirt, jeans, white running shoes. His shirt reads, "Support local music, sleep with a musician." I make eye contact with him and think, "Oh, God, don't let him hit on me." Other t-shirts in his collection say things like "I Put Out on the First Date" and "Lord of the Cockring." Paul, in his late thirties, has the kind of tan that comes from a tanning bed. He looks almost orange. He sports a hairstyle he works hard to achieve. It looks like a mullet—short on the sides, longer in the back. Except that it has some Farah Fawcett-esque feathering on the sides. The final result is a Carol Brady-inspired coif. It gives a feminine edge to his otherwise burly physique. He looks like a former high school football player whose body has atrophied with a beer belly and 20 years of couch sitting.

"It'll be five bucks," he tells me. When he speaks, I hear the two-pack-a-day habit in his voice. It's not so much a haggard voice that smoking causes, but the deep corroding of the lungs that brings a constant cough with every light-up.

In the dim glow of the bar, model airplanes hang from the stained ceiling tiles. The support columns in the bar have old framed photos of pilots and newspaper articles about the bar from the '50s. It's a Saturday night at ten o'clock and members of that evening's band, Dallas Alice, stand around the bar with a few regulars and a few fans.

While the regulars at ADI vary in age from twenties to fifties, each age group has its set of traits. Most of the folks are in their forties and fifties. There are some couples like Kenny, the daytime bartender, and his wife Patsy, but most of the older crowd is composed of divorced women who come in small groups and drink vodka and dance together to the band. There are some men who are married but leave their wives at home and come to hang out at the bar with the band and feel single and young for a few hours. The thirty-year-old pack tends to be young professionals, mostly couples who have recently bought their first house in the neighborhood near the bar. The twenty-somethings are usually dorky-yet-hip kids with fresh tattoos, goatees, or pairs of dark plastic-frame glasses. They are the kind of crowd that in one weekend will go to both punk rock and country shows.

Alan and Gina work the bar most weekend nights. Alan always wears a red, laundry-faded Hawaiian shirt. He's in his forties, or maybe his fifties. Who can tell in the backlighting of a Bass Ale sign? He seems to have a kind spirit and is always friendly. When the bar is slower, usually on a weeknight, he will quiz folks on politics or language trivia because he speaks five languages. Originally from Scotland, his accent has faded since he came to the U.S. in his teens. One night I was there and told him I was going to go home and write and he gave me pen and paper. "Only give it back to me after you write a good story on it," he said.

While Alan is efficient and kind in his service, Gina acts as if she would prefer no one come to the bar. If customers have to be there she would rather they speak to her as little as possible. I try to be pleasant and decisive and have cash ready when I go to the bar. She doesn't want to be messed with, and really she frightens me a little. A woman can wait fifteen minutes at the bar to order, no matter how empty the bar is in an evening. I don't even try to catch her eye as she's taking other orders down the bar. I lean in slightly and look interested in ordering, hold my money out to show I'm ready. I wait patiently, trying not to appear anxious, put out, or friendly. Nothing will get you ignored more quickly than actually trying to get her attention. As I wait, I practice my order in my head. She finally slows down as she walks by and points to my money.

"Bourbon and ginger ale, please," I say. She keeps walking and gathers beer bottles filling the order of the man to my right who came to the bar after me. It doesn't matter who got there first, or how long I've been waiting, it's Gina's call. She comes back, a bit exasperated. It's more of a general statement about people coming to the bar than about me.

"What was it?" she asks again as she sets down four beers for the man in a North Face vest and polo shirt.

"Bourbon and ginger," I repeat. "A tall one," I add. I realize it's best to order a double because I don't know if I will be able to get another drink later on, depending on Gina's mood. She nods as the man tries to hand her a credit card.

"Oh no. Cash only," she says as she points to the woman behind the customer who has taken her Rolling Rock. "Give me back that beer until you settle up." The man fumbles for enough cash, as he seems thrown off by the rules of the dive: Cash only. No tabs. After he settles up, she hands me my drink, charging me fifty cents more than Alan would for the same drink, $3 instead of $2.50 which strikes me as criminal.

She shakes her head, "Don't hand me a credit card and think you can take your drinks," she says under her breath. I'm relieved to know enough to play by the rules. I drop two bucks—almost the price of the drink—into the tip jar in a quick gesture hoping she'll notice.

Gina has bleached-blond hair with visible dark roots and loose curls that look like a home perm growing out. She wears a wide, red bandana to keep her hair out of her face, and a sleeveless tee, perhaps a beach-vacation souvenir, over a visible sports bra. She tucks the shirt into her cut-off jean shorts that stop above her thighs. I think she wears such short shorts to show her muscular legs, not to garner high tips from the men at the bar, but as a quiet warning that she can kick your ass if you get out of line. Instead of a belt she wears a low slung fanny pack. She sports Reebok high-tops with Velcro across the instep.

Gina used to be a champion kickboxer, and she has the physique to back that up. I learned this one night at the bar as a musician friend of mine whispered to me over a glass of Maker's Mark. "Gina used to have breast implants," she said, quickly looking up to make sure Gina couldn't hear us from the other end of the bar—or read my source's lips. "But she busted them in training. Twice." In an effort to keep my mouth from hanging open and to keep from staring at Gina's breasts, I slurped on a straw, extracting the bourbon-tinged water from around the ice cubes in my glass. "Finally her doctor told her she had to either quit kickboxing or ditch the implants," my friend continued. "She kept her third set of implants. Now she teaches yoga at Gold's gym."

I turn from the bar and look around to see whom I might know. I see a couple of the guys from the band Dallas Alice at the end of the bar smoking and a couple on stage doing a sound check. I see Brandon and Katie, two of my bar acquaintances, sitting on the opposite end of the bar. I see them at the bar two to three times a month. Eventually you start to say hi and become bar friends.

I move to a bar stool at the end of the bar on the edge of the dance floor. Nick, the lead guitarist, is leaning against the bar drinking a bottle of Bud, smoking a cigarette. He arches his eyebrows and lifts his beer to gesture a hello. At forty-five, Nick is the oldest member of the band, while the other fellas are in their twenties or early thirties. He always wears a dark suit with a coordinating button-down shirt and bolero tie. He heads to the stage as I settle onto the stool. There are a few tables on the edge of the small dance floor, but since I came to ADI by myself I don't want to sit right in front of the band.

The five guys in Dallas Alice don't fancy themselves a band for bikers, truckers or even the lonely old guy at the end of the bar. They see themselves as a bar band, or rather half-ass musicians that would be drinking at Air Devil's anyway so might as well get up on stage and sing some songs. Sean, the lead singer, has a voice that growls like a stick shift searching for second. The band's harmonies have an audible twang like empty beer cans rolling around in the bed of a pick-up. Sean writes most of the songs and his lyrics ride the line between country dirt roads and big-city blacktop. He's from southern Illinois, but he sings songs that could be about the small towns in eastern Kentucky where I grew up. The band's musical style could play in the background in some of the stories of my life, if I were to make them a movie. They weave together small town roots and the grown-up life of living in a city.

Sean has short blond hair he sweeps back in a miniature pompadour. He's wearing a short sleeve Steve Earle t-shirt that partially covers his tattoos. Most prominent is one on his forearm with his mother's name, Georgia, written across the shape of the state, fashioned like a vintage postcard with a peach in the foreground.

He sings the song "Free Coffee," the first track from their album. He begins a cappella:

All the fields around my hometown grew lima beans and corn
Now there ain't much but weeds and broken dreams
That grows there any more.

The rest of the band kicks in with a harmony:

It's just another small town. Small town slipping away.

The drummer and the guitarists pick up and the stage comes to life. Patrons start to turn from the bar and edge toward the dance floor without actually stepping on to it.

Nick plays a hard driving interlude on his Stratocaster. The younger guys he plays with cede the stage to him. His improvisational style lands somewhere between extended riffing and jamming. He moves the cigarette he is smoking to secure it under the guitar strings just above the neck of the guitar. A small crowd of eight or so people stands and watches attentively with drinks or cigarettes in hand. They sway to the music or bob their heads in time.

I require a live band with enough Red Bull in its veins to help me paint the town a particular shade of roots rock red. I dig Dallas Alice because they can balance twang with tattoos, guitar solos with bourbon shots, and smart lyrics with foul mouths. The five members are slightly scruffy, occasionally charming, reliably boozy, and guaranteed to be smoke-stained. They serve their music neat, no mixers needed. After seeing them play on a few occasions, their music stole my honky-tonk heart. It has become a welcome soundtrack to my evening. I enjoy the people-watching, the drinks, and the good company of friends always available at ADI. I answer the Dallas Alice altar call about once a month and I get doused in enough twang to keep me away from commercial country music until the next time I cross the threshold at ADI.

At the end of the first song, Gina delivers a tray of bourbon shots to the band. They each take one. Sean turns to the mike, as the applause slows. "We're Dallas Alice," he says raising the shot glass for a toast. "Social!" and the band's members knock their heads back and drink down the brown liquor. Regulars repeat Sean's call and tip back High Life bottles and glasses of whiskey. A table of young women in low-cut tank tops and tight jeans slam empty glasses on their table after finishing shots of Jagermeister.

People start to head to the dance floor. I leave my perch and move to a support beam plastered with posters for upcoming shows. It's near the dance floor, but back far enough that I feel comfortable and slightly hidden. I watch the guitar playing and sing softly to myself.

∞

The Name of the Place

Come on, let me show you where it's at.
Come on, let me show you where it's at.
The name of the place is I like it like that.

-Dave Clark Five

At the low-slung altar of her Magnavox console, I bowed
to their greatness, the ministers of my stepmother's music:
Louis Prima and Keely Smith, Roy Orbison, Joey Dee
and his Starliters, Mancini and Lanza. I jumped to their jive,
their strings and hangdog vibrato, popped my hips
to the peppermint twist. I wanted to be the pulse of bass
thumping, the verve of *I like it like that.* Whatever cool place
the beat sent her, I was the metronome tocking at her heels.
Dizzy and tuneless from my mother's discordance,
I wished myself into the turntable and scratchy revolutions,
into my stepmother's rouge and pancake makeup, fingers
snapping *Sweet dream baby, how long must I dream?*
The records spun dreams of waking her blood daughter,
with sapphire eyes and cucumber skin, our separateness
drowned out, our pitch pure as belonging.

Milkshake Run

Mossie Brantley first laid eyes on Garrett Long when he appeared out of thin air in front of their house one unseasonably hot June afternoon. She was sitting on the grass in the front yard, pouring water on her legs from an old Coca-Cola bottle. She had her pants rolled up past her knees, sunning her legs and listening to the radio on the front porch. She had plugged the radio into an outlet in the living room and run the cord out the window. She knew her Daddy would be mad if he came in from the field and saw her sitting so near the road with her pants rolled up and music blaring. The experience was delicious, and she decided it was worth the risk of getting caught. Her daddy didn't approve of her constant electric companion, but Mossie loved the music and she just couldn't help herself. Sometimes when their voices poured from the crackling radio she forgot that she didn't really know Hank and Loretta and Conway.

I go out walking after midnight, out in the moonlight.

"Wish I was like you, Patsy. Wish I'd been places like you have. I'd have plenty to talk about if I had," she said.

Sitting with her face turned toward the sun, she heard the car well before she saw it. She put her hands over her eyes to shade them from the broiling sun. A white cloud of dust was moving fast along the road. She stood up just as a green Ford Fairlane rumbled to a stop right in front of their mailbox. The door creaked open and out stepped a tall, thin man with the bluest eyes Mossie had ever seen. Keeping her mouth closed took every ounce of strength she could muster.

"Hey," he said. "You know where Jim Brantley lives?"

"Yeah."

"Is it far from here?"

"No."

Mossie stared at the man's face. His mouth pulled to one side in a crooked grin and he looked down at his feet. He moved a few large gravels around with his toe, then looked back at her.

"Well. How far is it?"

"How far is what?"

"Jim Brantley's place."

"Oh. It's here. I mean, this is Jim Brantley's place. But he ain't here. He's down in the bottom over there cutting hay with the Hargraves boys."

"Oh. Well."

"What do you want with him, anyway?"

"See, there's a man up in Luttrell told me he's got a good coon dog for sale. And I'm looking to buy one so I wanted to see if he still had it and if so what kind of shape the dog is in and how much he wants for it."

"You from Luttrell?"

"No, I live up in Tazewell. Back up on Cedar Fork Road, Little Valley. I got some buddies I run around with there in Luttrell. We coon hunt some on the weekends."

Goodness, gracious, great balls of fire.

Jerry Lee Lewis' raucous pounding on piano keys ran right across Mossie's spine. Her eyes widened and she turned and dashed toward the porch, throwing the half full bottle of water on the ground as she ran. She switched off the radio and turned around to look at the man, still standing awkwardly by the mailbox.

"What's the matter?" he asked. "Don't you like Jerry Lee?"

"Yeah, I like him fine." Mossie's face burned. "I just...I just got tired of it, that's all."

"So, you don't know if Jim Brantley has a coon dog for sale or not?"

"Well, you'd have to ask Jim Brantley about that. I know he's got some dogs, but I don't keep up with what he does with them. I could walk you down there to him. If you want to ask him your own self, I mean."

"You kin to him or something?"

"Yeah, I'm his girl. I mean, he's my daddy. So you want me to walk you down there or not?"

"Why, yeah, if you got the time."

Mossie started down the yard toward the mailbox. She stopped suddenly, turned her back to the man and rolled her pants legs down. She walked up beside him and motioned for him to follow her across the road and through the field. They walked in silence for a time, then he spoke.

"What was you doing with that bottle of water?"

Mossie felt her face burn again.

"Nothing."

She looked sideways at his face and saw he was smiling at her. She couldn't help laughing.

"If you must know, I was pouring it on my legs so they'd soak up more sun. That's all. Just sunning my legs. Don't people in Tazewell ever sun their legs?"

"I guess I just never took notice if they do."

She began to relax. Talking to the man was easier if she didn't look right

86

into his eyes. Her stomach knotted up if she looked too long at those long dark lashes.

"What's your name, anyway?"

"Mossie Elizabeth Brantley."

"Ain't you going to ask me my name?"

"I figure you'll tell it to me sooner or later if you want me to know it."

"Garrett Long. My name's Garrett Long."

It turned out Jim Brantley did have coon dog to sell and Garrett was interested in the trade. The two men wound up talking for much of the afternoon and Mossie tagged along behind them, sneaking looks at Garrett as often as she could. Much to her delight, her daddy asked him to stay for supper that night and he accepted.

"Well, I do have a hard time passing up chicken and dumplings, that's for sure," he said.

Her mother glowed when he shoveled second, third and fourth helpings onto his plate.

"Lord, Mrs. Brantley, them's good. Them's about the best dumplings I ever put in my mouth. I hope you teach your girls how to make dumplings like this. It's a talent that needs to be passed on."

Mossie was thrilled every time he looked across the table at her—not at her older sister Mattie—but at her. Once, when no one was looking, he winked. She just knew this was how she'd feel when Jesus come back for His church.

The best part was Garrett Long kept coming to supper. He and Mossie would sit in the tiny suffocating living room with her parents and Mattie. They all talked about everything from tobacco crops to the scourge of Elvis Presley. Her daddy said Elvis was going to be the ruination of the country. Mossie watched Garrett's face, watching for signs that her opinionated daddy was offending him. If he was offended by anything her daddy said, he sure never showed it.

Eventually, her daddy let Mossie sit out on the porch after dark with Garrett. She couldn't believe it. Here she was, sitting tight against a man right in the front door. Mossie knew a twenty-seven year old town man surely had better things to do than sit close to a skinny sixteen year old girl who had never been anywhere. On their second dark porch sitting, he laid his hand on top of hers. Her flesh melted and ran down her body like candle wax.

Before she knew it, August was pouring down on the holler. One close night after supper, everyone had gathered on the porch trying to catch a cool breeze. Mossie was frustrated they had company on the porch, but she welcomed any opportunity to be with him. She had come to measure her life by the time she spent with him. They had all sat quietly for a long spell when

Garret spoke.

"Jim, would it be okay if I took Mossie to ride around town a while Friday night?"

Mossie's heart went straight to her throat. She could swear even the big bull crickets in the thicket hushed as his words rang out in the still air. She held her breath until her daddy cleared his throat.

"Well. I reckon it's all right with me if you want to take her and she wants to go. Mossie, you want go to town with Garrett?"

"Yeah," she said.

And that was all there was to it. Mossie laid awake the next four nights trying to absorb the miracle of the whole thing. Her daddy didn't even stutter when he said she could go. They hadn't spoken of it since. Now here she was, pinning her black skirt over so it fit tight about her waist.

She heard the Fairlane skid in the gravels in front of the house. Her hands felt devoid of bones as she struggled to fasten the large pin in her skirt. The screen door creaked as her daddy spoke.

"Come on in the house. That girl ought to be ready to go by now."

Mossie started toward the curtain covering the bedroom door. She stopped when she realized she did not have her shoes on. She ran to the cedar chifferobe and pawed through the pile of clothes and shoes in the bottom until she recovered her black shoes.

When she finally emerged from the bedroom Garrett was sitting beside her daddy on the couch. He stood up and looked at her for a time.

"Hey," he said. "Ready?"

"Yeah, I reckon."

Mossie couldn't get her feet to stay on the ground as they walked to the car. She reached for the car door handle and smashed her hand into his as he did the same.

"Here. Let me get that for you."

They rode the length of the holler pretty much in silence. The smell of the gray dust swirled around them and Mossie began to worry about her hair as the wind whipped through the open windows. She was afraid to reach her hand up to touch it, afraid her thick curls had grown to twice their size.

People see us everywhere; they think you really care; myself I can't deceive; I know it's only make believe.

For the first time in her life she wished Conway Twitty would just shut up. She jumped when Garrett finally spoke.

"So, what do you feel like doing tonight?"

"It don't matter to me. Whatever you want to do."

Mossie hoped he didn't know that she had no opinion because she had no idea what the options were.

"Well, I thought we'd just go ride around town a while and then maybe make a milkshake run. How does that sound?"

"Sounds good."

"I ain't had a good one in a while. It's especially a fine thing in hot weather, don't you think?"

"Boy, that's the truth."

Mossie had absolutely no idea what a milkshake run was or what she would be expected to do at the onset of it. Her mind was racing. A milkshake run. What on earth could it be? What if it involved something she had never seen before and she didn't know what to do with it once she got it? She could only hope he would go first so she could watch. She didn't want him to know that she hadn't been out much and that there was so much about the world and town life that she had never experienced – never even seen. She frantically tried to decode the words, tried to assign some meaning to them. She felt her stomach knot up. What if it was something she shouldn't be doing with a twenty-seven year old man from town? Her heart sank as her perfect experience changed into a nightmare.

She should have been enjoying the ride and the sweet rhythm of the car radio. She could smell Garrett's Vitalis hair oil and she wished her mind would get off the milkshake run so she could memorize every movement, every detail. She was sure this could easily be the last time Garrett Long took her to town on a Friday night. She was going to need to hang on to every fragment of this one.

Once they got to town, they drove along the highway, circling back and forth between the truck stop parking lot on the north end of town and the bank parking lot on the south. They cruised down some of the side roads near town. He showed her the turn to Cedar Fork Road.

"It's about six miles up that way to the turn to Little Valley where I live. It's a bad old road once you get on up there, so we won't go. It's dark, too. No lights or nothing up that holler there."

"That's okay. I like this fine. Town's fine with me."

After a time he said, "I'm about ready for that milkshake run. How about you?"

"Yeah, boy," she said.

After much soul searching, Mossie decided her best defense was to fake it. No matter what a milkshake run turned out to involve, she would pretend she was an old hand at it. If it got ugly, she'd just call on her natural talents to help get her out of it unscathed. Going to town alone, even for this brief time, had given her a confidence she never thought she'd have.

Garrett wheeled the Fairlane into a brightly lit parking lot. Mossie noticed people sitting in the rows of cars lining the pavement. They were all facing a small brick building with large windows all around the front and sides. A huge, neon ice cream cone-shaped sign flashed yellow and blue, yellow and blue from the top of the building. Garrett turned off the engine, but left the radio on. Porter Wagoner crooned "A Satisfied Mind." Mossie could hear other people around her laughing and talking.

Soon a girl with a tight green sweater that left nothing to imagination twisted up to the open window. A small leather pouch hung from her belt and it bounced in time with her swaying hips. She leaned down and peered in the open window, a yellow pencil poised over a small green notepad. Mossie could see a huge wad of pink gum between her teeth. She wasn't sure she liked Miss Green Sweater hanging her large bosom so close to Garrett's face.

"We want two milkshakes. Chocolate for me, I guess. What kind do you want? Chocolate okay?"

Mossie shook her head in agreement.

"Thank you, Jesus," she thought.

Chocolate. So it had to do with eating. She hoped she liked whatever it was, but she felt better now. She knew the worst that could happen is she might have to choke down something she didn't like.

"If it's got chocolate about it, I'll get it down somehow, no matter what it is," she thought.

Sweater girl went toward the brick building and pushed her way through a glass door on the side. Mossie was more relaxed now, and she looked around at the other cars. Most of them were young couples, and they all looked like they were enjoying themselves. She felt her body begin to relax, sink deeper into the vinyl seat. She wanted to lay her head back, close her eyes and sing along with Porter Wagoner, but she knew that wasn't proper. A hot breeze passed through her window, across her face, then across Garrett's before drifting out the open window on the other side.

"Why don't you slide over here a while?" he said.

Mossie looked over and saw him pat the seat next to his leg. She could smell his hair oil again. The buttons on the front of his shirt shone in the flashing light of the sign. His eyes were right on hers. Her heart fluttered and she thought for a moment she might cough. Without thinking, she gathered the skirt tight around her bottom and slid across the seat.

He raised his arm and she slid right against him. She fit perfectly in the crook of his arm and she allowed her thigh to rest against his. She thought the heat from his skin might brand her, hoped it would, wished it would melt her to him so she would never have to be even one inch away from him again.

Miss Green Sweater walked up to the car and held out two white cups with green S-shaped squiggles around the tops. Two red and white paper straws stuck out from a creamy brown mixture. Garrett removed his arm from around her to take the cups and handed money to the waiting girl. Mossie held both cups while he counted out coins into the girl's hand. She tried not to stare at the contents. The paraffin cups were icy cold and she fought the urge to hold one against her cheek. After the girl left, he took one of the cups from her and wrapped his arm around her shoulder again.

Mossie watched his cheeks cave in as he pulled hard on the straw. She followed his lead. The sweet mixture flooded her mouth. So that was it. No wonder he looked forward to the milkshake run.

They drank in silence for a while. Mossie tried to savor hers, even though it was hard to hold back. She could feel the cool goodness of it slide down her throat. She loved the way it made her tongue feel numb and how the little puddles of melted liquid gathered around the edges of the cup. She used her straw to drain them off, working carefully not to disturb the solid mass in the center.

Garrett finished his before her and she was surprised to see him toss the empty cup out the window. She had noticed earlier that the parking lot was littered with empty cups and waxy squares of paper. Even though she had gathered it was acceptable to throw trash on the ground in front of the little brick building, she wondered why he didn't want to keep the cup. She fully intended to salvage hers, take it home and wash it out. What a fine remembrance it would make.

They drove for a short distance, Mossie settled against him like she had always been there. She sipped the last of her milkshake. Neither of them spoke. Soon they came to a dirt road and he steered the car off the pavement. When they came to a wide spot in the dusty road, Garrett eased the Fairlane into it. He turned off the key, again leaving the radio on. Pasty Cline was well into "Crazy" when he turned to look at Mossie. She clutched the empty cup, fixed her eyes on his face.

His hand sat easy on her skin as he stroked her cheek and titled her face upward to meet his. When his lips covered her mouth, it never occurred to her to worry about how to go about what she found herself doing. Her lips led the way, responding to his cool mouth as surely as if they belonged to someone else. As she melted into his embrace, she prayed that God would allow her to go on many more milkshake runs. Even Hank Williams couldn't hold a candle to the music Garrett Long made when he touched his mouth to hers.

∞

In the Basement

Each day the dance beat
sleeps in vinyl, lined up
evenly in basements. It leans
against boxes of chalk
and spare scooter parts.
Dust gathers under
wooden crates of records
the covers creased with dirt
the corners cracked.
Never has "The Twist"
stood so silent.
No one moves
to the frug, the jerk, the pony.
No jitterbug or rumba.
Only the ghosts
of smooch songs
and goodnight love songs
float above the baseboards.
Upstairs, unpacked from plastic jackets,
the CDs bass-thump, bass-thump
into a break dance
and shake the house down.

Jam

Col-trane
blowing life-giving *Naima*
and joined outside, now
by a raucous crow—
glossy-black praise and blame.

Nothing
                        improvisational about its
cawing contributions
but the crow's a witness, just the same—
absolutely for real
                        and testifying
like a hip some-body
scatting
                        to the booming pedal point
of a city-hall clock
                        only reversed
            as though the clock
    were
                        responding, in its
                        prearranged
                            one
                            way
to the genius
push
                        and probe of the scat each contributor
blowing
                        out of radically different, but shared
moments, needs—asserting   radically dis-similar
yet similarly commanding
rhythms
                        and timbres. An unlikely mix
that (briefly) works—a serendipity of co-incidents
till Col-trane turns
'round

                    to chase his equinox
and the peremptory crow

                                        (*simple* cat that he or she *is*)

packs up
and scats.

                              ∾

Rockin' With Red

The other day a friend sent me a Piano Red CD, a reissue of his classic recordings from the fifties. When I dropped it into the CD player and cranked it up and I heard Piano Red for the first time in years, decades maybe, and it all came roaring back—the whole experience of living in East Point, about a dozen miles south of downtown Atlanta, at the time when segregation was just beginning to show cracks in its foundation, the whole thing of learning to question the rules and assumptions that we were expected to live under. Rebellion was in the air and Piano Red, although he would have been shocked to discover this fact, was one of the prime movers, one of the causes of discontent in thousands of young white kids.

The kids I grew up with just couldn't get with the segregation program. We found the whole idea of hating people because of the color of their skin just a touch on the odd side. To be down on black people simply because they were not white was to assume that they were not as good as us. We knew better. We'd heard the music and that was enough right there to show that the white power structure was as crazy as a pickup truck full of drunken hunters.

The fact of the matter was that black people were, by force of the law, outsiders and we admired anyone who lived the outlaw life, whether it was by choice or by compulsion. Our own lives were circumscribed by rules, conventions and customs; we were being shuttled down a path that led to a huge cup of more of the same. None of us wanted to go there, so we admired anyone who lived outside the lines. That life was purer; as Bob Dylan wrote a decade later, "To live outside the law, you must be honest."

How did we come to elect black people as the embodiment of cool? Mostly through the music, and that's where Piano Red comes in. Zenas Sears, a local DJ and record producer, owned and operated WAOK, the soul station that introduced young impressionable white kids like me to the magic of the music of bands like the Midnighters, the Five Royales, Ray Charles, Clyde McPhatter and the Drifters, Chuck Berry, Bo Diddley—all of the songs that turned your head inside out, that had a power and a strength to them that made the music on the white stations seem as pale as our winter skin. Pat Boone covering Little Richard? Who could even listen to that without their head exploding?

When I first heard Ray Charles sing, I heard a new world coming into existence, as the old, settled and secure ways gasped once and died. The future was just around the corner, sliding in, arriving far sooner than anyone had expected. When Muddy Waters' voice and guitar came slicing through the speakers, I knew there was a heaven. But it was Piano Red, a fairly obscure blues and barrelhouse piano player, who changed my life.

He'd been born William Perryman in Hampton, a small town about thirty miles south of Atlanta. Growing up, he was known as Willie. Like his older brother Rufus, Willie's skin was the color of a catfish filet and his hair was white with a reddish tinge to it. Both he and Rufus were so nearsighted that folks thought they were blind.

And both he and Rufus became barrelhouse piano players. As a young man, Red followed his brother onto the Chitlin' Circuit, a string of southern honkytonks and clubs that were owned by black entrepreneurs and catered to African-American audiences. After a few years, he was able to cross over, to expand his touring to the resorts and clubs frequented by white audiences.

In the thirties, he met the legendary blues singer, Blind Willie McTell, and traveled with him. With McTell, he made his first records, a set of half a dozen or so songs for the Vocalion label that weren't issued during his lifetime. He continued to tour the South, working his way up, and when he made it up to Atlanta, Red got two big breaks: he got signed to RCA Records and he met Zenas "Daddy" Sears, who was at that time working as a record producer, DJ and talent manager. When Sears took over radio station WAOK and began building it into the most important rhythm and blues station in the South, he signed Piano Red to do a two hour program every afternoon. On his show, Red would spin a few records but mostly he'd play live in the studio and tell stories about his life.

I heard the first show. Red played his hits and sang in his raspy, rough voice. As a singer, Red didn't have what you might call great pipes but he could sell a blues tune. He was a master story-teller, either in a tune or when he was riffing between songs. His playing had a sophistication to it that the titles of his hit songs did not hint at: "Rockin' with Red," "Decatur Street Boogie," "Just Right Bounce." He knew a seemingly unending string of barrelhouse blues numbers, including his signature tune, "Right String, Baby, but the Wrong Yo Yo." The songs were familiar. He was a fixture on juke boxes all over town. You couldn't hear Piano Red's music without wanting to dance.

And laugh. His playing was as funny and eccentric as Laurel and Hardy. Just listening filled you with good feelings. In fact, later on, after he'd stopped getting air play as Piano Red, he changed his billing to Dr. Feelgood and his Interns and carved out another career, becoming famous all over again.

Hearing him on the radio knocked me out but it wasn't enough. I had to see him, to be there as he performed. I could not have said why it was so important and to this day I'm still not absolutely certain what I was looking for, but I knew Red's music offered something that a southern white boy couldn't find anywhere else, something that I had to have. So after school one day, in an almost trancelike motion, I walked across the railroad tracks to Main Street, stuck out my thumb, hitchhiked downtown, and walked down Auburn Avenue to the station. I was twelve years old.

Piano Red was pure spirit. A nearly blind albino whose skin was as light as mine, his eyes seemed to swim in an attempt to focus, so you could never be quite sure where he was looking. Far from physically imposing, he was fairly short, with a shuffling way of walking as though he thought keeping his feet flat on the ground would prevent him from tripping over things he could barely see.

He knew he had been touched by the cosmos, though. He told one interviewer: "I gets my spirit from the universe. Anything you gonna do, if you don't put God in front, you ain't gonna do nothin' to start with. And that's what I do. I be's prayin' when I'm drivin' in my car. I be's prayin' at the intermission of my show. God let me know a while back when I was making records it wasn't me but him and I never forgot that. From then on, I put God in front of me, and I been doin' good ever since."

The dialect is in the original quote but it's a pretty good indicator of the way he talked. Red was a lot of things but educated was not one of them.

WAOK was located right in the heart of Sweet Auburn, the artistic and commercial center for the black community. Daddy Sears, who was so immersed in black music and culture that people were shocked to discover that he was white, ran both the station and the record shop across the street from it. If you were looking for great soul music that you never heard on white radio stations—and all of us kids were—you went to Daddy Sears' shop. I'd spent a lot of time in the record shop, so I knew the neighborhood.

A secretary smiled as she saw me coming into WAOK. "May I help you?"

Piano Red's music came out of the speakers that hung on the wall. I shrugged. I couldn't really explain what had drawn me there. It wasn't just curiosity or a love of the music. It had nothing to do with being a fan. Some force far beyond my understanding had taken over. Today, I'd probably call it a spiritual drive but back then I didn't have the words to identify it.

"I want to see Piano Red," I said.

"Well, he's on the air right now."

"I know." I stood there stupidly. "Can I watch him?"

97

When she looked at me, I could see amusement in her eyes. Smiling, she led me down a hall and let me stand outside the studio, watching through the window as Piano Red, seated at a grand piano, banged away at the keys and sang, his eyes staring ahead at nothing in particular. I stood by the glass and took in his show, which consisted of one man in a room with a piano. At the far end of the room, behind a glass partition, an engineer fiddled with dials. Nothing out of the ordinary was going on, but there was magic in that room.

When the show was over, Red came out the door just a few feet away from me. I silently watched as he approached me with that funny little shuffle.

"Hey," he said, "you watched me through the window, didn't you?"

"Yes, sir," I said.

My parents had taught me that everyone older than me was addressed as "Sir" or "Ma'am." Little Joe, my uncle, claimed the rule didn't apply to black people. As young as I was, my rule for getting along in life was simple: if Little Joe advocated a thing, I did the opposite.

"You likes the music, do you?" Red still carried the rural south in his speech and manner.

"Yes, sir. It's great."

"Next time, you come on in the studio, you hear? The music's better in there."

I became a familiar fixture on Auburn Avenue. A few times a week, when I got out of school, I'd step out onto the curb of Main Street, stick out my thumb and head into town. I had it timed out; school ended at three, Red's show started at four. If I got a ride into town by 3:20, I could make it to the station before he started. No ride by 3:20, I'd hop onto the bus and ride it to Rich's Department Store and then hurriedly walk east the few blocks to Sweet Auburn. I'd hang out at WAOK, listening to Red on the air and sharing a few words with him when he got off the air. Then I'd comb the record shops for a half an hour or so before I hitched back home.

One day, the routine changed. When he came out of the studio, Red stopped next to me, pointed down the hall and said, "Come on back to the lounge with me." We walked to the end of the hall and Red led the way into a small room that had a couple of chairs and a sofa in it. The walls were covered with fliers advertising records and concerts. I remember one announcing a new forty-five from Elmore James.

Red grabbed a couple of Cokes out of the refrigerator and handed me one. Sitting heavily in an arm chair, he said, "It's good to know white boys likes my music."

"Everybody I know likes your show," I said.

"Music don't know no color. It ain't no black thing or white thing. It's an everybody thing."

"Yes, sir." This was church. This was religion.

I really don't remember what all we talked about that afternoon. All I know is he told stories and I listened. That afternoon started a new pattern. After his show, we'd go to the lounge and, over Cokes, he'd tell me stories and I'd listen. He told me about growing up in the small town South during segregation and how he and his brother Rufus, who later became the blues musician Speckled Red, used to try to outdo each other on the piano. The day he talked about traveling around with Blind Willie McTell, I ran across the street to Daddy Sears' shop to buy McTell's records but they were all out of print.

When my friends found out what I was up to, most of them thought I was crazy, but a couple, who were as deeply into the music as I was, began going down there with me. People quickly got used to seeing us running up and down the Avenue. If anybody was upset by what I was doing, I was too deeply into the music and the energy from the street to notice. The fact was I felt more at home on Auburn Avenue than I did in East Point.

After a couple of years, though, sports, chasing girls and getting into all the trouble that teenaged Southern boys got into took over, and even though I still listened to his show every day, I spent less time with Red at WAOK. Then I graduated and left Atlanta. That part of my life receded until the gift of a CD brought it back.

It's all gone now. Piano Red is dead, though his music is still out there and still holds up. Daddy Sears is dead too, and WAOK moved uptown and became a gospel station, and I no longer live in Atlanta. I took what Piano Red taught me to Maryland, where I now live. Just a few years ago, I took my daughters down to Atlanta to meet the southern branch of the family. While we were there, we went to the Martin Luther King Center and the Ebenezer Baptist Church, where King's father had preached before him. Although I hadn't even known it was there, the church was two blocks from where WAOK had been located on Auburn Avenue. My wife and I got to talking to the women in the church, telling them how I hung out around there when I was in school. One of the church women, a matronly gray-haired lady in her seventies, looked up at me in surprise and declared, "I remember you boys. You were all over the place."

I smiled. It's always nice to be remembered.

∞

New Orleans Ragging Home
Romare Bearden, 1974

The tuba's round eye of blackness
stares at you, burps and burps
again and the band blows slow
drag and rattle down the alley
where a brown woman leans out
from a balcony waving a pink
satin underthing, rippled, shiny
like a river. Play it harder,
she says as they shuffle
past. She knows that every night
about this hour a rooster flies
high over the milky windows
and the horns bleat like sheared lambs
missing their mama. She sways
her backside in rhythm, 2,500 miles
of slippery river if you count
the bends, all the way south
to the delta, muddy vulva
of a continent birthing
a vibration, jazz, like a flutter
of wings, four white doves
drifting across the blue darkness
in an arc below the moon's
yellow sidewise smile.

Sound Track

No songbooks in our house—Mother
remembered every lyric she'd ever heard,
sang endlessly while she cooked, cleaned,
ironed our frilly dresses, sang the old
ballads or World War II songs—*Don't sit*
under the apple tree with anyone else
but me, My buddy, your buddy misses you.
When the Philco radio scratched out tunes,
Mother danced, snapped fingers, swayed hips,
her house-dress as enticing as the get-up
of a fan dancer. Evenings after supper,
we'd sit in the swing,
sing the crickets to shame.

Years later, my sisters and I
danced to rock and roll, wild music
from the West Virginia hills
or Louis Armstrong's cadences
rolled into Elvis' swivel,
learned to shake to any beat,
the rest of the world scandalized,
Mother glad we had finally found our bodies,
rejoicing that the river of music
flowing in our DNA
had not been dammed
by the Calvinistic ice
of our father's forebears.

∽

Dancing

My sister's husband taps and steps
to a Motown beat, call and response,
a girl group singing *Baby Love,* forward
and side to side, his eyes bright as strobe
lights, his grin like an ecstatic child's,
rolling his shoulders, snapping his fingers,
tossing his head, he gasps and giggles.

Bill loved to dance, my sister says,
at clubs we went to Friday nights.
His mind fading like the end of a record,
his vocabulary reduced to *yeah, you, who,*
he finds grammar in motion, the need to catch
the beat, a language he can understand.

The song dies away like memories,
but Bill wants to dance. We look
for buttons to punch, pick a funky favorite:
rhythm section from Muscle Shoals,
horn chorus, night song, river coming home.
Bill blurts out a yeah, *another song,*
my sister says, *while there's time.*

My Promise to the Rolling Stones

This is a story about a promise. A promise that I made years ago. A promise I have struggled to keep. When you're young, you make all kinds of promises – some you make out loud to other people, some you just make to yourself. One challenge of getting older, it seems, is figuring out which promises you're really supposed to keep. For guidance, I look to the people who inspired me to make this promise in the first place: The Rolling Stones.

When I was little, my dad was a hippie with a convertible. We used to ride around the winding roads of east Kentucky with the top down, Dad's long hair all swirling in the wind. I remember him singing, "I Can't Get No-hmm-hmm-hmm – I Can't Get No – hmm-hmm-hmm – Satisfaction." He sang with joy and abandon, and in those moments sounded, despite the words, deeply satisfied.

The Stones themselves made their first impression on me when they got to MTV. By then, Dad had lost interest in them. He'd cut his hair short, replaced his convertible with a sensible hardtop – a car he drove every day to a sensible office job he didn't like very much. I hardly ever heard him sing anymore, and I knew at some level he'd grown up. This somewhat soured me on the whole concept of growing up, and sparked my interest in the Rolling Stones.

Mick Jagger and Keith Richards never cut their hair short. Never got sensible office jobs. Never completely grew up. Somehow these old British guys had escaped all that, and prospered. And I wanted to know how they did it.

I used to skip school and spend hours at the library with a stack of music magazines reading about the Rolling Stones. I learned, among other things, that Mick had been a student at the London School of Economics when rock'n'roll called. His father told him not to do it. Just because the band thing was going well, Mick shouldn't stray from the sensible path of business. But the boy loved rock'n'roll, and he believed in himself, that he could do something different. So he went for it.

I also learned that almost everyone who writes about the Rolling Stones feels compelled to work as many Stones' lyrics into their articles as possible, as in, "Mick Jagger hopes his bandmates won't be Shattered by his new solo album."

This seemed so fawning and obvious. I decided that one day, when I was a writer, I would do something different, shun cliché and write something original about the band. Of course, that would be tough because they've been written about so much. After all, they've been around since Jesus Christ had his moment of doubt and pain.

(Oh, crap. I just quoted "Sympathy for the Devil." Oh well, another promise Young Me made that Old Me hasn't been able to keep.)

I was twenty-four the first time I saw the Stones in concert. I was living in Japan, working as an English teacher, wondering what I might do with the next fifty years or so. The tickets weren't cheap – about eighty dollars worth of yen – but I didn't care. Life, as I saw it, was about collecting experiences, and money was just a means to that end. So as I filed into the Tokyo Dome, I expected to enjoy the show. I expected it to be kind of like a visit with some really loud old friends. I didn't expect it to change my life.

But it did.

It wasn't just the music, or the smoke and fireworks, or this giant jack-in-the-box head. It wasn't Mick's strut-dancing charisma or Keith's rapturous guitar work or their obvious love for playing live. It was the combination of all of those and something else, something I couldn't see or hear or name. From the opening riffs of "Not Fade Away," they had me handing over control of my eyes, ears and mind to them. For those two hours, they took away every doubt, every fear, every thought and replaced them with light, sound, energy and joy. And they made me grateful.

Afterward, somewhere on the Tokyo subway, I made a promise to myself. Actually two. The first was that if I ever got a reasonable chance to see them in concert again, I would.

The second promise was the big one. I figured that creating that kind of all consuming rock'n'roll moment must be how you avoid growing up completely. I decided that I would create those moments for myself and other people. And through that, I would live and work on my own terms. I would be no office monkey man. I would be free to do what I wanted, any old time.

There were some caveats. I wasn't a musician. And if possible, I preferred to avoid drug addiction and paternity suits. So my version of the rock'n'roll life would be telling stories. I came back to Kentucky and created stories based on embarrassing moments I'd had in Japan. I started performing these stories at festivals and schools and radio shows. I earned a little money, but mostly I was learning how to read and respond to the crowd, how to structure the stories and the presentation of them to maximize their impact. I strategically placed the biggest crowd-pleasers at the beginning and end. The Stones had "Jumping Jack Flash" and "Brown Sugar." I had "The Asakawa Christmas Party" and "The Attack of the Japanese Pre-Schoolers."

But life rolled me like tumbling dice. I was married by then and my wife got pregnant – which we'd planned. With triplets – which we hadn't. One night in 2004, I became a father for the first, second, and third time. Suddenly, we needed a bigger house, a minivan, health insurance. What's a poor storyteller to do? Why, get a sensible office job, of course.

The job – writing technical documents for a large corporation – really wasn't bad. It came with nice people and good benefits. I was earning more money than ever (though still not always enough). Even so, I felt like I had broken my promise to myself. It stung to think about how I'd imagined the future that night after the concert. It had felt so good to make that declaration and trust myself with it, that to abandon it, even for justifiable reasons (like triplet boys), felt like failure. I was struggling with the whole thing in the summer of 2006 when I found out the Rolling Stones were coming to town. They planned to stage the first rock concert ever held at Churchill Downs, just a few miles from my house in Louisville.

Yes! I thought. Here's a promise to myself that I could keep. Start me up, baby! Let's rock and – What? A hundred and twenty-five dollars for a decent seat? Whoa. Talk about making a grown man cry.

A hundred and twenty-five dollars is a trip to the grocery. It's three little pairs of shoes. But it's the Stones! If I went to the show, the kids would still eat, they'd still have shoes. I could put the tickets on the credit card. I'd pay it off. Eventually.

Oh, what a drag it is, getting old.

I looked up the set lists from the Stones' other shows on that same tour. Just like in the Tokyo show, almost all the songs they played were decades old. It occurred to me that in a way, the Rolling Stones were dealing with the same issues I was. What was each of those ancient hits but a kind of promise – a promise that the young Rolling Stones made that these much older Rolling Stones were obliged to keep? A promise to us, the audience, that for the duration of that familiar song, they would erase all our worries and obligations. They would make us wild and irresponsible. They would make us free.

Mick Jagger once said in an interview that there are certain songs they basically have to play or the fans won't feel like they've really been to a Rolling Stones show. He also said that sometimes, when they played their brand-new songs, "You get all these blank faces," he said, "Like everyone looking at you going, 'What the fuck is this?'"

So apparently, being the world's greatest rock'n'roll band doesn't entirely free you from obligation. Understanding that didn't make my decision any easier. What should I choose – responsibility or rock'n'roll?

Ultimately, I think I made the right call. The Stones put on an incredible show at Churchill Downs that night. Mick apologized for the rain, but they rocked the place so hard nobody cared. They closed with Keith ripping into his guitar, bringing "Satisfaction" to life with a fresh, vibrant, youthful energy.

That's what I heard, anyway.

I stayed home. Yes, I had made myself a promise. When you're young, you make all kinds of promises – some you make out loud to other people, some you just make to yourself. But some of the most important promises are ones we never put words to, like the promise you make to your children the day they're born.

I had wanted to emulate the Stones and that night, in a small way, I did. I held each boy for a minute before putting him in the crib. But instead of the usual lullaby, I offered him this:

No, you can't always get what you want.

But if you try sometimes you'll find,

You get what you need.

∾

The Boss

Mounts the stage alone, minimal
Beams of white light swallowed
In a black cavern of black
Back drops, black clothes, a simple
Black guitar. Thousands of souls keep
A close watch as he strums:
A then E7 then A
On a late summer evening
In North Carolina.

A voice the texture of a brick
Sings another man's words.
My questions for God are lost,
Echoing in the stadium,
Lost in E7s and As. Thousands of
People with eyes wide open fail
To see the shadows for the dark,

Fail to see the mystics standing
In their midst. Better to sing with
Eyes closed and strum A then D then A
Where bound ends outweigh the limits.

More E7s as members of the
E Street Band join in this offering to
A silenced voice (E7 to A). Black
Clouds threaten the moon, as I
Try to walk the line, the ordained
Path which leads to the same silence.

THE DECEPTIVE CADENCE

"To be played with both hands in the pocket"

– Erik Satie
(direction on one of his piano pieces)

Two Singers

1. Pop Princess

Her sound man, soused one night, confessed
    her stage act's just a mime:
"She wants to give the fans her best.
    They get it every time."

2. Old Crooner

His plastic surgeons rightly beam with pride,
but two or three bars in
                        you'll wish he'd died.

Playing the Piano

Like a horse, it had been led in
beside long planks of sunlight.

When I was done with it,
years later, my stepfather
wanted the piano out of the house,
out of my room, the once-garage.

All the pedals stuck, three keys
stayed down when plunked,
and mildew had eaten the varnish
off one flank.

The fall opened by screwdriver.
The lid would not lift.

I was handed an ax to put the old
Campbell out of its misery.

First stroke took the front leg off;
body clamored to the cement floor.
My grip
raged at the nights of not learning "Nocturne."

I chopped away through screeching
rosewood and black and white keys.
An old secret, its harp lay sprung and forlorn.
I expected to find something occult coiled among

the wires and metal frame. I chopped
it into bell-shaped pieces
and carried music out one clang at a time.

I barely fitted them through the new door.
From the center of the wreckage, I hacked at a heart

that pumped out notes connected to light,
the way bad children dissect
cats in alleys expecting
the core of death to purr god.

Joyful Noise

Evie yanked the garden hose to the front of the house where her mother-in-law Betty Jo was on the porch keeping an eye on every move Evie made. "Did you water the tomatoes?" Betty Jo asked.

Evie nodded, turning the spray toward a bed of day lilies decorated with solar lights that were meant to look like flickering hummingbirds come dusk. Two gazing balls, one red and one blue, stood in the middle of the geranium and begonia beds, and across from them was a resin lighthouse, two feet tall, nearly the same height as the wooden windmill in the middle of the hostas. Betty Jo decorated for summer more than most people do for Christmas.

"Any of the tomatoes ripe?" Betty Jo rested her cast on her knee. She'd broken her right arm last week, and that's why Evie was in southeastern Kentucky rather than nine hours north with her husband Brad. He'd been born and bred in the county and, after twenty-five years, still regretted leaving it.

"A couple," Evie said. "I'll pick them in the morning."

Betty Jo nodded. "That's the right time of day."

Despite all the old jokes about mothers-in-law, Evie liked Betty Jo, maybe even loved her, although distance kept them from visiting often. When Brad's sister Diane had called to tell them about Betty Jo's fall, Evie had immediately wanted to send a card, flowers. But even though Diane lived no more than thirty minutes from her mother, had taken her to the hospital, and stayed with her for several days, Diane's grandchildren were coming this week, and, besides, she thought she'd done her share.

"Mom doesn't want me," Brad had said when it became obvious that someone had to go to Henley County to care for his mother. "She thinks she has to have a woman to do for her, and she asked for you."

Evie supposed she ought to feel flattered, but the challenge of running another woman's house in a part of the world she hardly knew was a daunting one. She remembered the first time Brad had brought her down to the county. His father, Dewey Gillespie, had chortled, "You got you a Yankee this time, didn't you, boy?"

"Beats that flirt-assed piece of trash he married the first time," Betty Jo had muttered. Evie figured that she'd started loving her mother-in-law from that very moment.

Of course Betty Jo didn't talk like that any more. When Dewey had died three years ago, she'd gotten religion and didn't hold with cussing any more, she said, even though just this afternoon Evie had hidden her smiles when Betty Jo caught herself, turning "damn" into "dang" and "ass" into "hind end."

Evie flopped into the chair by Betty Jo's swing. More decorations hung down from the roof of the porch: whirligigs, plastic light catchers, and wind chimes decorated with seashells. A puff of breeze came down from the wooded ridge across the road, setting into motion all of what Betty Jo called her play-pretties. The air felt good, Evie thought, as she let the tiredness seep out of her legs. One trouble with old people – and, at seventy, Betty Jo qualified – was that they didn't differentiate between twenty-five and forty-five. Younger was simply younger. Although she'd been polite and sweet-natured about it, Betty Jo insisted upon an immaculate house and had filled Evie's day with laundry and cooking and gardening. And the day wasn't over yet, Evie thought, sighing a little as the creak of the porch swing lulled her into sleepiness.

"And you don't mind going to choir practice with me this evening?" Betty Jo asked. Her left hand worked at the gnarled fingers peeping out from her cast. She'd commented that her arm itched like the dickens inside that plaster. "You're sure?" The woman had already asked this four times since lunch.

So for the fifth time, Evie reassured her. "I'm looking forward to it. I love singing in the choir at home." Which, she imagined, was a completely different proposition. First Presbyterian was a big, downtown church constructed of weathered stone with a bell tower and double wooden doors like something from an English tour book. Evie's choir was forty voices strong and led by a music professor from the university. In the winter, their organist sometimes wore a flowing black cape like the Phantom or Dracula, and once or twice a year played solos with the symphony. At Christmas their big production was usually Bach or Vivaldi or, of course, Handel.

"Do you reckon we should go on and eat?" Betty Jo asked. "We wouldn't want to be late."

Evie heaved herself out of her chair. "Sure. I'll get it ready."

She went in the bathroom to splash her face and wash her hands, forgetting yet again that the hot tap was on the right and the cold on the left, the opposite of any other faucet she'd ever used. Old Dewey had installed the plumbing, and like many of his projects, hadn't gotten it quite right. This morning when she'd searched for tomato stakes in the shed he'd built, Evie had noticed that the rafters didn't quite meet, the walls weren't quite square. But the faucet didn't leak and the shed had been standing much longer than the five years she'd been married to Brad. She remembered Dewey shrugging when somebody questioned his work. "It don't have to be pretty," he'd said. "It just has to work."

Evie wondered how Betty Jo, so orderly and neat, so delighted by figurines and ruffles, had tolerated Dewey's bone-deep sloppiness for nearly fifty years. But some couples seemed to ride out their differences. She and Brad had their different quirks, but somehow marrying in their forties after divorce on his part and widowhood on hers had made them more willing to wiggle a key in the lock until the door opened or to sand a board until it was smooth. She guessed it was all a matter of flexibility.

Sunlight poured through the sanctuary windows of Pisgah Baptist Church turning everything golden except for up in the front where there was a shadowy painting of Jesus standing beside the River Jordan. It was a peaceful picture, soothing for troubled souls, Evie supposed, and an appropriate backdrop for the baptismal tub or whatever Baptists called their dunking place. Presbyterians sprinkled.

Eight or nine people hovered around a piano, all calling out greetings to Betty Jo as she walked down the aisle. With the exception of a tall man with a guitar who was introduced as Kenny, Evie was the youngest person in the room, and she was forty-seven. Betty Jo, as neat and fixed up as her house, was more than willing to repeat the tale of her fall and trip to the emergency room even though she talked to most of the women on the telephone every day. She introduced Evie who smiled back at the worn, wrinkled faces and asked, "Do you all sit in sections?"

"What do you mean, honey?" This was from a heavy, grandmotherly woman.

"You know: alto, soprano." Evie's voice trailed off.

"Nah. We sit anywhere we want," said one of the men.

"What do you sing?" asked June, an elderly woman with a deep booming voice and hair as red as Reba's. Even after all that time up north, Brad still liked country music, and Evie had picked up a little just like she'd learned to make what her husband called "passable" cornbread, with buttermilk and no sugar.

"Alto."

"Me too. Sit by me," said June. It wasn't like Evie would've ever taken June for a soprano. Her voice sounded like she'd inhaled way too many Marlboros.

After they all settled, Evie understood why sections didn't matter. Accompanied by the man with the guitar on "What a Friend We Have in Jesus," the choir sang only melody. From listening to June, Evie figured out that singing alto meant doing the melody down an octave. Well, she could do that.

They mostly sang songs from xeroxed sheets of words, many of which Evie didn't know. Kenny complimented the choir, saying they were sounding real pretty, but Evie didn't hear much of anything she'd call pretty. Out of tune, with no harmony or musicality to it, the singing was dreadful, and she was fairly

116

sure one of the sopranos was tone deaf. Evie'd been expecting country singing, but good country singing, like the Carter Family. Brad was always bragging about them.

When Evie sat silent on one of the songs, June asked, "Why aren't you singing?"

"I don't know this one."

"Don't you go to church?"

They were all listening, craning their wrinkled necks to hear what Evie'd say.

"Yes, but I'm Presbyterian."

This got a collective murmur. "Oh. Well, I reckon the Lord'll forgive you," June said, croaking like a bullfrog. A smile tugged at the creases around her mouth.

When they switched to the hymnal, a tiny wisp of a woman played the piano, surprising Evie with the strength and verve coming from her arthritic fingers and bird-leg wrists. Here Evie had something to work with, singing the written alto parts on "Just As I Am" and "Softly and Tenderly." She didn't know the songs well but had some dim recollection of her grandmother singing them as she washed dishes in a dented aluminum pan.

June noticed. "We got one singing harmony over here."

Again, all their eyes rose and focused on Evie. "Should I not? I can quit," she faltered.

"It's okay. We just don't hear it much," June said.

Betty Jo reached across her cast and patted Evie. "You're doing fine."

Then they chose their "special" for Sunday and discussed what three songs they'd sing on Tuesday when they went around the county singing for shut-ins. Evie tried to imagine her choir at First Presbyterian doing something like that. One of the men, Howard, insisted on a song the guitar player didn't know. "That don't mean we can't sing it," Howard declared. "We'll just do it *a, a*. . . ."

"Acapulco," Evie said without even thinking. It was an old joke in her choir.

They all laughed like she'd thought it up, although she could tell it was an old joke for most of them too. The choir vetoed Howard's choice, and he sulked, making everybody uncomfortable until the tiny woman said in an equally tiny voice, "I do believe Evie's going to fit right in."

Betty Jo preened.

During prayer time, more foreign territory for Evie, the choir members held hands, the grandmotherly woman squeezing Evie's until her rings pinched, and, as they called it, lifted up their concerns and joys. Howard prayed that

117

they'd bring healing and save souls on Tuesday, and Kenny added that, if not redemption, the choir would at least bring the joy of Jesus to those who heard them. And as the circle broke up, at least four of the choir members asked Evie if she'd be joining them Tuesday evening. Betty Jo never missed it, so Evie said she would. "Besides," Betty Jo said as they were leaving the church, "The choir always goes for ice cream afterwards."

So, on Tuesday, the choir piled into a car, a van, and a pick-up and drove narrow, winding roads to the top of a hill where they crowded into a double-wide with a sleepy mongrel laying by a hydrangea, or snowball bush, as Betty Jo called it. Evie wondered if the hound would howl when they sang. As the choir gathered around a pale woman recovering from surgery, Betty Jo whispered to Evie, "A female operation." The singing was no better than it'd been at practice, but the woman smiled as they went through their repertoire and pleased Howard when she agreed to a prayer.

Evie caught on to the routine. After three songs, Kenny asked the shut-in whether he or she would like to hear another song or pray with the choir. "What if they ask for a song we don't know?" Evie asked Betty Jo as they passed the hound out front. He hadn't moved.

"I reckon we'd substitute something else," the woman said. "Sometimes they do pray with us, but I don't remember nobody ever asking for another song. Strange, isn't it?"

At the second house, a tidy, brick box situated in the heart of the county seat, an old man sat in his recliner watching Andy Griffith re-runs while they sang. Nobody bothered to turn down the volume. The only person paying much attention to the choir was the chubby toddler who'd answered the door, sucking on a red popsicle. He never took his eyes off Kenny's guitar. Evie heard someone in the kitchen clattering pans and running water, but no one came out. Distracted by the loud television, they sang particularly badly there, but nobody seemed to care. The old man never flickered an eyelid and paid no attention to Kenny's offers of another song or prayer. "Stroke," Betty Jo murmured as they got back into the van. "So sad. He used to teach Sunday School for us."

Their final stop was at a white frame house similar to Betty Jo's but without all the gewgaws. The choir crammed into a small living room and circled the oldest woman Evie had ever seen. "She's a hundred and one," June croaked in what she probably thought was a whisper. "And never says a word. Alzheimer's, I reckon."

The old woman's sparse hair was scraped back into a bun and she had an afghan over her lap even though the room was stifling. She looked as though she ought to be wearing a bonnet and apron, like those dried-apple dolls Evie had seen at the Mountain Crafts Store. Her eyes were lowered, focusing on her knitted up hands. A middle-aged woman, evidently a member of Pisgah Baptist Church by the way everyone greeted her, sat on the sofa. The choir sang the same three songs with the same mistakes, June bellowing and one of the men singing about a half-step flat most of the time. When Kenny asked if there was a special hymn the old woman would like to hear, nobody expected a response.

Kenny repeated his words, and the middle-aged woman got up to hover over Granny and holler, "Do you want them to sing something special for you, Mamaw?"

Evie figured it was time for the Dairy Dip, but suddenly the old woman's eyes lit up. "Rudolph," she croaked, her voice as cracked as old glass. "Lord yes, Gene Autry. Rudolph."

Howard muttered, "We don't know that."

A soprano hissed, "It's not even Christian."

And June boomed, "Maybe she thinks we're Christmas caroling."

Granny kept nodding and mumbling, "Rudolph. Gene Autry. Lord yes."

Holding up his hands, Kenny said, "I don't know it. Don't know the chords."

"Come on," Evie said. "We'll improvise. You'll remember it." She smiled at the choir and raised a hand to start them. "We'll do it Acapulco." And with an encouraging grin, she started singing, "Rudolph the red-nosed reindeer, had a very shiny nose."

Most of them had forgotten the song, if they'd ever known it, but Evie pressed on. She was no soloist, more of a utility alto at best, but she could sing loud if she needed to. Granny didn't seem to care whether they were in tune. She tapped her old fingers against the arm of the rocking chair and finally broke out in a big grin that showed startlingly white dentures. At the end she clapped her hands together and cackled, "Gene Autry, Hi Ho Silver, and away!"

When they exited the house, most of the Pisgah Baptist Church choir members were shaking their heads and murmuring. Kenny slung his guitar case into the van.

"There wasn't a thing spiritual about that," Howard complained.

"Poor old thing," the tiny woman said. "I wonder if she's a Christian."

As they moved to their vehicles, Evie took hold of Betty Jo's right arm, just above the cast, and felt it shaking. Alarmed, she looked at her mother-in-law's face and was relieved to see that the trembling was from laughter. Between giggles, Betty Jo whispered, "Damn," and fumbled in the pocket of her lilac slacks for a tissue. She wiped at her eyes and took a deep breath before saying, "Well, I reckon we brought her joy, Howard."

The old man sniffed.

Kenny raised his chin. "It wasn't one bit pretty."

At this Betty Jo burst out in great guffaws, infecting Evie until both of them were leaning against the car, trying to catch enough breath to speak. When their giggles died down, Evie caught Betty Jo's eye and said, "You know, it don't have to be pretty. It's just got to work. Ice cream?"

∞

The Part Where the Guitar Begins to Bleed

Stop searching forever. Happiness is just
next to you, the fortune cookie gloats, as if

cartons of Buddhist Delight, infinitely meatless,
could know me so well. Spring rain rushes

all sins down marked storm drains, stenciled
fish imploring: *please, no poison*. I will try.

I will fail. I will fall, skidding palms rough
on the slick black street. Gravel-torn skin,

I'm knocked out of my shoes, sabbatical from
grace, a dank river smell: around me, on me,

every primordial remnant soaking my jeans.
What if we climbed from the swamps and

this is all we did with Eden? Stumbling crazy
into holly trees, tangled spiny leaves, faces

scratched faint, hungover from impossible
last loves: true, I stole this story. Are we fallen

brothers, cut from one alphabet? Forgive me.
Forget fortune. This is my song and yours.

I Dreamed of Patty Loveless

Driving home from far away,
I pull into the lot of a new building,
Just missing fresh stripes.
This restaurant is not open, but I enter.
White-uniformed workers prepare fixtures;
Through openings between the counter and the kitchen,
I see Patty Loveless, directing workers surrounding her.

Why am I here? She never asks,
But instead dishes up a meal
She has prepared, perfecting
Recipes because,
I come to understand,
This is her restaurant
And pride requires her food be good:
Ah, catfish delicately fried
With a batter light as mama's best biscuits,
Hand-cut French fries,
Crunchy outside and flaky inside,
Hush puppies of irregular ovoid,
Obviously spoon dipped
And deep fried to gold
Surrounding yellow aureole
That bobbed above hot oil,
Coleslaw, shredded, creamy,
With a spicy bite,
And fresh-brewed sweet iced tea.
Eating here is like saying grace and meaning it.

I want to tell her
That in a market crowded with Faith's,
Shania's, and backslid pop Dolly's,
She and a few others commune
With Kitty, Tammy, and Loretta.
I tell her, "*Mountain Soul*

Keeps every promise you made
In 'If My Heart Had Windows.'"
She smiles, and I shake her hand.

I lie next to my wife, who dreams of Sean Connery
In trim tuxedo and a head full of hair,
Burring her name like innuendo.

∞

Women's Voices

My husband and I are closing in on forty years of marriage, a milestone our children and many of our contemporaries find amazing.

"What's your secret?" they ask as though we were one hundred years old and had happened upon a patent-worthy tonic.

I wish I had something wise to pass on to them, but the truth of the matter is so mundane it's downright embarrassing. My husband hasn't heard a word I've said in the past thirty-five years. About the time the honeymoon glow began to fade, his hearing went south, and the rest, as they say, is history. It's hard to argue with a person who can't hear you.

When I go on a nagging jag, he sits there and smiles fondly at me as though I'm discussing, say, the weather or the remarkable qualities of our grandchildren. When I pause in my rant, he asks sweetly, "Would you like another cup of coffee?" and passes the front section of the morning paper to me. Lately, I've taken to making my "here's how you could improve" and "honey-do" speeches via email, but I can't muster the same energy electronically as I do face to face.

For the longest time, he's insisted it's only my voice he can't hear, and I admit I do speak in soft tones. Allergies, vocal nodules, and what-you-may have taken a toll on my volume control. And I have to admit, too, that he does seem to hear his friends pretty well. Still, this seemed like a cop-out to me.

Lo and behold, he now has science on his side. With a triumphant look, he waved a newspaper article under my face the other day and said, "See, I told you." It seems that a university study conducted in Great Britain confirms that men do not hear women's voices in the same way, or even in the same area of the brain, as they do men's voices. In fact, when a woman first begins speaking they don't hear speech at all but instead (are you ready for this?) they hear music.

But since it's not music, the poor male brain gets confused. He has to convert to a different computer software package in his head to figure out that his wife is not Patsy Cline singing the blues in her terrycloth bathrobe. Instead, she's lip-syncing a ditty that sounds vaguely like "Don't forget to pick the kids up after soccer practice, o-o-o, because I'm taking your mother to the doctor-o and can't do-wapity-do-it."

According to this study, men were not biologically hard-wired to hear women's voices. (So much for Adam blaming Eve for talking him into eating that apple in the Garden of Eden.) Men process other male voices quite easily in a large (the study uses the word "simple") section of the brain near the back of the head. In fact, since that "simple" section of the brain recognizes the other man's voice as being like his own, the man first thinks he's hearing his own voice when another man speaks. Maybe this explains how men can sit for hours watching football games grunting the same phrases back and forth at each other without having a real conversation. It's hard to talk to yourself.

Women's voices, however, must be processed in the section of the male brain that decodes music. This is not because of the softer pitch of the female voice, but because of her "more complex range of sound frequencies." The number of sound waves and the vibration of the female voice are much more intricate than a man's due to the gender differences in the size and shape of the larynx and vocal cords.

"So see, honey," my husband said, "your voice really is music to my ears."

I wonder if I'm too old to get a gig on *American Idol*?

∞

Molluscicide

Caruso, the spaniel, howled
in the tenement above
when Pearl, a mezzo,

hit high C
after taxiing up and down
both major and minor scales.

The potted delphinium
rattled petite mal,
a jack hammer duet

of quake and canary
that ceased when a broom handle
beat the floor into submission.

Pearl's gig was up, the curtain fell,
and Caruso slept at his master's feet.
The world was his oyster.

JOHN SIMONDS

Selling the Song

Ojai, California 2000

In the Ojai darkness
we sit with others of more faith
and watch Sir Simon Rattle
lead string-scrape and reed-drone,
bows screeching across
the melody nerve
of stifled brass,
beneath the trees
on numbered benches,
sitting as notes on a score,
listening as though some
hidden blend of noise
had fused a secret sound
to make us feel the millions
spent to sponsor yet another music fest
were worth applause
allied to foreign cars
to show the customers
their rare tastes matter.
White-jacketed cellists
and busy violins,
quiet turning of the pages,
moving to the moment
when the drum sounds
or the cowbell tells all.
A composition strides
to screed a tune
in the dark festival
of orchestral precision,
wild hair and arms askew,
groping for a sound
we might hum
through a night
in which other music
has mined all the good veins,

leaving us with a wish for a song,
that is almost a prayer,
to spread light from the stage
into the crowded dark of trust.

∾

Beautiful Dreamer

Sometime that morning before school, after dressing in the aqua pleated skirt, matching tights, Peter Pan collar blouse, and aqua vest with the appliquéd horse on it (comprising my best third grade outfit), I must have stolen the sheet music from the piano stool. Perhaps Mother was gathering up her pocketbook and car-coat, or cleaning up after a French toast breakfast she somehow managed to stir up while getting two girls ready for school and herself ready to teach.

In my plaid book-satchel with the leather straps, I had secreted it away—the piano score to *Beautiful Dreamer*. My plan was simple. Ask Miss Janet, the music teacher at school, to play it on the piano in the cafeteria, after everyone finished lunch and went back to their rooms.

If only she had not agreed. Had not played it through patiently, without criticism, adulation, or the slightest showing on her face of what she thought when I sang it, the solo that was to be my first step to stardom.

Beautiful dreamer, queen of my song, list while I woo THEEEEEEE with sweet melody! I wanted to *woo* Miss Janet, *lull* her into a complete state of love for my great undiscovered talent. I was coming out, and Miss Janet was the person I chose to witness my song.

She didn't question me when I handed her the piece. She took it and played it in her quiet way, no showiness, never looking over at me. As I stood there by the piano, singing the words I'd memorized, I wasn't so sure how things were going, since Miss Janet wasn't letting on, wasn't changing characters suddenly as I'd hoped, stopping the music to yell, "Hey, kid! Why didn't you TELL us we had a Shirley Temple on our hands! Who'd-a-thought right here in Burkesville! Boy, wait till America hears THIS!" Miss Janet was not taking on the persona of a talent scout character from a 1940's musical, and I was not turning into Shirley Temple.

Miss Janet simply began to slow down rather significantly at the end of the first verse, and there was no intro into the second. There was just that ritard, that ending so sudden and terse to me, no matter that she played it, I'm sure, as appropriately and generously as could be done.

And I'd sung as well as any third grader schooled in the Baptist children's choir might sing, sliding comparably well to the high notes, voicing the antiquated and romantic words so out of context from my world at the time.

But the *starlight* had dimmed considerably, and the *dewdrops* had not

129

glistened so as anyone would notice.

Not too long before that, we had moved from the little white rental house with the uneven floors to a brick ranch-house on the main street in town. Perhaps this upward mobility was what gave me the hope that I might make it big, might move from the shows we held standing on the picnic table, twirling open umbrellas flirtatiously toward imaginary audiences.

Our parents were not show people. They were teachers. Mother had worked in her college drama department some, and Dad was known as a fine speaker at civic functions, but they weren't people who thought at all of seeing their names in lights—not like my sister and I did, having been won over by Annette Funicello, the Lennon Sisters, Bobby Darin, Connie Francis, and my favorite, Little Miss Shirley Temple.

Their emphasis was right, I know now. The big Revised Standard Bible was what had the special place on the pretty table in front of the picture window at the new brick ranch-house. George Beverly Shea records were much preferred to the ones my sister and I might buy at the record store downtown with our allowance—her "All Shook Up" and my "El Paso." Mother and Dad agreed on "Ave Maria," "How Great Thou Art," "My God and I" and "On the Wings of a Dove," though their tastes ran differently. Dad's preferences were more hillbilly, Mother's more spiritual and refined.

Besides the piano Miss Janet played in the school cafeteria, there was the one at Burkesville Baptist, which Miss Janet also played, and the one in the neighbor's basement up the street. I had tried these out and not been impressed or inspired. But at some point I began to believe that when they delivered our new, our very own piano, which was shortly after we moved to the brick ranch-house, there might be a great miracle involving music.

When it took its honored place at the end of the long, narrow living room with the perfectly level hardwood floor, opposite the end with the TV, I was beside myself with anticipation that when I sat down at the new piano there would be no effort, no thought to this. The piano would magically respond to me, and all the music in my childhood soul would flow forth, in beauty and splendor, and the public would hear me and be flabbergasted at how unbelievably talented I was.

What actually happened was that the piano was very difficult to play, and was not usually enjoyable at all. The beginning books with songs about birthdays, wooden shoes, and little Indians, even with the simplest rhythms and melodies, proved much too challenging. My teacher (Miss Janet) listened, pointed out problem areas, penciled dates on the pages, and made me repeat the awful pieces time after time. The daily half-hour practice sessions seemed to last forever, making dusting or dishwashing chores a welcome relief after twenty-eight minutes. That piano allowed only the most boring and laborious tunes, and there was no magic in it.

Dad didn't play the piano, except once a year to take his index finger down the scale, laugh, and claim that he was playing "Joy to the World." Mother knew a few chords, and would sometimes play a fairly complex and flowery version of "We Are Climbing Jacob's Ladder." But by virtue of her other talents, which were quite real, well applied, and not based on such fantasies or vanities as mine, she was often called on to direct the senior play or help with the local talent show.

Burkesville was home to Druscilla Cooksey, who looked and sang just like Loretta Lynn. It was worth sitting through tone-deaf twins swaying and singing "In Them Ole Cotton Fields Back Home" or big, rough boys stumbling through dramatic monologues to get to hear Druscilla Cooksey at the end. Thanks to Druscilla Cooksey, we had quite a few talent shows until she got married and moved to Marrowbone.

One involved a number that called for someone to be a ballerina, if only for a minute or two. I know full well now, having been told fairly often by the most generous and gentle of family and friends, and from the falls and bruises, nearsightedness, and odd shape that's mine, that I am awkward and uncoordinated. I have no ballerina in me. And I know now that Mother probably did the casting. What I did that night was wear one of her perfectly sewn creations that made me look the part, stand perhaps a few seconds up on the toes of my large, flat feet, and as gracefully as a tomboyish third grader could, walk from one part of the stage to another, pointing my long arms here and there in time with the music. But what a remarkable success! One lady, I remember, thought surely I must've had dance lessons! I assured her I had not, thinking to myself, "I don't need lessons. I just have tremendous talent. These things come naturally to me."

I have not come so far, and am as yet deservedly undiscovered. I write this in a small town a few miles from Burkesville. As a hobby, I play second fiddle, literally, at another First Baptist Church, with no Miss Janet to hear me, keep a straight face, fold the music up, and hand it back. Just a retired band director stomping his foot and banging his conducting baton on the music stand to drum the beat to us. I have no plaid book-satchel, but a burlap tote bag my niece got me in Nashville, with "Music City USA" on the front, from which I can pull out any number of pieces.

My imaginary audience is not as often summoned anymore, but when it is, with its imaginary thunder of applause, *sounds of the rude world heard in the day, lulled by the moonlight, are all passed away.*

∞

Morning Jazz

After a long winter,
they sit in Adirondack chairs.
She tells him
she needs to hear the saxophone
now, in the morning—
Coltrane or Parker.

Its voice belongs out here
on the deck with coffee and scones,
out here where crocuses
push through moist soil.

Yet she knows the minute
its clear tones resonate,
she will be back in some smoky bar,
the taste of gin on her tongue,
a strange man's fingers tracing
a path between her open
silk shirt and her lips.

She pushes up against him,
up against the clear notes,
their feet moving over the tiles
of the grimy dance floor,
over the rough boards of the porch.

The notes ebb and flow, the morning
sways, the sun does a sidestep,
the crocus petals lean
toward the sound.

∞

Rhonda Hears Dolly Parton Sing "The Silver Dagger"

Flying with knives, Dolly,
are you going to kill me?
You do it well,
floating high next to yourself
in thin air
and landing just right
with those daggers,
those very sweet blades.

Times, Dolly,
when air presses in
I am brought to live under water.
I listen to you,
my heart breaks back into life
and I too can take off,
body or no body.

Meds

1. *Perphenazine*

no more layers of loud disc jockeys
broadcasting nothing intelligible

but the music, O Music!
still plays over the air

conditioner, a perpetual encore
faint as vapor.

2. *Fluoxetine*

without it, she lived in a cocoon
of cotton where every move

was premeditated—
to roll over in bed,

to open her swollen eyes,
to push away the light

gauzy sheet, the thin blanket,
to pause to hear the music,

to stand up, shower
to linger in the shower,

even the brief effort
to smile in the mirror.

3. *Trazadone*

chords cast themselves around her
the way clouds drag vast shadows

down the Tomoka River.
She makes herself ready for this—

wades into the cool shallows of sheets
so that tomorrow, on the opposite bank

she'll wake curled up like a treble clef
under a swamp tupelo, not sad exactly

but wishing she could have been
awake to experience it—

to be part of the river
without having to go under.

∾

NOTES

"And when the wind blows high and clear
A line or two pray send to me
That I may know by your own handwrite
How times has went with thee."

– *"My Dearest Dear"*
(folk song)

From The Jim Reeves Museum with Love

(Author's note: The Jim Reeves Museum at Evergreen Place operated from the early 1980s until 1995. The property and all of its contents were sold to a carnival owner who later filed bankruptcy. Evergreen Place was allowed to slip into ruin and, in spite of the best efforts of local historic conservation groups, was demolished in 2005 to make way for a Home Depot.)

June 28, 1985
Nashville, TN

Hey there Denton,

Hello from Music City USA! How's my favorite brother? Well, I'm happy to report I finally have some good news to tell. I got a job! It isn't exactly the show business gig of my dreams but the hourly wage is pretty good and it is not just an ordinary job like being a bank teller like I was back home. I am working as an official tour guide at the Jim Reeves Museum!

You're probably thinking "Jim who and why does he have a museum?" Well, I didn't really know much about him either before I got the job but I'm going to be an expert soon. Just so you know, he was a famous country singer from a long time back who died really tragic, then his wife opened up this museum for him and now they are paying me to tell people all about him and his life.

You might remember from my last letter that I had been answering just about every classified ad in *The Tennessean* for weeks without a bit of luck. I'll tell you, I was pretty desperate by the time I got to this place. I work five days a week but have Mondays and Tuesdays off so I still have a chance to look around for something better.

The museum is up on Gallatin Road not all that far from Opryland Amusement Park. It is in an old house that is really beautiful with a big wooded yard, white clapboard siding and green shutters. It looks like an old plantation house to me. Lots of folks come down here and look around after they're done riding the roller coasters over at Opryland.

The lady who owns the Museum is Mary Reeves Davis, Jim's widow. I met her the other day when she came by to check on the gift shop and she was real friendly. She's remarried to a man named Terry Davis, and he is some sort of preacher, I think. The manager is a guy named Buddy. He's kind of cranky but I'm starting to think it is just a show he puts on to keep the staff in line.

The first thing Buddy handed me after he hired me was a script for the tour. I had to memorize this whole long thing that must be at least ten pages. I spent my first week working in the gift shop with these two older ladies, Juanita and Doris. They are really nice and showed me how to work the cash register and fill out the daily money report and sell the tour tickets.

Doris is the main tour guide and she had me follow her on her rounds for a few days so I could watch and learn the right way to conduct the tours. I was so nervous when she made me do one all by myself. I was sure I was going to forget everything. In between tours when the house is empty I just walk around by myself trying to figure out where things are that I'm supposed to be talking about. It is a lot to remember.

The funny part about this being the Jim Reeves Museum is that Jim Reeves never even lived in this house. We have a whole big speech we give at the first of the tour telling about how the Rev. Thomas Craighead, a Presbyterian minister who was president of one of the first schools in the county, built a log home here in 1785. The school he started turned into the Peabody College and then was made part of Vanderbilt University later on. He's buried at the Spring Hill Cemetery that is right across the highway from the house.

Over the years all the other owners built onto the house to where it looks the way it does now. The story goes that Jim and Mary used to drive by and say to each other "oh, what a pretty house" but Mary only bought it after Jim died and put all his stuff in it and opened the museum years after. Like I said, it is a really pretty house from the outside but they have it crammed full of so much stuff that it's hard to tell when you get inside.

They have one room full of radio memorabilia because Jim Reeves started out his career as a disc jockey in Texas and then in Louisiana. He got his big break as a singer when some other act didn't show up for the Louisiana Hayride radio show. Some folks say it was Hank Williams that Jim filled in for that night.

Anyway, he got a record deal right after that and had a bunch of hit records. Poor guy died in a plane crash only a few years later in 1964. Can you believe anyone would still be coming around to look at a house full of furniture and other junk after you'd been dead for over twenty years? I have a terrible time remembering all the radio station call letters in the radio room and the only two song titles I can ever remember are "He'll Have to Go" and "Distant Drums."

Another room is set up like a living room with a couch, a chair, a coffee table and an old fashioned TV set. All the pieces in there look like they came

140

out of Roy Rogers' house, cowboy looking stuff made up around wagon wheels. Even the lamps on the side tables have little wagon wheels. I sure wouldn't want it in my house, although since I don't have a couch in my place yet, I suppose I would take it after all, wouldn't I?

There's some crazy stuff in the museum. One room is set up with Jim and Mary's bedroom furniture. There's a big wardrobe in there with a few clothes hanging up in it. It's really embarrassing because they have one of Mary's lacey, pink nightgowns in there and you have to point it out to the tour people. But that isn't even the strangest thing. There's a big photo of Jim with his dog up on the wall over the bed and part of the script is to tell everyone that Jim's buried in Carthage, TX, his hometown, and that his dog is buried only ten paces away from him. That's kind of nutty, don't you think?

Another weird room is the one they call the Plane Room that isn't a room at all. It is just a wide hallway between this real big room with a high ceiling that was probably the dining room and what I'm guessing was the kitchen of the original homestead since it has a brick floor and a big old fireplace. Anyway, there's a glass case built into one wall of this hallway. It's probably about four or five feet long and three feet tall and about a foot and a half deep. The back wall is covered with that photo wallpaper like Aunt Sally has in her Florida room. You know what I'm talking about? That long wall opposite the front door that looks like a beach scene with palm trees and a sunset? The wallpaper at the museum is just of some woods like up behind the house at home. They have this little plastic model airplane hanging from some fishing line off the ceiling of the case and a leather wallet with some money laying on the floor of the case and that's it. When you're giving the tour you tell the guests this tale:

"Before you is a scene much like the landscape where Jim Reeves' plane crashed near Nashville on July 31, 1964. He was a pilot and was flying the plane himself when he ran into bad weather. He and his keyboard player and good friend, Dean Manuel, were killed. When the plane was discovered, the searchers found Jim's wallet containing three ten dollar bills which are displayed here in the case." Is that kind of creepy or is it just me?

I tell you what else is creepy is they have this duet song they play over the stereo in the house and gift shop all the time and it is of Jim Reeves singing with Patsy Cline. They play Jim Reeves records all day long there. Anyway, the both of them died in plane crashes which is bad enough but the way they did these records is that they took Jim's record and then Patsy's record of this same song and they cut them together and made one record after they were both dead. That just seems gross to put two dead people on a record together so long after they were dead. What if they didn't like each other at all and now they

141

have to spend eternity spliced together at the Jim Reeves Museum? I'd hate that if anyone decided to do things like that with my stuff after I was dead, but I guess since I can't sing a lick, I won't be worrying about that, will I?

The last room is called the Jewel Room and near as I can tell has nothing at all to do with Jim Reeves or his music. It is full of statues, glass cases of jewelry, an ivory and gold chess set and some other odds and ends. No one seems to know where all this stuff came from so we just say, "Here is the Jewel Room" and let them look around for a few minutes before we herd them like cattle out a back door and into the gift shop.

The gift shop is full of souvenir photos, mugs, magnets with either Music City USA or Jim Reeves printed on them and hundreds of Jim Reeves albums and 8-track tapes. The rest of the shop if filled with what looks to me like stuff Mary must have picked up at yard sales. For some reason, folks going through the museum seem to think Jim and Mary owned and used these cracked dishes and rusty buckets and other junk so they buy the junk right along with the coffee mugs and records.

Before I finish up, I have to tell you about this character that hangs around the museum. His name is Jimmy Angel and he is an Elvis impersonator that Mary Reeves Davis has taken in and let stay there as some sort of overnight security guard. He doesn't really do much guarding, though. He mostly spends the night sleeping on top of one of the desks in the office. Poor guy is completely bald so he wears an Elvis-style wig that is really old and ratty looking. He touches it up with black shoe polish. The lady that does the housekeeping is always fussing at him about getting black mess everywhere. He even wears a polyester jumpsuit all the time. I should get a picture of him to send. You can't even hardly imagine what a sight he is.

Well, I guess I better close out for now. I'm going out tonight to see some music so I need to go get cleaned up. My next door neighbors, Janet and Chris, are songwriters and they are taking me down to the Bluebird Cafe to watch some of their friends do a show. Lots of record company and publishing big shots hang out there so maybe I'll meet someone famous or find a way to get a really good job at a big company. I just know in my heart that things are going to turn out great and everyone back home who thought I was crazy to come to Nashville will find out they were wrong. I'm going to be the first woman to run her own record company and then you all can come down here and live with me in my big house and I'll get each of you a Cadillac all your own to drive up and down Music Row. Think you'd like that?

Anyway, before I forget again, thanks as always for being there for me and cheering me on. I can't tell you how much I appreciate you loaning me that money to get my apartment. Now that I've got work, I can start sending you some back a little at a time and will get you paid back in full as soon as I can. Please give Momma a big hug from me and tell her I'm doing great and will write her shortly.

Maybe soon I can get me a phone hooked up so I can call. I sure do miss the sound of everyone's voice.

For now I'll just send you all my love and hugs and kisses from the world famous Jim Reeves Museum!

Yours for true,
Sissy

∾

God's Key
for Sue

For wherever two or more are gathered in my name, there am I in the midst of them.
—*Matthew 18:2*

She picks that banjo like a woman
reading Braille. Listen to the ancient
tones, those clucks and pops. She pats her foot
to the beat of stories waiting there
in her fingers. *Belonged to my great-
grandfather.* She pauses, spreads one big
hand out over the worn skin. *Bird's-eye
maple.* We are silenced by her goodness.

She is an Appalachian from the
Middle West, a child of the plains who
had the mountains in her memory.
I miss Kansas sometimes. Her voice
is like a cool rain. *I miss the sky.*
And I think she pictures
that big blueness, those bruised clouds
swelling, the plum horizon of dusk,
stretched out like time. *I once saw seven
thunderstorms, all in one day.*

She tells us how she lost use of her
pointing finger. *A rabid cat.*
That simple. She studies her own hand.
*But it's better to play with your
middle one anyway.* She holds
out her ruined finger, beautiful
in its inflexibility,
lovely in its inability.

Then she is launching into another
song and we are all taken away
from this place, away from the war and

144

the badness we know lives in this world.
And all at once we are floating
right here, right now, in this holy place.
We are a family now, a people
joined by music, by words. *This one
is in D*, she says as she picks the
opening lines so we can join in
if we want. *This is in God's key.*

I believe God made the world for nights
like these, when we are safe with our kin,
with people who have mountain blood
in their veins, with banjo players who
speak poetry each and every
time they put their fingers to the strings.

∾

Jewel Case

Which holds no jewelry but the disc
itself, silvery side down and label
in boldface up. All the literature
of creation: candid photos of the artist
and session players, original lyrics,
copyright infringement warning,
credits and dates. Plastic rainbow
circle inside clear squares of covers,
an open book on breakable hinges.
Thumb and index finger pry the disc
by the edge from its touch-lock hub
and place it on the laser carousel.
Press Play. In the given of song,
I listen for the diamonds ringing.

Cante Rosado

Hand-clap and castanet call
above the clink of toasts
in the cantina,
and Rosa,
café-skinned,
slowly spins in place,
a gyrating flower,
girasol,
her golden arms stretching
for that sun she left
in Sevilla.
She fans her hands,
palmas opened;
palmas closed;
they flutter
from hip
to lips
to that hanging lantern
flickering
above her head.
Her hair,
a saffron glow, wisps
the air. She sandals
the dust. It's skirting up
ruffled – flamenco swirls
at her ankles.
¡Bravo! and *¡Vale!*
She corrals the stallion-men.
They clomp
their boot heels
but fail to break
the reins. Her sway
promises:
a suck of olive,
a sip of wine.

The Trumpet

Jimmy Tanner positioned his fingers on the ivory insets at the top of the trumpet's valve stems—a long stretch for a twelve-year-old.

His reflection in the curvature of the brass was distorted as in one of those trick mirrors at Coney Island. His face flattened horizontally into a thin line under a wide band of black curls and stretched vertically as he turned the instrument, his hair becoming a narrow pompadour, his cheeks hollowing above puckered lips, his chin dropping out of sight. Somewhere between these images was the real boy— small for his age, and thin, but muscular.

"How much is it?" he asked Charlie Belcher.

"Twenty-five dollars."

"It's got a dent in it."

"So take it to a body shop." Charlie's chubby fingers headed for the trumpet as if by retrieving it he might prevent the boy from discovering further blemishes, but Jimmy stepped back beyond reach of the pawnbroker.

"I'd like to play it," Jimmy said.

"Sure, kid. As soon as I see the money."

Jimmy placed the trumpet into its worn velvet-lined case, closed the lid and thumbed the latch.

"Can you hold it for me?"

"How long?"

"A week maybe?"

"I'll need a deposit."

"How much?"

"Fifty percent."

Jimmy reached into the pocket of his corduroy knickers and came up with a tattered five-dollar bill. "It's all I've got."

"That'll hold it for five days. Then it goes back into the window."

It was snowing when Jimmy stepped out into the December chill. His empty newspaper sack hung loosely over his shoulder. He fisted his hands into his jacket— twenty-seven cents in one pocket, a receipt for five dollars in the other.

When he first spotted the trumpet in Charlie's window, Jimmy was reminded of a photograph pasted inside the lid of his father's Victrola. It pictured Louis Armstrong cradling a trumpet and the words "Good luck, Ed

Tanner." It was signed "Satchmo." Below the photo a dog barked into a lily-shaped amplifier in response to "His Master's Voice."

Jimmy was five when his father wrapped his Plymouth coupe around a tree coming home drunk from an Armstrong concert. He left behind a crippled widow and a son.

Records that Ed Tanner collected were stored in the Victrola cabinet, some scratched so badly that the needle skipped across their grooves. Jimmy had cranked up the machine countless times, closed his eyes and pretended he was in his father's lap.

He sensed a connection between the wounded recordings and the trumpet. Perhaps the West End Blues were trapped within intricacies of ivory and brass waiting to be released.

Even with Christmas tips Jimmy couldn't afford the trumpet. He remembered a movie in which James Cagney etched a circle into a windowpane and without a sound removed the glass with a suction cup and stole a precious jewel.

He knew he couldn't do it. He'd already been caught down at Woolworth's, and for what? A lousy nickel's worth of LifeSavers. And there was the matter of Willard Fenster's bicycle. The rich little snot didn't deserve it, leaving it in the middle of the street like he did.

He could count on Phil's Barbershop for an extra two dollars, but others along his route, well there was no telling. It was a poor neighborhood.

But circumstances miraculously changed one morning when Carl Dodd from the *Herald Statesman* called, explaining that one of the boys was sick, and asked if Jimmy could take on an extra route.

When Jimmy arrived at the pick-up point, two other boys were blowing on their hands and passing a cigarette between them. The temperature had dropped and the roads were glazed with ice. They waited until Dodd's archaic station wagon chugged to the top of the hill. Even with chains it was doubtful it could have made it without the weight of the bundles. Carl rolled down the window and summoned Jimmy while the other two lowered the tailgate and dumped their papers onto the sidewalk.

"We're in a pinch here, Jimmy," Carl said, "I don't like to pull this on you but I'm sure you can handle it."

Jimmy knew what was coming.

"You understand I'll need ten percent. I hate to do it, but I've got the wife and kids to feed."

"Sure," said Jimmy. Ten percent of six dollars in the small yellow envelope each week was the price you paid. That was the system for you.

Carl raised the window and cranked up the heater while the boys stacked their papers against the wall under the awning of Flink's Pharmacy.

Jimmy could leave one of his bundles in the barbershop while he delivered the other but he'd have to double back to get it before five. It was already three-thirty.

For three weeks Jimmy got home after dark, feet frozen, shoulders aching from the pull of the strap. He went to bed exhausted, got up at five, and huddled over the kitchen table in his flannel robe, hands tucked under his armpits, oven door open to deliver what little heat it could as he agonized over homework.

The trumpet was Jimmy's Holy Grail and the quest for it kept him trudging up the hill. Fear that it might be sold drew him to the pawnshop window every morning on his way to school. He didn't trust Charlie.

Four days before Christmas, when school let out with a promise of sleep, he dumped his coins from the coffee can onto the kitchen table: quarters, dimes, nickels, pennies, carefully separated into piles, stacked neatly, and finally counted . . . twenty-eight dollars and twelve cents. That plus five dollars and forty cents in the yellow pay envelope totaled thirty-three dollars and fifty-two cents— enough for the trumpet and a breakfast tray for his mother that had side compartments for books and papers and a top that tilted so she could read in bed.

On Saturday morning the pawnshop was crowded. Charlie spindled Jimmy's receipt, rang up the twenty, and tucked it into the register. He took a key from a ring on his belt and unlocked the access panel to the window. *Real trusting*, Jimmy thought. *Spends his life within ten feet of the window and still has to lock it.*

Charlie laid the trumpet case on the countertop. "You're twelve short, kid."

"You said twenty-five dollars."

"It's gone up. You weren't back in five days. You're lucky somebody else didn't get it. I had an offer for thirty but I said I was holding it for you."

"You kept it in the window the whole time. I saw it there the day after you said you'd hold it."

"Look, kid, I didn't have no other place to put it. You want it or not? Take it or leave it. I got other customers to take care of." He turned to lock the window.

That was when Jimmy grabbed the trumpet, latching its case as he headed out the door.

"Stop, you goddam little hoodlum!" Charlie shouted as he scrambled from behind the counter. By the time he reached the door Jimmy was halfway down the block. Charlie could never catch him and, besides, he wasn't about to leave his place unattended.

Jimmy rounded the corner, shaking and out of breath.

Not ten minutes after he got home an officer knocked on the apartment door. "I'm Sergeant Harris. Is your father here?"

"I don't have a father. My mother is sick." Jimmy's stomach was churning and he was shaking again.

"We had a report about some trouble down at Belcher's pawnshop. I need to talk to Jimmy Tanner."

"That's me."

"Mr. Belcher didn't indicate that it was a . . . a young fella." Harris searched the boy's face. "I don't suppose you'd happen to know anything about a missing trumpet."

"I didn't rob anybody," Jimmy blurted, "I paid twenty-five dollars for it. That was the price he wanted, but then he changed it. So I . . . I guess I kinda ran out with it. He was trying to cheat me."

"Slow down, son. Now that wasn't the way to handle it. You shouldn't have run off like that. Mr. Belcher has filed a complaint and, right or wrong, we have to follow up on it."

"He'll keep the trumpet and my money too!"

"We'll hold the trumpet down at the station until this thing is settled. Don't worry, you'll get your money back."

"It's the trumpet I want."

"I'm sorry, son." He handed Jimmy a card. "You come on down to the Sixteenth Precinct tomorrow morning, and we'll see what we can do."

"You mean I'm not under arrest?"

"We're not in the habit of arresting kids. Besides, we know where to find you."

Judge Haywood was in his chambers when Donna, his clerk, ushered in Officer Harris.

"Looks like I caught you without your robe," said the sergeant. "Planning to go fishing?"

"Ice fishing maybe. Robe's hanging on the back of the door. I'm not about to model it for you. What's up, Jeff?"

"Well, Tom, we've got a problem and I'm hoping you can help us."

"What's this *we* stuff and who is *us*? Just because I did your homework for you back in eighth grade doesn't mean I'm going to fix your traffic tickets."

"Nothing like that. A local loan shark, Charlie Belcher, has filed a theft charge against a twelve-year-old kid."

"You know that's out of my jurisdiction. Our juvenile division handles small claims and petty theft."

"I know, but hear me out. Charlie promised to sell this kid a trumpet for twenty-five dollars. The boy gave him five-dollars to hold it and worked his little ass off for three weeks to pay the balance. When he went to pick it up Charlie hiked the price to thirty-seven bucks. The kid panicked and bolted with the trumpet. But he left the twenty dollars."

"Where are the boy's parents?"

"There's no father and his mother's an invalid. They barely squeak by on welfare and what little the kid scrapes up delivering papers, running errands, cutting lawns . . . whatever. He doesn't want his mom to know about this and I haven't told her. I know that's wrong, but there's more to the story, Tom."

"I'm listening."

"The kid has . . . well, not exactly a record, but there are some notes about him down at the precinct."

"What do you mean? I don't understand."

"Well, he's been in trouble a few times, nothing serious— shoplifting, he borrowed some kid's bicycle, broke a few windows, stuff like that. Thing is, Tom, nobody has pressed charges, but the Chief thought it might be a good idea to keep an eye on him.

"I still don't understand. Why haven't charges been filed?"

"When people find out his mother's an invalid and there's no dad, they feel sorry for him and drop the matter. He's had a lot of responsibility dumped on him and he's trying to handle it all by himself."

"That's exactly the kind of situation we have agencies for."

"But the thing is, Tom, the boy knows that if Child Services gets involved he'll wind up in a foster home.

"And what am I supposed to do?"

"Talk to him. His experience with cops hasn't been good but he'll look up to you. This kid's at a point where his life could go either way. He could really mess it up, and I'd hate to see that happen."

"Well, I'll talk to the boy, Jeff. And I'd like to talk to Mr. Belcher, too."

"I thought you might. He's outside with your clerk and not too happy about it."

"Send him in."

Charlie Belcher, exuding defiance, overflowed the heavy oak chair facing the judge's desk. "I want you to know, Judge, I got a business to run. Every minute I sit here I'm losing money."

152

"Well, I'm terribly sorry to inconvenience you, but I'm sure you can make up the loss by raising your prices. In fact it appears to be a habit of yours. I understand you told Jimmy Tanner he could have the trumpet for twenty-five dollars. Is that correct?"

"That was a month ago. Times change."

"And when he paid you that amount, you raised the price?"

"It's a free country. I can charge anything I want. The little bastard had no right to steal it."

"Well, let me tell you something, Mr. Belcher. Taking advantage of a child like that may not be outside the letter of the law, but from now on we'll be watching you, and if I see so much as a hint of unethical business practice we'll yank your permit and shut you down. Do you understand what I'm saying?"

"Lotsa luck. I run an honest business."

"Sure you do."

"Gimme my trumpet. I gotta go."

Judge Haywood stood up, drew a wallet from his pocket, and laid twelve dollars on the desk. "The trumpet is mine. Fully paid for. Now get the hell out of my chambers and take your small claims charge with you."

Charlie took the money and turned as he reached the door. "Thanks, sport. Good doing business with you."

It was the closest His Honor had ever come to hitting someone—a target that would be difficult to miss.

The same chair Charlie Belcher had occupied an hour earlier now swallowed Jimmy Tanner.

"What's your name, son?"

"James Tanner . . . sir, Your Honor, sir."

"And how old are you, James Tanner?"

"Twelve, sir."

"And you go to school, James?"

"Yes, sir. Seventh grade, sir."

"And Sunday school?"

"Yes, sir. Sometimes."

"Well, Mr. Tanner, what you did was wrong. You know that don't you, or you wouldn't have run the way you did?"

"Yes, sir."

"You've been in trouble before, son, and I understand you have a mother to worry about. You can't be of much help when you're in trouble. So I'm going to try to get you out of this mess, but I can't promise anything. I'm sure you're smart enough to figure out what will happen if you don't straighten yourself out, and you'd better do it before it's too late."

"Yes, sir."

"Are you a musician?"

"No, sir."

"Why did you want the trumpet?"

"I don't know, sir. I can't explain it. It's beautiful. I'd like to learn."

"Well, you go down to Precinct Headquarters and get the trumpet from Officer Harris. It's paid for."

Jimmy paused for a moment. "I've got twelve dollars, Sir. I wouldn't give it to Mr. Belcher, but I'll give it to you."

"Let's just consider it a loan. You can pay it back some day.

Tom Haywood wondered if he had done the right thing, just handing the trumpet over to the boy like that. Catherine always said he was too soft. He wondered if he was ever really cut out to be a judge. He was never comfortable with the trappings, never wore his robe in his chambers.

He leaned back in his chair, his hands behind his neck. The late afternoon sun streaming through the window from behind transformed his silver hair into a blazing halo. When Donna entered to say good night, his face was swallowed in shadow. When she closed the door he stared at the robe hanging from its hook. He thought not only about the Tanner boy, but all the others who came before him. They appeared one by one, projected against the back of the door and across his robe like a show that started before the curtain opened. He began to nod.

When he awoke, the room was dark. *It won't be long now, three more weeks.* His replacement had already been appointed. Judge Haywood saw little of himself in the eager youngster. Things had changed over the years. Too much politics, too many appeals and delays. Men outside that belonged inside, inside that belonged out. The system was rife with flaws.

Tom Haywood was not going to miss the bench.

Riverview was a vast estate that had fallen into bankruptcy. It was purchased by a conglomerate of doctors who converted it into a retirement facility for the well to do. Its manicured gardens stepped down to the Hudson. Judge Haywood's quarters had been one of the libraries. It boasted a fireplace and French doors that led to a small terrace with a view of the river, the Palisades and, on a clear day, the Catskills.

The judge detested television and spent much of his time listening to music on his radio or talking to himself and to Catherine who had passed away almost ten years ago. He was fully aware of her absence, but indulged in harmless fantasies. He sat on the terrace, the Sunday *Times* in his lap. Music drifted through the French doors— something called CBS Jazz Masterpieces. The host introduced a young musician, Jimmy Tanner.

Jimmy Tanner? —The name rang familiar.

The Judge prided himself on his ability to recall cases that had come before him, but where was Jimmy Tanner in the picture? The music moved into what they called Miles Davis modal jazz when he suddenly remembered.

It was not a case at all, but an incident. He tried to picture James Tanner as a grown man but could only conjure the image of a frightened child swallowed by a huge chair, an image now clear even though his only encounter with the boy had been for ten minutes. When was it, fifteen years ago? The Judge smiled. Two weeks later Donna had handed him that pitiful yellow envelope, wet and bursting at the seams. It contained a five-dollar bill and seven dollars in quarters, dimes and nickels. "The kid left this on my desk," she said.

2

Tender

Loving him is too much
cereal and milk
when what she wants is

platters of fried eggs and ham,
biscuits and gravy, fried apples
in big steaming bowls,

sudden storms of sliced
potatoes and slivered onions
hitting hot grease

in heavy black skillets–
and someone
pushing it all at her, saying,

Eat, eat.
He's a tune that devils
her, whose words

she can't recapture–
something
about two sisters,

dreadful wind
and rain; he's a poem
she wrote in a dream,

that faded like bruises
from the page. His eyes like
windows of a second-hand store

in a strange town, with the exact
quilt, one of a kind pitcher,
out of print record

she has been wanting
for years
just closing as she pulls

into the lot, shades drawn
before she's run halfway,
even though she is willing

and has money to pay.

∞

After the Gig. Before the Blizzard. 1973

Eight of us—a trumpet section, two tenors,
a third of the trombones, one wife—
rode back to Boston in Richie Cole's bus
sweeping across the river under pale snow
sifted out of bulky skies.
Scrambling from the van, we laid claim
to Tremont Street, strung ourselves
across four blank lanes aimed
deep into midnight dark.
Funnels of light marked off a city
surrendered to the promised blizzard
and to us.

The tenors scatted,
shooba-dweeoo; the trumpets
mimicked high notes; someone
hummed a bass line intricate
and dark. You reached a hand
to brush the crystals scattered in my hair.
"I know what you'll look like old," you said
and kissed me.
I remember eight erratic lines of footprints
fading under snow, and all our voices
—strong, melodious, and young—
flung against the cold electric current
of the oncoming storm.

∞

Feeling Sound

Had it not been sequestered around bends and between towers of trees, the school would have seemed dissonant with that sprawl of city just up the river. The land rolled in unassuming waves, smoothing a gentle cadence along the bottom of the sky. Quiet hovered like mist, soaking into the ground and trilling down like dew from tree leaves. While here the land lulled, the city above stole air in panicked breaths, short and spiked like Lamaze. Life was there. The symphony of streets and sidewalks and pitch-purple alleyways was staccatoed with drones of similar sorts of people. It sang. Get too far from this place, and that life-blood Tennessee River would not carry the pulsing tune. It would drown out before it reached your ears.

I drove from west Knoxville to the residential school for the deaf all that summer. The campus was gated, but once the security guard recognized me I passed through to scale the small slope toward the house where the girls lived. They were there for camp, and I volunteered to visit them in the evenings after their activities, to help what I could.

Until I had been there a few times, I had difficulty finding the house I was assigned to. They were all brick and similar to the point of parody, with tin roofs that made music of rain. Their long-eyed windows were blinded in the daytime, shutting out the outside light. These houses were spaced and planned, as if placed there by design by a higher hand.

The front door of their house was solid, as heavy as a pedal tone, swollen and unbroken and more movement than noise. The girls knew I was there. They could feel it. The door trembled into its frame, bothering their floor.

Julia swayed her way to me. With her left arm parallel to the floor and bent in at the elbow, her left palm facing herself, she united the heel of each hand, her right palm pivoting as if she were waving. *Cheese you want?* She curled one eyebrow and cradled a smile. I did not want cheese. But being that my signing skills were far from deft, I wasn't entirely sure that's what she was offering.

Again. Slow. At this request, Julia's hands fell in broader, smoother sweeps, replacing the quick movements of the previous expression. Her hands touched and pulled and glazed something I couldn't see, as if she were strumming a secret harp.

It took me a second. Oh, movie! Do I want to watch a movie. *Fine.*

I shied my eyes toward Cilla. She was slightly bowed, her spine like the neck of a guitar warped under the imperceptible weight of strings. Summer, and she was draped in a blue sweatshirt with embroidered black cats. I had seen her in it a few times. In these, her end days, the veins of her hands had pushed to prominence. They were mountain ranges skimmed with skin, her once taut flesh sinking down to fill the valleys. That flesh flowed out to the beds of nails that were neglected and hinted at curling. Cupping her mug with both hands, she muttered syllables over her coffee and waited by the back door, impatient for the Tuesday paper and news from outside.

Cilla was boss. I would seek her consent for fear of somehow doing something wrong and incurring her ire. I wouldn't leave a room until I looked her way and made sure she saw what I was doing.

Determining her wholly taken with her muttering, I stole away.

Julia flitted from the kitchen with me behind, her sometime shadow. She landed in the living room, her tall, lithe figure finding respite from a phantom breeze. She was one of those people you hoped would let you love them. Her face glowed warm and wide, like the first suggestion of a close sunrise. I envied her ease.

The others were there, semi-circled around the television, the six of them, on the floor and on chairs. Julia and I sat on opposite ends of a couch, and Laura sprang from the floor to plop between us. She and Julia started discussing something. Maybe anything. Maybe they were talking about the aurora borealis or Beethoven or the way popcorn kernels get stuck between their teeth. Or maybe they were staring at each other, manipulating their fingers and hands and faces, with no intention of meaning anything.

I still wasn't sure what to do around them. Continual smiling can be friendly only so long before it becomes suspect. But what else was there? One-on-one I could understand some of what they said. They would slow down for me. But together, they signed allegro, so fast I couldn't distinguish. All their words were one long movement.

I devoted myself to the study of the couch cushion. The earth-brown fabric bristled against the bald bend of my knee like the beginnings of a beard. Parallel navy lines thin as thread raced across its length, throwing themselves over the edge, each unaware of the other or their nearness.

I had never been so conscious of quiet. Even the furniture seemed stiff and unmoved, guards of silent secrets. Tables, chairs, and couches were still without the hum of conversation. There was no vibration to stir them. Every atom was fixed. I cleared my throat and looked to see who knew it. The couch had heard me more.

The first week I was with them, I had talked to test their ears. Said their names, asked questions. Once I stole around a corner and sang to them. Part of me wanted to believe they could hear something. I couldn't fathom a world of all silence. Sitting in silence always felt like waiting. Waiting for something to happen, for something to be said. But I learned that in my waiting was their world. And I had no access to it. I was visual fodder. A table. A chair. Something still to sit your eyes on.

I had grand plans to come to the school and be a bridge from the outside. I knew how separate our two worlds were. When I was working back home as a cashier at a pharmacy, I met a deaf lady who had been coming there for years. No one had attempted to communicate with her until the day we met. When I tested the sign my tenth-grade English teacher had taught me, she lifted and brightened, like coming out into the sun. She was so excited that she started scrambling at signs and telling me stories I couldn't understand. And when she left, she hugged me full and tight. Soon after, I excused myself to the back to mourn for something so rare—that beauty of connection.

In this house, the only one I felt I had reached was Laura, who would stand out with her long, paprika hair even before you knew she was the only one who could hear anything. We would often have conversations, with me speaking in what felt like shouts and her moving her mouth around indistinct echoes. I think she enjoyed talking with her lips and giving her hands a rest. It can hurt when you're first learning to sign. I often wondered how the others, especially Cilla, signed so much without being in pain. Cilla was so old. Surely she had arthritis.

I learned that Laura was from a family of musicians. She liked to talk about how high her momma could sing and how her grandpaw had his own bluegrass band.

"I can play the fiddle a little bit."

"Oh really?"

"Yeah, my grandpaw has been teaching me since I was ten. I like how you can play real fast or make it sound like a train."

Except for Laura, all the girls were profoundly deaf. They had never heard a sound. Though she could hear a little now, Laura wasn't far behind them. Someday she wouldn't hear a thing. I wondered which was worse.

For the time being, Laura wore hearing aids. When she walked through the house wearing her blue headphones, you could hardly tell she had ears for all the plastic on top and behind them. "Are those things attached to your head?" I mussed her hair and smiled.

"It's my grandpaw's band. I want to remember his songs." I smoothed my hand down her hair before she went to be with the other girls.

Following her, I found them as they usually were, cozied around the television with the sound off. I glanced at the screen and found familiar faces.

They were mimes this time, though, figures floundering toward meaning without sound. It was a movie I had seen before. Johnny Depp was the lead. I could almost fill his empty mouth. I almost knew what he was saying. But there was no friendly reminder for my ear. Only scrolling sentences. My eyes were held captive by captions, missing much of what was going on behind the words.

And there they were in a semi-circle, half distracted. They were much the same to me. Only without captions. No friendly anything.

They weren't always so quiet. The girls could get rowdy. They especially enjoyed horseplay, which was explicitly restricted. One evening they had started at it, pushing and shoving and rolling around. They were playing. I could understand this, although Cilla apparently could not. She charged into the room and bombarded them with indiscriminate yelling. It was certainly indiscriminate. And I was certain it was yelling. Her hands beat against each other and against her face. She paused, looked right at me and signed, then stomped off.

"What did she say to me?"

Laura looked up, and just after hesitating said, "Cilla said she can't believe they allow a hearing person who can't sign to work with the girls. She said you can't control them. And she did the sign for *stupid*."

Well. I didn't pretend she liked me, but I didn't expect that.

Not worry. Julia continued, but I didn't know all the signs.

"Can you interpret?"

"She says that Cilla was mean to the last woman who was here, too. Cilla does not like hearing people because she went to a public school and they made her feel bad about being deaf. Like she was handicapped."

How do you know?

Cilla my friend.

After a few weeks with the girls, I started feeling guilty. I'm sure some of it was from not being able to communicate with them as well as I had wanted. But more of it was from my ability to hear. I heard everything. Doors closing, pages turning, the ceiling fan circling. In their silent rooms I heard floors creek, and I heard them laugh. And I wanted to. But it was all so heavy on me to know they knew none of it.

It's hard to harness hope when you're a neighbor of affliction. Even when your good sense says there's no way, hope runs right past reason. I didn't want to accept that there was nothing to be done for these girls. I asked and looked, and what I learned was the option of cochlear implants. They required surgery. While they didn't restore normal hearing, they would allow the profoundly deaf or severely hard-of-hearing to have some semblance of sound.

I didn't search for a segue. *Do you know about cochlear implants?* I spelled it with my fingers and pointed to where it might be if I had had one.

Julia smiled and nodded, then pulled back her hair. I iced to see her scar. I pictured how they had prepared the spot, shaved the hair then sliced the skin that joined her neck and scalp. The thin brown circle was almost hidden in her hair, but the part that looked like a hearing aid was missing. She kept it detached.

Why don't you use it?

I not use cochlear because I accept be deaf. She was so good to sign slowly for me. I didn't have to ask anymore. She told me how her mother had taken her to get the implant when she was three. Now that she was older, she could decide what she wanted.

Laura stepped in to where we were and motioned us into the kitchen. When we arrived there, I saw Cilla helping two of the girls bake cookies. She was kneading the clumped brown sugar into a measuring cup. This was the softest I had seen her. The girls eyed her to learn.

I jumped like something electric passed through me. There was nothing, then everything. Silence to sound in an instant. I thought of that gospel song that talked about the trumpets of the Lord sounding and earth time being no more. I snuck a peek at my watch to make sure I was still safe.

Laura had put her grandpaw's album in the stereo. He was singing "A Voice from on High," and she was helping him. All the girls gathered to feel his voice. They touched the speakers and the countertop that held the stereo, feeling the vibrations. One girl pressed her ear directly to the speaker. I went to stop her, then remembered it wouldn't hurt. But it hurt me. The music was blaring. The speakers heaped sound into my ears. It was hot and sharp, aching the tender lining and filling me full to the lobes.

They talked over top of the music. Julia stood at the countertop, her elbows resting as she signed, stuttering as she spoke.

I felt ashamed there in the music, fat and full on food they couldn't eat. Julia looked to me, her brown eyes like long-worn river stones. *Can't hear.* She pointed to the stereo like she was tipping a solid space between. She only wanted to tell me. I wanted to say I know. Let my lips spill those same soft tones my mother had used. Try somehow to make it bearable.

She leaned over and closed her still ear against the countertop. Both palms flowered against the quaking surface. Eyes shut. Her body hummed in unison with the music. Facing me she cradled her lips in that smile again. I understood.

This is enough.

∞

Music Lessons
for Frank & Peggy Steele

I write poetry
when what I really want
is to play Beethoven
      on the piano
like Peg does
on tissue paper mornings
when Frank shuts his voice
      flat as a note
behind the bathroom door
and whistles, follows ebony
and ivory depressions
between beard and teeth.

Repairs

The day an appliance repairman petted both my cats
then squatted beside my purring refrigerator
to say "This motor's really shot" before he pulled
the cord, the purring did not stop but slid
into his voice as he talked of cats...belts....
Just one morning I would like
to keep on working when a stranger comes.
This time, a piano tuner, highly recommended,
sets down his doctor kit, eyes
my Kawai as if a long-lost friend.

"I've seen this one before. Used to be
in a bar, didn't it? I think I played it once....
I never touch pianos anymore."

And then he touches mine. Plays only tuning
chords and carries the melody in his voice,
singing of flooded Wurlitzers, a broken
baby grand, paced by my exclamations,
"Oh" and "Really," and my percussive
"Yes" while in the laundry room
the well-tuned dryer whirrs its harmony.

∞

Beth's Hands

Beth's hands on the keys never remind me of ivory-
tickling cliché. Not just clever fingers amused
with the naturals, the accidentals, the true thirds

spanning thumb and little finger, they are
instruments themselves, enjoying
deft inspirations released from a willing heart.

No discord diverts the compass of sound.
I watch Beth's hands moving over the octaves,
and when I listen to the music, they are what I hear.

Nashville

The best days were always acoustic
and usually on the floor. Leaning
against a speaker, unplugged, ashes
tapped into empty bottles as a full one
made the rounds. Scant plates of stew,
corncob pipe, we never scorned
the coughing. Joy and sorrow alike
floated on currents from the screen door,
ebb and flow of conscience and kisses.
The jam would go from stiff to tight to
loose then looser, sun down, moon up,
then put to bed. Huevos rancheros, sun
rise and go our ways.

The Call

Like a human voice, the cello called my daughter to play.
As a little girl, she squeaked out *Twinkle Twinkle Little Star*
Over and over and over and over and over
As I cooked dinner, yelling to the next room, "*Bravissima!*"

Now we speak of Janos, Yo Yo, and Rostropovich as
If they live next door and wave to us as they walk their dogs.
First movement, second opus, *schneller,* and *forte* are
Everyday words like *getouttahere, what's for dinner*, and *whassup.*

Out on the deck, we squint in the sun and sip our Crystal Light
While we deliberate on cello polish, cello postings,
Her latest gig. She blooms with future auditions,
Thousand dollar bows, and perfect pitch.

Bach cello suites weave through tales of Jacqueline du Pré,
Poor thing. Musings of bass clefs and Brazilian *pernambucco*
Wood become *molto agitato* as we hum Bach's Prelude No.1
To the maple tree, and she follows the low notes.

Country Gold

The static from the radio seemed to make my eyelids even heavier as I lay across the backseat of our 1979 Dodge St. Regis. I felt the gray corduroy upholstery marking my left cheek. Chilling, I pulled my winter coat up from the floorboard to use as a blanket.

The streetlights from Cumberland Avenue, coupled with the distinctive whining of our nine-year-old gray car, ignited a rhythm in my head. Instead of lulling me to sleep, I turned over on my back and began humming the melody I'd made up a few months before to accompany the car's percussion. Tonight, I added a couple of lines of lyrics: *I'm on the way home/All the way through town.*

My father and I were driving back home to Dorton Branch from visiting my aunt Jeanette at her house in nearby Middlesboro. Despite the frosty mountain weather, I'd insisted on playing outside all day in her big backyard, chasing a red bird with a salt shaker. It was a trick I'd tried all year but to no avail—both my Mamaw Howard and my chosen grandmother, our neighbor Myrt, had told me that if I poured salt on a red bird's tail it wouldn't be able to fly away. Somehow I figured one might be easier to catch on a winter day, but of course my luck wasn't any better. My skinny seven-year-old legs were exhausted.

As we turned on to Highway 25E, passing Service Merchandise and Roses in the darkened strip mall on the left, I recognized the familiar radio jingle:

Country Gold Saturday (Saturday, Saturday, Saturday).....NIGHT!
Then the trumpets started.

I sat straight up in the backseat. This sure wasn't Jim Reeves, a favorite of my dad's. As a rollicking guitar and piano chimed in, I found myself tapping my foot on the clear plastic floormat.

Then a voice growled: *Love is a burning thing/And it makes a fiery ring.*

I didn't understand what that meant, exactly, but I felt like it must be something good. And scary. Words like "wild" and "fell" and "fire" kept coming out of the radio. By the time he started falling *down, down, down,* I was relieved to hear three new voices floating upwards through the car, humming in place of the trumpets. *Burns, burns, burns,* they sang sweetly, as if they were saving him from the flames.

The blonde hair on my arms stood up. I couldn't take it anymore.

"Who is that?" I asked my daddy.

"Johnny Cash," he said from the front seat.

"No, not him. Them women!"

He gave me a funny look in the rearview mirror. "Oh, those are the Carter Sisters," he replied. "He's married to one of them. They're from over the mountain in Virginia."

I was a little disappointed by that. I'd wanted them to be from Kentucky. But since I'd been to Virginia and it looked a little like Kentucky, I figured that wasn't so bad. Regardless, they didn't sound like they were of this world. The little upward curve they made in their voices during the final ooh of the chorus gave me the same feeling I had when I heard Jimmy Swaggart play "This Is Just What Heaven Means To Me" on the piano.

It made me want to be a musician. I'd started taking piano lessons the year before, but I was already bored with Bach and Beethoven. Reading those notes and squiggly symbols and foreign words on a page didn't feel anything like "Ring of Fire." This was liberating, exciting, honest.

I wondered what those Carter Sisters looked like. *Their looks must match their voices*, I reasoned. *Sounding like that they had to be pretty.*

I imagined them resembling the pictures I'd recently seen of Jackie Kennedy in my little Step Into Reading book *Who Shot The President?* I saw them walking forward to the microphones each time the chorus came around, swaying gracefully in their matching A-line dresses, dark hair perfectly flipped and lacquered, as they looked up through false eyelashes towards the heavens while singing of being burnt alive by something called "desire."

As a piano player in the Holiness church, I was required to forsake the things of the world. Fearful of burning in my own teenage desires, I shunned wearing shorts and listening to secular music, including Johnny Cash. I took to fasting regularly. I was taught that these sacrifices would bring me closer to God, a part of Paul's exhortation in 1 Corinthians to "desire spiritual gifts." They would rid me of any impure or unnatural thought or yearning or attraction. They might also increase my talents as a musician, playing for the Lord.

I'd given up formal piano lessons for on-the-job training. After quickly figuring out the basic chord system, I took over on the piano when everyone was too busy shouting to notice any flawed notes or chords. While much of the congregation was running pews and laying hands on one another, I hunkered down behind the keys and developed my own style.

I found myself being influenced by piano players who combined the old-time honky-tonk method with black gospel and blues chords. Slurs and sevenths and diminished triads became my obsessions. The sounds I craved were rough and rowdy and raw, songs that showed old Satan who was boss:

It's a long, long road
But I'm gonna make it home on time
It's a long, long road
But I'm gonna make it home on time
Ain't no devil gonna stop me
I've got a made up mind.

I was determined to be a good musician. It was my calling, after all, my way of reaching people for Christ. When the piano was taken, I made sure my hands weren't idle; I began to learn the bass guitar. And then the organ.

The more I could do, the more I pleased God, I thought. The more I pleased the Lord, the less chance I had of going *down, down, down* and being consumed by my own carnality.

It was an impossible standard. Even after moving to Washington, D.C., to attend college and joining a less overtly legalistic congregation, the pressure to please and measure up was overwhelming.

After one last fierce effort, I gave up to work out my own salvation.

I created a church of the heart while displaced in our nation's capital. My congregation, I decided, would be filled with a theology of love and acceptance and grace. I added new hymns to my repertoire, the robin's song on my back deck or a doe running down Wisconsin Avenue in Upper Georgetown in the middle of the night. Friends and strangers and literature and nature unknowingly preached the sermons. Tithing became simply donating time to help a friend or supporting a worthy cause. In short, I adopted a belief system that recognized spiritual value throughout my own environment, one that embraced doubt as an essential part of faith and rejected enslaving rules.

I began making my own kind of music at coffeehouses and bars throughout the D.C. area – Jammin' Java in Vienna, Virginia, the Iota Bar and Café in nearby Arlington. The reception was enthusiastic; people weren't used to hearing just a guy and his piano. I covered songs by Elton John, Ryan Adams, even Morrissey. But something was missing.

Terminally homesick, I yearned to perform mountain songs onstage, but as I didn't play guitar, that seemed impossible; traditional Appalachian music generally doesn't translate well to the piano.

During this time, I began to rediscover the Carter Family. While browsing the music section at Borders in Fairfax, I spotted an intriguing CD:

Press On by June Carter Cash. Recorded in 1999, it was her first solo album in over twenty-five years, featuring songs of the Carter Family paired with originals. One of those tracks was "Ring of Fire."

I bought the recording, tearing off the shrink-wrap before I was even out of the store. My fingers were stiff from the cold as I popped it into my car's CD player before merging on to I-66 to go back into the city.

With the first strum of her autoharp, I was mesmerized. No trumpets, no piano, just an autoharp, guitar and fiddle.

Her voice moved me. Gone were the sweet harmonies created with her sisters. This was all June – rough, soulful, emotional – written at a time in her life when she burned, burned, burned for Johnny Cash.

Bound by wild desire/I fell into a ring of fire.

This version wasn't wildly frantic or erotic. Instead it was quietly sensual, vulnerable.

This must be how it sounded when she wrote it, I thought to myself as I drove across the Potomac on the Key Bridge.

I pictured her sitting at a yellow Formica-top dining room table, lined notebook laid out in front of her, cradling an autoharp. There were no false eyelashes or bouffant hairdo in this daydream. Instead, her eyes were wet with tears from falling *down, down, down* into the torrid pit of love for a man who wasn't hers. A few of them fell onto her simple sky blue cotton nightgown. Ignoring them, she began strumming.

Those warm strums became the solution to my challenge of not being able to play mountain music onstage.

I'd learn to play the autoharp.

A descendant of the German zither, the autoharp is the only instrument native to America. The concept is quite simple: the player presses and holds the desired chord bar with the left hand while strumming the strings using a thumb pick on the right hand.

Picking out a melody is more difficult. Based on the piano scale with each string representing a single note, players use finger picks on two or three fingers to play melody to their thumb's rhythm.

Immediately, I began researching my options before settling a month later on a restored 1969 Oscar Schmidt from an eBay seller in South Carolina. I spent each day anticipating its arrival, tracking it by the hour on the UPS website.

It was waiting for me on my front porch on a Tuesday evening. Dragging it inside the house, I cut through the tough packing tape with my keys. Peeling back the layers of bubble wrap and Styrofoam peanuts, I lifted it out of the box.

I ran my hands across the honeyed wood, pausing to feel each foot peg on the back. Turning it over, I studied each of the fifteen chord bars, memorizing their positions with my fingertips. I cradled it against my chest, fantasizing about its history.

What songs had it played? Where had it traveled? Where would I take it?

Fishing out a thumb pick from a container in the box, I took a deep breath and strummed it for the first time.

The sound vibration felt tingly against my stomach. Warm, mellow, vulnerable. The blonde hair on my arms stood up.

As I idly plucked each string, savoring the warm tones, I instinctively knew what I'd call her.

June.

∞

L YRICS

"Blest pair of Sirens, pledges of Heav'ns joy,
Sphear-born, harmonious Sisters, Voice, and Vers,
Wed your divine sounds, and mixt power employ"

– John Milton
(from "At a Solemn Musick")

Song Trajectory and Weight

A pound of warmed song
escapes gravity,
shimmers out of a throat
like visible heat above the road,
insubstantial and moving
toward transparent collision
with a listener
one beat away.

Roy

*They say Don Gibson wrote "Oh Lonesome Me" and "I Can't Stop Loving You"
the same Sunday afternoon in Knoxville, Tennessee. And I knew this old boy
who knew the old boy. . . .*

Roy was a wino by the railroad warehouse
He worked for Bud Whedbee doing maintenance jobs
Just a coming and a going in his green GMC
A bottle full of troubles and a pocket full of keys

> Hey Buddy, are we friends?
> Do you like me all right?
> Let's drink some this morning
> We'll be home by tonight
> Do you like country music?
> Hell, it's come pretty far
> I used to know Donny Gibson
> Before he was a star

He was laying in the front seat as evening turned to day
Eleven days running just wasted away
Once there was a family, a wife and a son
And forty years of trying before it was gone

> Hey Buddy, are we friends?
> Do you like me all right?
> Let's drink some this morning
> We'll be home by tonight
> Do you think you could learn me
> That flat top guitar?
> I'm too old, I reckon
> But you could be a star

Now some folks are wealthy and some folks are poor
Some folks love money while some never care
Old Roy was just a drunk, one drink at a time
And he never cared if you done the buying

Hey Buddy, are we friends?
Do you like me all right?
Let's drink some this morning
We'll be home by tonight
Do you like country music?
Hell, it's come pretty far.
I used to know Donny Gibson
Before he was a star

Hey, do I talk too much?
Let me know if you mind.
And would you sing that one again:
You Are My Sunshine?

2

Care of Birmingham Jail

Write me a letter
care of Birmingham jail.
I have the picture
curled and yellow,
her lap hugging a Gibson,
his gift from the pawn shop,
moonshine money.
She filtered his song
in tune with the guitar

if you don't love me
love who you please
spilling memories of bubbling
mash vapors cooling in copper
coils to Mason jars.
Revenuers.
A dead man at his feet.
Hang your head over
hear the train blow.

Voice clear and soft,
plucking magic on strings,
she answered *roses love sunshine*
Angels in Heaven know I love you
care of Birmingham jail.

∾

lullaby of birdland

listen to the sigh
sleep little baby don't you cry

mama, where does the winged horse sleep?

in an old beech born with the moon
limbs cradle fast and firm

where will we go if storm shakes
branches tremble nest falls?

we will enter tree heart lightning opened
long long ago the song was lost

how dark, mama?

when clouds cloak starshine we huddlewarm
night storms teach black   teach whip and brace   teach holy songs

mama, does the willow weep for me?

willow whispers love
whispers low and sweet

mama, can we fly on moonglow?

on clear nights we light on the stone lady
her arm upraised   her robe ripple   in frozen place

mama,   tired so tired

sleep my turtle dove
listen to the sway of leafshushshshsh

∞

My Niece and I Listen to Jazz

It's *round midnight*
and Cannonball Adderley's
deep sax mines dark matter
of the heart, and my niece
starts singing the words.
"I lose the music when
you sing," I say. But she
wants to *know what love is*,
she wants to be a *funny valentine*,
she wants to sit on Chet's lap
and put her ear to his chest.
I want to hear his trumpet.
I want the slant keys of Bill Evans
plinking the bones in my spine,
I want to feel Coltrane count
neutron stars before they implode.
She asks why they write lyrics
if you're not supposed to sing.
She really doesn't need my reply.
She wants to sing *let's get lost*,
she wants *her love here to stay*.
I need to hear maestro Monk
share his stage. "I'm *kinda blue*,"
I tell her, "I've got Miles to blow
before I sleep." But we settle on
Ella scat, Mel scat and listen
to Sarah Vaughn whose shrill vocals
tempt musicians to case their horns.

∾

In Memory Of My Heart

Light a candle in the rain
Sing a sad song in the dark
Throw a flower in the river
In memory of my heart

You were such life to me and so sweet to me
For my heart you were breath and blood
Now I'm in misery
Cause I can't live without your love

Light a candle in the rain
Sing a sad song in the dark
Throw a flower in the river
In memory of my heart

I'll go on like before
And look the same as I've always been
But my heart's gone for sure
Since forever's come to an end

Light a candle in the rain
Sing a sad song in the dark
Throw a flower in the river
In memory of my heart

Dance in the Dawn

Join the circle that's never been broken.
Color each red feeling blue.
Break the one bread into many pieces.
And dance just once in the dawn in the dew.
Dance at least once in the dew.

      For maybe the sun will stop shining.
      Maybe the moon will go out, too.
      So break the one bread into many pieces.
      And dance just once in the dawn in the dew.
      Dance at least once in the dew.

Marry that lonely-eyed stranger.
Sleep with your backs to the moon.
Let your lives grow bright as a diamond,
And feed your first-born with a spoon.
Feed your first-born with a spoon.

      For maybe the sun will stop shining.
      Maybe the moon will go out, too.
      So let your lives grow bright as a diamond.
      And dance just once in the dawn in the dew.
      Dance at least once in the dew.

Set your home down in a forest.
Care for the wild and the tame.
Bury the seed with the apple.
Your name will be found in the Book of Names.
It will be in the Book of Names.

      For maybe the sun will stop shining.
      Maybe the moon will go out, too.
      So bury the seed with the apple
      And dance just once in the dawn in the dew.
      Dance at least once in the dew.

Gather the flowers while they're blooming.
Pick the bone of sorrow clean.
Praise the straight road for turning.
Welcome back the green of spring.
Welcome the green of spring.

     For maybe the sun will stop shining.
     Maybe the moon will go out, too.
     So praise the straight road for turning.
     And dance just once in the dawn in the dew.
     Dance at least once in the dew.

Song for Type 1 Diabetes

Could be blues,
harmonica lip-crushings,
a healthy body walking out,
cells pivot-turning
with chins in the air – an inside job,
a hard-luck soft-sell
and it isn't going very well.
Hard times
don't always look hard,
and blue is blood's true color
before it hits air.

Could be a campfire round
sung below
an orange heel of moon,
beside the cabin, above the dock –
a harmony of luck, on-and-on
between the bright bellies
of lanterns and what
could be more chronic?

Metal, possibly, and heavy,
a drumstick-snapping, bass-hurling,
knees-on-the-stage,
wet-necked wail –
the thousand-sticking screams,
not pain, but repetition, just.

Could be a jump-rope-rhyme
hand-heels churning air,
bangs in the eyes,
a chant from memory, from habit,
the staccato double-dutch slap
of rope on sidewalk.

Could never be a lullaby.
It's a psalm, after all.
That's no small thing.

Blessed be the test-strip vials,
        O my soul
the cartridges, each ultra-fine fang,
the experimental pig
        O my soul.
Blessed be the finger stick
and each twig of history
on insulin's family tree.
        O my soul.
        Blessed be –

∾

Lullaby

Her throat raw from cradle
song and cold,
hush my little one

she keeps on singing.
The snow sets on the barred
window like white coal
dust stirred

around the mouth
of a mine.
now that evenin's come

Under her mended shawl
a thin baby sleeps, coughs,
mama shakes the dreamy tree
and sleeps.

Mother Jones said sing
to keep the jailers
awake sing
the baby through the night sing
the brutal moon
to the other side of winter sing
this strike
to the next coal town
and catches for you a sweet dream
on icy anthracite wind.

Stiff and numb, she
rocks
on the jail cot,
hush-a-bye hush

the song a lull
in her tiniest miner's ears.

∞

Up On Sexton's Creek

Lately I don't even hardly want to go out
Half the world's too mean, other half's too devout
I tell ye now, I'm ready to pack up and leave
I need away from traffic – I need to believe

We've gotten too far away from the giving land
Sometimes you have to make your own kind of stand
I want to eat from my own fields, wade in the creek
I need a beech grove where I can lay and think

> Way up on Sexton's Creek folks really got it made
> Twilight on Sexton's Creek – hear whippoorwill serenade
> I want to live up on Sexton's Creek when evening turns blue
> Wanna live on Sexton's Creek with you

All the little houses and their gardens of dark green
Up on Sexton's Creek the water's good and clean
We'll sit on the porch and watch the mornin' roll in
I know where I'm going, want to forget where I been

We'll grow big 'maters and our own sweet corn
We'll gather blackberries, sing hymns and get reborn
In summer we'll open windows, in the winter build a fire
We'll fall asleep every night to a katydid choir

> Way up on Sexton's Creek ....

I'm going to live on Sexton's Creek till the day I die
Tell this old modern world that I've said goodbye
If we don't have it we'll make it – if we can't, we'll do without
Our entertainment will be the redbuds blooming out

Let's go to Sexton's Creek where the days are long
If we need something new we'll just write a song
Enough is as good as a feast, that's what my mama said
We'll live on poems and lovin' and cornbread

> Way up on Sexton's Creek ....

∞

Appalachian Refugee

Lay your head upon my knee,
I'll drive a while so you can sleep.
And you get ready for the place we're going to:
So blue, so new and so deep.

It's like you love your father so—
And you know it that he knows—
And it's been years since you have seen his eyes
So blue, so new and so deep

And heard the voice of by-God West Virginia
Speaking through the fog that lies between the
Oldest ridges they call "Blue"
The oldest river they call "New"
Can only reach a place so deep to Appalachian Refugees.

Slowly lower the body down
Six feet beneath the frozen ground
Although its time has passed it passes on to you:
Eyes so blue.
Old life as new.
And love so deep.

After Sunset, What the Woman Sings to Her Babies

Tomorrow I will shape clay dolls,
shape clay dolls to look like you.

The mountain days dry and clear,
lambs are barking at the stars.

Tomorrow I will shape clay dolls,
shape clay dolls to look like you.

Your father's name soft as skin,
soft as skin I wrap you in.

Tomorrow I will shape clay dolls,
shape clay dolls to look like you.

An island hangs in the sky,
hoof prints on it big and dry.

I don't want to go there,
what my arms hold now, that's my sky.

Tomorrow I will shape clay dolls,
shape clay dolls to look like you.

Tomorrow I will shape clay dolls,
shape clay dolls to look like you.

∽

Burgundy Shoes

We wait for the bus that's going to Bangor
In my plaid dress and burgundy shoes
In your red lipstick and lilac kerchief
You're the most pretty lady in the world

  Sun

The bus driver smiles a dime and a nickel
We climb on our seats the vinyl is cold
"Michelle Ma Belle" a song that you loved then
You hold my hand and sing to yourself

  Sun

The leaves are green and new like a baby
Tulips are red now I don't miss the snow
It's the first day I don't wear my big boots
You hold my hand I've got burgundy shoes

  Sun

NOCTURNES

∾

"Chopin, in his poetic Nocturnes, sang not only the harmonies which are the source of our most ineffable delights, but likewise the restless, agitating bewilderment to which they often give rise."

– *Franz Liszt*

A Little Night Music at the Olsens' Cabin Near Deary, Idaho

for Lance & Andi

The cows are playing their bassoons
in the next pasture, the long low notes

round and golden as the moon.
The man and woman who tend the cows,

I happen to know, are lying together
upstairs, making a more corporeal music,

or dreaming corn into heaven. The moon,
meanwhile, strikes a brilliant chord

and drives a scruff of coyotes, far off,
into free-for-all a cappella—half music,

half hunger. I sip the last bit of fire
from this glass and start singing, off key,

an old Dylan song. The coyotes hesitate.
I can hear them listen. They wonder, perhaps,

what animal would make such a noise.

∾

Let Me Down Easy

We took the back roads toward Saltville. I steered her old Dodge pick-up with one hand across gravel roads. Amanda leaned up against me, our bodies riding the bumps in the road together. I was coming down from the drunk, and our talking, which had been feverish for a while, had settled into something quiet and calm like the night around us. Except for her telling me where to turn, there was only the noise of the motor and static from the radio as she searched from one station to another.

"Seems like there ain't no good stations anymore," I said.

Her hand paused as we heard Johnny Cash for a second. The station went out as fast as it came, and she finally gave up.

"Don't matter. We'll be there soon." She switched on the CD player, and I recognized the band that had been playing earlier at the Mill, their fiddle noises floating around the truck and into the surrounding hills as if their music belonged out there.

A couple of the guys from the band were driving behind us. My brother Noah was back there somewhere too. It was the middle of the night, but we made a train of headlights through the dark country, on our way to somewhere else where we would try to keep the evening from ending.

Amanda told me to turn left, onto another gravel road. This one sloped uphill before plummeting down in a curve. We passed an ancient farmhouse with a dim light coming from the first floor. The moon above was nearly full, and I could tell the house was in bad shape like most of the others we had passed. Barbed wire fences lined the road. We crossed a cattle bridge and entered a field of tall grass ready to cut for hay. On top of another hillside, I geared into park. Amanda pulled a blanket out from behind the seat as she stretched her legs to the ground.

"Bring that Thermos with you," she said over the other car doors and people's voices. "I stole some of the Mill's secret punch tonight. Ever had any?"

I shook my head no and followed her out into the middle of the field. She spread her blanket on the ground and motioned for me to take my place beside her. We were out in the middle of nowhere, high up on some ridge. It was the kind of night when you look at the stars and think no one else could ever have seen them be so bright. You know it's crazy, but that's how you feel.

"Be careful," Amanda said. She opened the Thermos and held it under my nose for me to get a whiff of its strength. "It's full of fruit. You eat too much of the fruit and you'll go blind crazy." She smiled as she took a sip, careful as she swallowed. Then she flashed a piece of cut-up apple between her teeth, before handing the Thermos back to me.

I wouldn't have been out that night if Noah hadn't forced me. I sat perched at the bar at the Mill, feeling sorry for myself and watching Noah with admiration as he negotiated through the crowd towards Janie and Joy Hopkins.

"Those girls are just plainly the finest pieces of ass in Smyth County," Noah said before moving in their direction.

They were good-looking, but I never could tell them apart. I haven't talked with either of them enough to be impressed by any sort of distinguishing personality traits.

"Girls like that make you reckless," I said.

"Girls like that'll sink you to hell, but you'll have a good time going." He took a long chug from his bottle of Blue Moon. "If you'd come out more often, you'd remember why girls like that are fun. Why don't you come dance? There's two of them and two of us."

"You got me here tonight, but I ain't dancing. Don't push your luck."

"All right, but you mark my words. Move on or rust out."

Noah handed me his empty bottle and left me for the girls. He entered their conversation and made himself the focus of their attention in an instant. He stood between them with his arms wrapped around their shoulders. They all smiled and laughed and waited for the music to start.

Those actions weren't Noah's alone, or at least they didn't used to be. I was half proud of him and half humiliated at him showing me up. *I taught that boy everything he knows,* I told myself. *But I was someone else back then.*

I slammed back the last of my Miller Lite and waited for someone behind the bar to notice I was empty. The Mill was packed though, and the thunk of my empty bottle didn't register in anyone's hearing. It was while I was waiting that I first recognized Amanda. I had known her a long time ago, back when I was that person I used to be. She had worked at a couple of different bars in Abingdon, all places I quit frequenting when I met Michelle. We flirted a lot but it never went any deeper.

Amanda was still a pretty little girl with dark skin and hair and big, brown eyes, not much different from the other girls I had seen that night. She was prettier than a lot of the others, but it wasn't her looks that really set her apart. She smiled so genuinely to everyone. I knew she was having a better time than those she served. Shuffling down the bar from customer to customer, she mixed liquor, filled pitchers and opened bottles in a furious pace.

The band came on stage to begin their first set with the fast rhythm of a guitar, immediately calling people from every side of the building to the big wooden dance floor. I watched the crowd mix together in the center of the room. Some people stayed in the back to give themselves more room to dance, but others pushed their way through, wanting to get close enough to the stage to feel the pulse of the music blast through the speakers. The fiddle player raced his bow back and forth to give a piercing quality to their song. I turned back to the bar, and waited for Amanda to get to me. When she saw me waiting, she winked.

"Been a long time since I've seen you," she said, taking my empty bottle and replacing it with another. "Why ain't I ever seen you in here before?"

"I stopped going out when I got married." The bottle met my lips, and I felt the coldness of the beer run down my throat and all through me.

"I didn't take you for an old married man."

"I'm not married any more. Now I'm just old."

The expression on her face told me she already knew my situation, or maybe there just wasn't much that could surprise her. She looked down and reached under the bar for a fresh, white cloth. With one hand, she wiped down the bar, soaking up other people's spilled beer and the water rings left from cold bottles.

"I'm sorry to hear that," she said, still swabbing down the polished bar top. Then, she looked up, directly at me. "On the other hand, I guess that means you and me are free to have a good time tonight." Her eyes met mine straight on, and I was somehow afraid to look straight at her.

Most of the people who had surrounded the bar earlier were out on the dance floor. Amanda went back to pouring drinks and collecting empties. She kept a fresh bottle in my hand while I watched all the couples on the floor. Noah danced with both of the Hopkins girls. He occasionally caught my eye and motioned for me to come out, but I ignored him. After a time, Amanda came around the bar and sat on the empty stool next to me.

"You like the band?" She propped her elbow on the bar, giving away the first indication I had seen all night that she wasn't tireless.

"They're good," I said.

I had never heard them before, but I liked them. I understood full well why Noah liked them. They used a harmonica in most of their songs. Some of it was fast and fun and gave their music a rough edge like my little brother. And some was long vibrating drones, full of melancholy and the kind of sorrow I wanted to wallow in. The big double bass kept the song's steady beat. I could feel every pluck of the strings as if they ran up and down my spine.

"You got plans for later tonight?" she asked.

"I don't have any plans. Period." I turned my body toward her, and my knee bumped into her before I could move it around her. "Sorry," I said.

"I'm not hurt." She smiled. "Stick around until we close, and we can talk more. I think a bunch of us are going out to a place I know afterwards. We'll sing and dance under the stars and go to sleep where we fall."

"I probably won't be much company."

"Why don't you let me decide that for myself?" She leaned into me and looked at me again like she had earlier. I felt her trying to pull me out of myself and into her. I knew at that moment I was supposed to kiss her, but I couldn't. I couldn't kiss Amanda because, even though Michelle had left me, it seemed so wrong. Amanda must have realized I wasn't going to follow through, and finally, she took her hands off me and grabbed the bar.

"Chuck," she called to one of the bartenders. "We need some shots over here." Then she turned back to me. "You gonna do a shot with me?" She smiled, and I knew I hadn't completely blown it with her. Even more so, I knew I wanted another chance to get it right. There was something so open about her when I looked in her brown eyes, something about the way she looked into me when we talked.

I knew Amanda saw my pain, knew I was different than I use to be, but she saw past that too. When Amanda dispensed drinks at the Mill, she wasn't just covering up people's problems with alcohol. She was truly interested in those people. She was the kind of girl who wanted a real answer when she asked how a person was doing.

"What do you want to do?"

"How about an Irish car bomb?"

"That sounds the way I feel, so why not." I tried to smile back at her.

Her eyes studied me again, and for a moment, she looked as if she were the one in pain. "Never mind. No Irish car bombs for you. You need something to get the blood flowing again. How about a Jager bomb? You ever had a Jager bomb?"

I shook my head no and took a drink of Miller.

"I think that's just what we both need to get going tonight," she said. She pulled her hair behind her ear with two fingers.

Chuck handed Amanda a Red Bull, which she opened with a pop and fizzing sound. She split the can between two tall glasses while Chuck twisted the top of the green bottle of Jagermeister. The dark liquid filled two empty shot glasses, and Chuck walked away. It smelled like cough syrup.

"Drop the entire shot glass in the Red Bull and drink both," she said. I followed her, allowing the two liquids to mix together in my mouth. Instead of a medicine taste, the two drinks formed a minty flavor in my mouth. It was something fresh and new and delicious. "What'd you think?" she asked. "Not what you expected, is it?"

A warmth flowed through my face. I was smiling, and even my smile felt different—sincere and real. "Yeah. That's not bad."

The music from the band stopped with a long screech from the harmonica and a few final licks from the guitar. Everyone on the dance floor clapped and hollered. A few people stomped their feet, begging the band not to quit.

"Time for their break. I better get back behind the bar." She stood up, reenergized. Her hands went again to my knees. "Promise me you'll stick around and talk to me later," she asked, but she already knew I would stay. This time, when she leaned in, she kissed me.

We lay in the hay field, warm from the heavy summer air, the Mill's secret punch and the heat of our bodies. I discovered kissing Amanda was like flying. The dark skin on her arms and neck glowed silvery in the moonlight. Her body seemed even more unblemished and perfect.

The others had dragged limbs from the woods and built a little fire. Their shadows danced around the flame, but we had moved far enough away it seemed like we were alone. The guys from the band had brought their instruments, and if it was possible, they sounded even better out in the open field. At the bar, the band had performed their own songs, but here they pulled out their old favorites. Someone sang Bob Dylan's *Don't Think Twice, It's All Right*, with everyone joining in on the refrain. Their sounds settled over the field like the dew.

After a while, the music stopped, and then too their talking. Amanda and I settled into the stillness, no longer kissing. So much of the past few hours had gone between us without words. Our eyes had spoken for us at first, and later our ever-seeking hands. The silence between us had been comfortable and natural, and I didn't want to break it. We held each other and listened to the natural lullaby of the Saltville countryside playing around us – crickets and frogs trying to out-call each other, an owl at the edge of the woods, and the gentle roar of an occasional vehicle crossing nearby, hidden ridges. We were surrounded by a new kind of music that was wilder and more beautiful in its own way.

My fingers played across her flesh, but I still couldn't banish Michelle from my mind. Not completely at least. My fingers traced the length of Amanda's arm, and I couldn't help but to compare these two women, impossibly measuring one against the other until I realized tears were crawling down my cheeks.

I cried because I remembered the first time I had made love to Michelle and how it seemed to always get better for me every time afterward because it was familiar and common. I cried because I felt something with Amanda I never thought I'd feel again. And I cried because I felt ashamed. I was ashamed for crying like a child and more than anything for crying in front of Amanda. Before I could stop, her small voice, hardly more than a whisper, drowned out the night noises around us.

"She hurt you so bad," she said. "I'm so sorry."

It was the reaction I should have expected from her. She would never laugh or think less of me. She was too compassionate.

"You should tell me what Noah says. 'Everybody has problems. Deal with it.'" I pulled away from her, wiping the tears away with the back of my hand. "I'm sorry. I didn't mean to do this."

"What? Cry? Nothing wrong with showing a little bit of your soul every now and then."

I didn't know what to say. So I said nothing. She moved closer. Her arms tightened around me, unwilling to let me loose.

"I know you're thinking about her," she said. "It's all right."

"I *am* thinking about her, but I'm thinking about you too." And I was. "Mostly I was wondering if I could ever survive another broken heart."

"And now you wonder if you can trust me. Right? You're afraid I'll hurt you too." Her hand brushed my forehead and ran through my hair.

"When Michelle left, she said I didn't know who she was. When she said it, I thought she was crazy, but later, I began to think she was right. But now I think, maybe we can't really ever know someone else."

I lay completely flat on the ground and stretched my arms up to the heavens. I closed my eyes and blocked out the stars above me. She kissed me again, her warm mouth called me to movement.

"What if I let you down?" I asked, unable to leave it alone.

"What if I let *you* down?" she asked back, smiling. We both knew that was really what I wanted to know.

Her eyes caught some light from above. I pulled the blanket around us, and we fell asleep in this field in the middle of Saltville, under the biggest sky I had ever seen.

∞

Every Saturday Night

There's square dancing in the old opera house
out from Boneville, up Ruby Hollow.

We shuffle and stomp on the hardwood floor
that's as *tee-total perfect* for dancing
as Billy's linoleum rug ever was.

Outside, the rain and evening air.

In here, bright lights and loud
Laughter; banjos, fiddles, and guitars
tuning their tunes.

Sashay and *do-si-do—allemand left.*

We clasp hands, skip and bow,
clasp hands again and whirl around.

The current war seems faraway and only on TV.

Somewhere else—no, not here—

someone's pulling a black hood
over someone else's frightened face

∾

Aria on the Boulevard

I concluded my last conference call of the day and peeked out my home office window. At five o'clock, just a stubborn scrap of light clung to the bleak November afternoon. I'd been running every other day. If I ignored the blinking instant messages on my computer, I could get my miles in before dark.

I live near a superb running trail—Cherokee Boulevard in Knoxville, Tennessee. The graveled path is nestled in the Boulevard's tree-lined median, with stately old homes to the north and a riverside park on the south. Walkers and joggers from all over the city bask in the natural beauty and patrician elegance of the area.

I hit the Boulevard and broke into a run, but the frantic pace of my day oppressed me. My heart rate climbed, but instead of exhilaration I felt exhaustion. The brittle coolness of late fall exacerbated the jostling of my body. I felt dissonance, not an endorphin rush, but plodded on.

After a mile, my legs ignored my robotic, schedule-oriented brain and slowed to a walk. I was frustrated with myself, but the energy to resume even a modest trot eluded me. That demanding computer, with its incessant trickle of beeps and alerts, had eroded my stamina. My body wanted to walk, and I acquiesced.

I often spoke of my good fortune to live around the corner from this scenic route, yet my praise was rote. I seldom truly noticed my surroundings. Now, instead of gasping shallow breaths, I inhaled deeply of the crisp air, and the coolness tickled my lungs. The sun faded as if the horizon were sipping it, and I watched the cliffs on the far side of the river reflect the rose-colored hues of ebbing rays. Bare tree branches proliferated into delicate tributaries that emptied into the deepening purple-blue sky.

Other joggers and dog walkers faded away with the light, but I wasn't nervous, not in this part of town, not even when I heard faint footsteps crunching behind me, and certainly not when a passionate, off-key rendition of *Don Giovanni* wafted through the twilight.

> *Mi trada quell'alma ingrate,*
> *Infelice, o Dio!, mi fa.*
> *Ma tradita e abbandonata,*
> *Provo ancor per lui pietà.*
> *Quando sento il mio tormento,*

Di vendetta il cor favella;
Ma, se guardo il suo cimento,
Palpitando il cor mi va.

I turned. An older gentleman in a leather jacket and jaunty wool scarf trucked along at a spirited pace, singing a duet. His partner, an opera only he could hear, piped through earphones clamped over an Einstein-like nest of long gray hair. His shoulders were broad and unbowed by the evening chill; his palms stretched out with the yearning of the aria.

I kept walking, smiling now. This vision of pure, unselfconscious immersion branded me, as if I'd stared at the sun a second too long. Arriving at my corner and turning toward home, I stopped beneath a shadowy maple and leaned my cheek against its scabby bark. My wild-haired Southern Pavarotti serenaded himself down the Boulevard, dissolving into darkness, his crescendos fading shortly after. Pinpricks of stars twinkled their applause, and leaves shuffled around my feet as if roused for intermission.

I smiled and continued my leisurely walk home.

∾

Binary Measure

How it was only one measure
but yet held two beats,
separate and apart,
was mystery
and music,
was longing,
and memory that hung in the night,
the slack face of a haunted moon.

If her name was Mick
or Carson, if the letters
were confused about making
nouns and verbs, if the sentences
were hard and calloused,
discord that rose up angry,
and a trombone took over
and denied the flute,
and *băy* boong *băy* boong came
out of the night like flashes
of lightning, if a storm
played across Georgia,
moved west, moved into Alabama,
without definition, the heart,
its four chambers wanting,
became rite of passage,
became need,
became the struggle to love.

DAVI WALDERS

Ladino Concert at Spoleto

Lute, flute, rebec, psaltery,
Ladino melodies plucked from history
in a language almost forgotten.
"*Alta Es La Luna*" – love and sorrow

float again through alleyways
of the *Juderia*, where Sephardim
welcomed the Sabbath between
mosques and cathedrals. Gentle elegies

that sweetened the Golden Age,
before the terror and torture,
the masks and forced becoming
Marranos, Conversos.

We lean into the melody hungering
for what was – a long-ago language,
a sweet life. A people of so many
diasporas. who learned to hide,

to disappear at dusk taking only
the scent of vineyards, love songs,
and loss. Now the hush of hundreds
sitting, standing, hugging sanctuary walls,

spilling into a hot synagogue garden
half a millennium later, listening
to the whisper of those who carried
their melodies and stories into the night.

Ladino:
      a mixture of Spanish and Hebrew spoken by Jews in Spain and Portugal before the Inquisition

Re-choreographing a Discordant Dance

In my mother's study every Saturday morning, I clicked open my violin case and breathed in the familiar scent of old, varnished wood. Finding my cube of rosin in its velvet-lined compartment, I took my time rubbing it back and forth across my bow like I'd seen her do so many times. Then, studying my image in the mirror, I mimicked her stance, her posture, her wrists, everything straight yet supple. At eight, I longed to be a professional violinist, too.

But, as our lessons progressed, I couldn't learn vibrato, the violin's chin rest rubbed raw a spot on my collarbone, and my fingers were disloyal, behaving as if they belonged to someone else. More and more, my mother would stare out the window and quietly sigh.

"That's out of tune," she said one Saturday as soon as I started playing.

"I can't help it," I said, fighting tears. "I don't know how to do it."

"If you practiced a little harder—"

"I hate practicing!" I shouted. "I'll never be good enough!"

My younger brother, studying piano with our father, was giving recitals, while my scales on the violin still sounded scratchy and shrill. Around this time, my brother got a walk-on part in a Puccini opera that our father conducted. Dressed in a white choir robe matching his white-blond crew cut, my brother played an angel, a ghostly vision appearing center stage. Following our father's cues with the baton, he descended a staircase while the soprano, lamenting, threw herself on the ground in front of him. My mother, the concertmaster, played from her chair in the orchestra pit, I sat between my grandparents in the concert hall, squirming through the performance, wishing my brother would miss one of his cues or, better, fall off the top step and break his leg.

Back at home, my mother and I battled over lessons and practicing for a year before she let me quit. And, for a long time after, I believed I had failed.

One night, years later, I called my family together. "Watch this," I said. For three weeks I had been practicing a high school cheer in the garage, whispering the words and memorizing the long series of arm bends, thigh slaps and kicks that I'd watched my school's cheerleaders perform.

"C, H, A-R-G-E!" I shouted. My arms flew, and I executed the kicks precisely. I finished with a hop in place. I hadn't missed a step.

But instead of applauding, my mother, father and brother exploded in laughter, first with a little sputter and then, after exchanging glances, a crescendo of howls. "She didn't even get the rhythm right," my brother said, hooting. My face flushed, I turned, and without a word left the room. I didn't know what they were talking about; I was not a part of their private club. "That was a good try, honey," my mother called after me. But I never performed in front of them again, and to people who wondered why I didn't play an instrument when I came from a family of musicians, I explained with a forced smile, "I'm the audience in my family."

I didn't sing in front of anyone until my children were born. And then, in a rocking chair that squeaked out the beats with each push backward, in a room lit only by a soft night-light, and with my arms wrapped around a baby in fuzzy soft pajamas, I tested my voice. I invented melodies and words as I rocked (*You are my sweet, sweet love…*) and sang songs I remembered from summer camp (*Kumbayah, my Lord, kumbayah*). When I couldn't remember all the words, I hummed to fill in the blanks. My first baby clapped his hands and smiled. My second nestled his head into my neck and fell asleep. No one laughed.

One day, I couldn't get a melody out of my head; it repeated in an endless loop. It was a classical piece I'd heard in a movie, maybe in a scene with soldiers on horseback riding in full armor. The music haunted me, and I wanted to buy the CD, but first I needed to identify it. I called my mother and described it to her.

"The chorus really belts it out," I said. "The bass drum booms in a few places, and the music is so moving it gives me goose bumps."

"I'm sorry," she said, regret in her voice. "I don't know what that could be."

I remembered my family sitting around the dinner table humming parts of orchestra music to each other. "I played the section that goes dee da-da-da dum," my brother would say, humming a few bars, and my parents would immediately recognize the pieces. I sat in awe at their secret language.

On the phone with my mother, I said, "If you promise not to laugh, I'll try to hum a little of it for you. I'll probably botch it, but here goes." After a couple of false starts, my voice began to sound like the notes playing in my head. But I wondered what it sounded like to my mother on the other end of the line. I hummed it once more and waited.

"Oh yeah, that's Carl Orff. 'Carmina Burana'. You carried that tune nicely."

It was what I needed.

In my living room, I began to sing with my sons (*Yellow Submarine, Down by the Station*), and I didn't stop anymore when my brother visited. I twirled my boys around as we drowned each other out, our voices sometimes rough and ragged, other times soft and dulcet.

I got pajamas on my four-year-old by making up a song (*Jump, Jump, Jump into the Jammies*), and while we waited in traffic, my children and I sang songs from the preschool (*Puff the Magic Dragon, The Ants Go Marching*), the pleasure of making music carrying us away and bringing us all back together.

∞

Chamber Music

She fingers a phantom violin,
elbow up, wrist poised,
like her recital in third grade
eighty years ago.
An invisible horse-hair bow
saws air, slides across
unseen cat-gut strings, wound taut.

The moment passes. She slumps,
claims, *this is a living hell,*
her sweater stained deep
from mystery salad served at lunch,
someone took my clothes, she mutters,
and I have no arms.

She lifts her hand to her face,
palm set like the chin rest on a violin;
again, she works the bow and strings,
sways to music she hears
in some deep labyrinth of her mind,
a chamber still intact.

Nocturne: Rogersville, Tennessee, 1947

Come the stillness of late summer dusk over blue cedars
when the rasp of jarflies hangs like musk
& already bullbats have begun their dazzle
of swerve & dive & the last Greyhound whines
into the distance, its tail lights winking like stars:
now near the station from the edge of shadow
comes the first note of Ned, chores done & loafing at ease:
low, lonesome freight train wail
calling us home into the circle of his song:
we gather, boys in tee shirts flocked around the gleam
of silver cupped in his hands: what slips through
the black barred cage of his fingers
is melody liquid as the meadowlark's
notes, each breath an escape, sweet rush of summer
held & then surrendered to the lift of wing over wing,
beyond street & arching elms, rising above wires thrumming
with talk, over house & barn, beyond yard & field,
into that faraway blue-dark home of song & gone.

Talking Blues

"The blues is the truth.
You'd better believe what they're telling you is the truth."

– *Buddy Guy*

I Sing Blue to You

It was a phone call Ola Mae Wilson almost didn't pick up. The Silver Sands Café's operating hours began at 7 a.m., and the last drop cord light flickered out by 6 p.m. Ola was working an unexpected double shift because Barbara Jean called in sick with the flu. It was the third time in a month she had been infected with germs. Ola knew it was the late nights at the bootleg house with a new boyfriend that was inching Barbara closer to the unemployment line. It was only a matter of time. Ola was thoroughly pissed that her boss, Charlie Birdsong, demanded she stay and work the vacant shift. Charlie wasn't going to do it, or so he informed Ola before she was about to clock out at 2 p.m. So here she was trying to hold on to the little piece of job she had until something else came through.

Answering the phone meant she had to stop wiping down tables and booths. The first five rings went through one ear out the other. "Damn it, can't I get the hell out of here?" In five long strides she picked up the phone next to the cash register.

"Silver Sands and we closed!" Ola waited for something apologetic to be whispered in her ear. Nothing but silence, then a draw of air, then "Tonight. Big Moe's—7 p.m. Be ready. You on." There was silence again. Then a click.

It came rushing back to Ola Mae. Two Thursdays ago she went to Big Moe's for jazz night with Sugar Maple and Pepper. Liquor and curse words flowed freely for hours. Thursday nite brought out amateur singers to improvise along with the house band. Big Moe's establishment rested on 16th Street, between 4th and 5th Avenues and you had to walk down a flight of stairs to enter all the sinning that went on in there. Most of the patrons of Big Moe's weren't legal-abiding citizens, but the confidence men, bootleggers, prostitutes, and gangsters dressed sharper than a broke-dick dog. Several brown-skinned men with wax-downed mustaches caught Ola's eye, but she failed to let those same eyes meet hers. Men like that were intimidating, but she loved the smell of juke joints.

Before they left that night to go home, the three women stopped by the bar and Sugar Maple grabbed a thin piece of paper by the fishbowl and wrote down Ola Mae Wilson's name along with her work and home phone numbers. With the night diluted by Kentucky Tavern straight no chaser, there wasn't much protest about putting her name in the drawing for weekly amateurs who took the stage to try and hang with the house band.

Sugar Maple held the paper up to Ola Mae's carmel face and screamed over the loud noise and saxophone hollers, "Girl, you know I done heard you down at Ebenezer Baptist on Sunday morning and how you be having the whole congregation feeling the spirit, believing they actually getting one step closer to Jesus." Sugar Maple was dead serious, "Ola, five hundred goes to who can ever hang with the house band all of fifteen full minutes. Now, ain't nobody ever done that, but you can. Child, please."

Pepper, her coal black skin shining from sweat and alcohol, conferred like the amen section of Ebenezer, "Yeah." She said, "We seen all these no-talent having people from Smithfield come up to the stage and get booed off. Shit, wait til they get a taste of Ola Mae Wilson."

That was the last time Ola thought about Pepper and Sugar Maple's words. Between work and taking care of her Daddy, there was hardly time for anything else. Cecil Wilson had worked thirty years in the coal mines, in the colored section. He gave the company his muscle and sweat and pride until there was nothing else to give. It was just him and Ola. Cecil's wife died the day she birthed their only child. The doctor warned it would be a difficult pregnancy and delivery, with Shirleene being forty-five years old. In the end, Shirleene bore life, and hers was taken. Ola felt an obligation to never abandon her Daddy, who had been ten years older than Shirleene. Schooling stopped at the sixth grade in the colored high school, and that was the last time Ola held a Blue-Back Speller in her hands. Her first job was washing sheets for Muro's Laundry Service. Ola had to scrub the sheets until they were bleach white and then hang them on a clothesline until air dried them stiff. Nothing hard about that. This went on for seven years until one day Charlie Birdsong caught her walking down 8th Avenue and rolled down the window of his black Packard with fancy running boards and said, "If you tired of smelling them dirty sheets I got a job for you little lady. Two dollars a day plus tips."

Ola reached in the wood grain chifferobe and pulled out a dark wool skirt and white silk blouse and placed them on her bed. She powdered her face carefully, thinking how silly it was to go down to Big Moe's and try to sing. To move a congregation to tears was one thing, to move the crowd at Big Moe's was something no one had ever done. Ola ran some ruby red lipstick over her lips and put a dahlia in her ear. At 6:30 p.m. her black heels *click-clacked* coming down the linoleum hallways as she stuck her head in Cecil's room. At eighty-five Cecil could sleep whenever the need came up. Sometimes Ola thought he was waiting patiently to die. Ola kissed his forehead. By the time Cecil woke up, Ola was walking down the steps into Big Moe's.

Sugar Maple and Pepper were sitting in their signature corner both.

Ola squeezed her way through the crowd dancing to Louis Jordan.

"I was hoping your Momma gave you the message, Pepper. And since Sugar stay next door, why I figure the word spread soon enough," Ola said, sliding into the soft black leather seat.

"Girl, why is you late? They getting ready to start. Now you know Sugar need this money. Hell we all need it, and here you bout to mess the whole thing up," Sugar rattled the ice cubes in her bourbon.

Ola ignored Sugar. She breathed in the mingling bodies and their laughter. She wasn't even thinking about the money. No one ever got the money at Big Moe's. The house band was too good. It was all a hoax to get people to spend their money and cheer for someone to take home a dream, that's what Ola thought. She was about to order a drink when Two-Step, the announcer, hopped up onstage and raised his hands, meaning everyone had to take a seat and shut up. The curtain behind him spiraled upward and the house band appeared. The audience roared and clapped. Two-Step quieted them down again, as he raised the fishbowl high.

"And the first person to challenge the house band is Ola Mae Wilson" Ola swallowed hard. There was absolutely nothing in her brain to draw from. Pepper pushed her out the booth and damn near to the steps leading to the stage. Two-Step reached out his hand and brought her all the way up. He then whispered in her ear like he did on the phone earlier that day, "Tonight. Right now. It's all you." And he was gone.

The band consisted of Piano-Man on the piano, Claw-Hammer on drums, Sleepy on stand up bass, Stutterer on trumpet, and Gut-Bucket on sax. They gave Ola a quick eye-over and immediately went into the tune that would send her hurling back down the steps to her friends in the corner booth. Piano-Man started it off, leaning his solid black porkpie toward the eighty-eights. His wiry fingers came down on the high notes, a contrast to his signature start of low and guttural. He immediately pressed a set of pond rippling notes. It was soft, a quiet storm affect, yet addictive. Suddenly he riffed strong and quick, pulling pieces of watery waves towards a new kind of sound. The audience was still. They could see Piano-Man meant to make short work of Ola. The band members eyed Ola again, moving with subtle intimidation next to their instruments. Ola stood too scared to move, too scared to run.

After rolling his eyes away from Ola, Gut-Bucket found harmony as Piano-Man sailed the cool waters. He brought a piece of memory up from the curvature of his saxophone. It was nails hammered into hands, a cat-o-nine tails digging to flesh. It was the chokecherry tree on a mother's back when she'd tried to escape and paid the penalty. What escaped the horn were also rhythms, beautiful like the first buds of the dogwoods in April, so then Stutterer joined in the fray, for melodious backup. By this time Claw-Hammer was riding the slow nod from the quarter gram of heroin that ran up through his nose and was now draining down his throat. Without taking his eyes off Ola, he crashed the cymbals one time and found the entranceway Piano-Man had created for him. Now he was in four/four time. Simultaneously with Claw-Hammer, Sleepy, all six-nine of him, soft-plucked the bass. He became the glue of the composition being composed in Ola Mae's ears.

There were a few whispers from the audience. There was no way Ola could even jump into that tune, let along hang with them. Even Sugar Maple conceded defeat along with bourbon that she slid down her throat. Ola was about to run offstage, then she heard something that sounded like a mother's voice in the riff Piano-Man played every time the band met back on the one. The voice said, "Memory is the key to the future." Ola had never heard the voice before, but now she felt strength coming over her. It sounded the way she imagined her mother's voice would sound. Looking at the band members, she noticed how they were all lost in their own blues. They were remembering. This is where their sound came from. Ola moved toward the microphone and a guy sitting in the audience started to laugh, and smiles came over other faces in the audience. Ola was moving toward her own embarrassment.

Ola closed her eyes and concentrated on Piano-Man. He was the wild card, the one person who could push the band in any direction. "Master him and the rest will come," the voice said. Her hips began to sway to Sleepy's soft pluck, while her ears rested inside the erratic playing of Piano-Man. She could tell he was coming around to the riff he had played in the beginning, and, when he did, Ola slid to the microphone, "I sing blue to you."

The words had been easy. Piano-Man's rumble on the ivories brought back her seventh year of life on October 10, 1939. News had spread quickly through the colored section of town how Bo Willie was strung up from the tallest oak in the square and hung by the neck until it snapped like a dried-up twig, and death had pushed all the shit and piss out of his body. His neck was set to one side, tongue slithering, eyes almost out of their sockets, the palm of his hands turned open as if to ask the question *why?* The answer lay in his refusal to sell his land, land his grandfather got from the Freedman's Bureau. Cecil walked all the way home to get his little girl and bring her back, for her to see what kind of world she was living in. That day he showed her how hate brought out the ugly. "Look girl, look good and hard at what you see. Study the hate, and know it before it come round the corner."

Ola knew hate when she saw it, but she also remembered Bo Willie's eyes turning blue. She never forgot those eyes, and here was Piano-Man playing those blue eyes right now. So when Ola said, "I sing blue to you," she immediately followed Piano-Man as he took her on a journey up and down the scales with full and half notes. He then reached back to his boogie-woogie training, allowing the left hand to improvise while the right hand played guitar-like. Ola kept up with Piano-Man's back and forth swing to blues to jazz while working through her own memory as she belted low, her voice raspy and angelic. She sang different shades of pain: cobalt, azure, cerulean, and like Piano-Man, she too had found the beauty.

Ola's back and forth wordplay did not go unnoticed. The same group of onlookers who once laughed silently now strummed their fingers on the red tablecloths, moving in time to Ola's ruby-red lipsticked mouth. Ola tapped into something familiar. The strangeness of it overwhelmed them, the words salved their suppressed wounds. The attention did not go unnoticed by Stutterer, who decided to put an end to the novice trying to hang with seasoned professionals. Unexpected and without provocation, Stutterer revolted against playing the expected chord Piano-Man came around to; instead he screeched, long, erratic screeches, counter to Piano-Man's tempo. Stutterer became entangled in his own self-consciousness, but in a strange way the two men on stage gelled into one booming sound. Stutterer segued into a rainbow of color, climbing the spectrum of life, then riffing in a primeval language as if he were trying to speak. With each utterance, Stutterer's inability to articulate his complaint made the everforming composition more complex, his search for a language almost blew Ola Mae Wilson back into Sleepy's standup bass. But her hips found the rhythm and again she steadied herself.

Ola closed her eyes to Stutterer's manic rant and how he gasped breath and spat it out. He too was wailing a memory not yet reconciled. Ola re-remembered the day she saw James Earl, all 17 years of his youthful body, coming out of the picture show with Lula Jean, her best friend. The way he held her hand, and how her body leaned into his, caught her off-guard. He was staring inside her eyes lovingly, just the way he had done to Ola the night before, and she had believed him. She believed him so much she gave herself to him, willingly. She had given her milk for free. No need to buy the cow now, at least that was the expression James Earl gave her when he walked by with Lula who was too ashamed to meet her wet eyes. There was still a scab on Ola's heart that hadn't healed and so she informed Stutterer of this when she started out high and eased back into a strut, then the narrative of her blues.

Stutterer read between the lines of her comeback, although her voice was serene, Ola really was saying, "One good turn deserves another, one bad deed begets another. Show me your pain, I'll show you mine."

Pepper stared at the person she knew to be her friend, but Ola was transcending to a higher level of herself. She had taken fatback and collard greens and brought out the sweetness in them. Her wails were layered with pig ears and ham hocks, and the audience couldn't get enough. Out of the corner of her eye, Pepper caught Big Moe standing in the back with a cigar dotted to his mouth. He'd come from his back office. It had been too quiet for him. Usually when Two-Step brought a singer to the stage, the noise and boos soon followed. Big Moe was chomping down on his unlit cigar. He too was looking at the young lady, dressed in black skirt and white blouse with a funny flower behind her ear, sing down Piano Man and Stutterer. She was giving as good as she got. Claw-Hammer and Sleepy were only passengers on this ride, could not change the direction in which Piano-Man had gone, so they just kept time.

Gut-Bucket pushed his soft tan Dobbs back on his forehead, took out his silk handkerchief, and wiped the sweat running down his leathered skin. He then took center stage next to Ola. He blew in short pulses—his finger variations moving in slow motion: then he cried long and hard on his axe. The wail was reminiscent of the first cornfield holler in Old Town, Virginia. He then blew intermediary arwhoolies, fluttering them to one long whine. Gut-Bucket gathered his breath and broke into a hot silver flow, smooth and even, his lips pressed tight to the reed, his eyes staring Ola Mae down, producing a series of oohs and aahs from the audience. Gut-Bucket was getting low down dirty—right nasty with his axe. The band played up-tempo now, attempting to confuse Ola Mae. They were wilting Ola away into the background. To add insult, Piano-Man inserted a butterfly ripple. Stutterer stuttered on the trumpet and Claw-Hammer doubled up on the cymbals and snare. Big Moe smiled. Nobody came back from that.

Just as Big Moe was about to return to his office, Ola pressed her eyes tight again and listened as her mother helped her to re-remember the story of her great-grandmother hiding in the mulberry bushes when the patterollers came to get her Daddy. Luckily she had gone to draw water. And how they drug him and her Momma out of their lean-to, and then watered it down with kerosene. The lit match flew through the air and flames crackled against her Daddy's moist face. The men unzipped his pants and castrated him right there on the spot. This was the yell that Ola let out as she reached inside Gut-Bucket's saxophone and brought up her own throaty pain that sounded like a horn, each harmonizing chord echoing her challenger. She fluttered and scatted, and, at that moment, the band acknowledged defeat. She had duplicated and exceeded anything they laid down. Rather than keep on playing the band melted down slowly, like a sun relinquishing its power. Ola looked up, and the audience refused to breathe, waiting to see what she would do next. As she had started, she ended, "I sing blue to you."

∞

Blue Jazz Dream at New Year's

Yes, you had this dream and you were in it, but being a dream you didn't even know that you were that quiet-eyed woman listening to jazz musicians play a jazz that was blues out under summer sun in a field like the one in Bethel where you used to walk barefoot every August during Woodstock anniversaries in Catskills you left when you still had long dark hair like this woman in your dream now beginning to slowly dance inside the sultry sad jazz, this grave woman pressing her feet naked to earth, her face lifted unsmiling to sky, hair glinting red in the hot light.

And the musicians were improvising, playing her far back into music of her own skin, bones, genetic code, and how *sweet sweet sweet* it felt to be swaying like warm end of summer breeze rifting through trees and air tinged with wild chicory and Queen Anne's Lace, *yes*, and the black trumpet player sauntered over to her, whispered, "You are beautiful when you are serious like that, inhabiting the blues so fully, not bothering to smile when you have nothing to smile about," then pressed his horn back gold to his golden mouth and you woke, your silver hair crying across your pillow, thinking how it was New Year's and maybe the dream of the woman had something to do with you, and the trumpet player was Miles playing how to turn your back on the crowds and step haughtily into your own blue solitudes.

∞

Tempo

Mother. You were always music. Played the organ at the church services. I clutched the cold metal of my chair as the music crescendoed. The congregation was drowned out by the booming chords. You nodded toward the choir, fifteen of them, seven men, eight women, as they sang the harmonies of the hallelujah chorus.

Because of your music, you would not know. You would not know the wispy gray fog, always in my periphery, creeping slowly around my ears, ready to turn to smoke. You did not know the muffled sounds, whispers, cold, quiet, soothing, like snow softly begging me to sleep. The white snow and the white closets, heavy and light, rolling into fog that circled my throat. And then I smelled smoke. So I ran.

I won't bore you with how I got there (plane, train, tailwind), but I was there, in San Francisco, that city of ruin, temporal, winding, like the past I never had, a city that at any moment can shake and quake and tumble to the ground.

You did not understand what it means to want to run, that manic bright burning desire to leave by whatever means possible to save your life, to save the voices, and once you are there, there, there, you don't know how or why you did it, only that you no longer care or have the energy to save yourself.

I ran toward water, the ocean, San Francisco. There in the Castro, I went to one of the gay boy barbers and got my hair cut above my ears, the bangs long.

I will tell you, mother, that I bought a motorcycle, that my hair was cut short, that I carried a knife tucked into my boots. I tell you this so you know I live in the city, not a town, that I have to protect myself from robbers and rapists, from staring down the barrels of guns, metal pressed against the temple of my head, from being robbed at gunpoint at the library as I step out at two in the afternoon on a Friday into the fog and rain and wind. That I usually can't reach for my knife, but I know it's there, the cool metal blade against the hot leather of my boot.

The guy at the café. He was not handsome, but he was my type. The openness, the work horse face. Loose jeans. I had talked to him only once, yet there was something I projected onto him, a future, my life, with his rolled up sleeves and self-assured smiles, his talk, passionate, focused, a chef who sliced. The garlic skin, faded jeans, circles under his eyes. His restaurant, a cafe with freshly ground coffee and sandwiches with vegetables from local farms.

The man was my future. Us. Old, warm, together. I knew it, and because I knew, I waited. Waited for when I was ready for him, to meet him, look him in the eye, and then someday, marry him, someday have a child with tired brown eyes like his. I saw him holding our child, a girl, as she ran up and down the aisle of the cafe, demanding our attention. I would be their shadow goddess.

He would be a person whose name I'd say over and over, just to hear the sound. Just to calm myself at night.

I avoided him because of this, the timing wasn't right, and I thought he would wait, frozen, unchanged, for years behind the café glass.

I must tell you how happy I was there, how alive I felt in a city that is grown up. This wind shakes me awake, and I move with a rhythm that makes all of the desperate cries, close calls, worth it just to hear the snap and the water and the hills, a roller coaster that I'm always riding.

How do I know this was not projection, wild fantasy, or even idle speculation? How do you know when the significant person, event, emotion appear before you like an outstretched hand? How do you know when life opens and then folds in, pointing toward the light, a beam that you will float on, the wave that will carry you to your grave? You know. You know the difference between desperate longing and accepting the fate that is yours.

We both moved slowly because there was all the time in the world.

It was not so much a result of who I was. It was more like who I'd chosen to become. I would never be able to realize all of the possibilities. And I saw this one, my life with this man who ran a café by the ocean. I am much better by water, by salt, by that rhythm; it calms me, soothes me, keeps me cool. Only there could I stay with one person, have a life, the shape of a life like many others, and only in the details would I make it mine.

Finally, when I was ready, I went to the café. I applied for a job. Our eyes met, he took me aside, pressed his palm in mine. He knew, just as I did, the choices we were to make, the possibilities that we would have to throw away, discard like dried flowers. He told me to come back Monday. I could start then. Busing tables, taking orders, pouring coffee.

This man at the café. He is not you and he is not not-you. He is someone else, a stranger I could live with in an old house of this city, and one day, a baby, a child. I am not projecting. I am creating. Me with my short hair and big eyes, one day I will have a child, a daughter, who will look just like me. She will look like her mother. Not you. This does not have to do with you. This is mine. This man in the cotton shirt and sad eyes is mine.

My future with him, calm, stable. A future with a future. With a baby who burps and spits and strains our patience, a baby who will grow up to hurt us, remind us of our mistakes, our humanness. This is what I wanted with the man in the restaurant. Our child would not be beautiful and that was a blessing.

In the future, if I saw someone else I was attracted to I would turn my head, shut my eyes, put them on the sidelines because that is what you must do when you choose marriage and a child because that is what I'm talking about.

But when I came back that Monday, ready to begin a new life, ready for this chosen self, I saw the crowds and the smoke and my stomach fell when I heard the word fire. We grow green and red and then it's ash, fuzzy gray, nothing but death.

Fire is not good, the heat makes me wild, brings out my frantic side, fire brings panic, claustrophobia, death. Fire is too many memories, too much pain, dry skin, parched leaves, snapped twigs. Everything bursts into flames.

They said arson. Rags soaked in gasoline. I could not bear to find out if he had started it or someone else had. So then, not too long ago I was in San Francisco, surveying the singular certainty of my future for the first time. By fate, destiny, or mathematical probability, my life had become something by virtue of what it would not be.

But before that, before my desire for separation, rebellion, before that was the church. Tradition, the small wooden church with its choir balcony, stained glass, and old wood smells. After the service, you would gather the music, slip your feet back into your pumps, shake your hand with the choir members, and then, holding my hand, through the back way of the church, work your way to our old Chevy, parked in the back. You wanted to avoid the minister's hand shake, the chit chat. Your work was done.

Despite your playing at the church, there was no Bible in the house, no prayer before meals, no crosses above our wooden twin beds. There was only music, music played on the phonograph's scratched records, on your piano when we pretended I was asleep.

Your music. How could I know that passion? I wanted to be like the other girls, wear makeup, eat cookies. I wanted to be the most important thing to you. But many times when I walked in and found you humming, scribbling notes on white paper you jumped when I tapped your shoulder, then focused slowly on the girl in front of you, curled and ribboned, trying to discern who I was.

Your mouse-colored hair falling past your ear, covering your eyes, your nubbed pencil, the eraser dust, dark notes pressed into songs, your secret language. What were those songs? Loud deafening, a crescendo, the way you lifted your arms in the air, quickly, violently, then silence.

My piano lessons. Every afternoon after school. You were not a martyr. You were a spiritual person, as evidenced by the clean, simple, bright, two bedroom house we lived in. Only the shiny grand piano, dusted daily, tuned regularly, was money. Everything else was secondhand, scraps, noodles, cheese, powdered milk. The piano's sound, so soft then loud I wanted to cry, seemed hedonistic compared to our surroundings.

I wore the gingham and floral dresses that you sewed, dresses pressed and starched every morning. When I was young, the socks turned down, little anklets and patent leather shoes. Later, knee socks and lace ups, short dresses vulnerable to a flip, a gust of wind that exposed my underwear, my bare thighs. I wanted pants like the other girls wore, girls whose hair was neatly combed or pulled back with a ribbon, girls, who, if I looked closely enough, had purple crusts of jelly around the corners of their mouths.

Most of the days of my life are forgotten; most of my moments are not even a dream. I will not remember the days I must have been quietly happy. The days I woke up, went to school, and kissed you good night. Yet I can recall each night of torment, euphoria, and obsession. Still I must ask if even those moments were real.

In high school I wore jeans like the others and put my makeup on in the girl's bathroom at school. I'd scrub it off before I came home. By then I knew that you were strange and eccentric with your singular passion for church music. I was embarrassed and mistrustful of you. I told you that I would no longer go to church because I didn't believe in God.

But what about the music, you asked.

It does nothing for me, I said.

I know that's what made you cry sometimes, that I didn't love music, your music, the sounds of saints, the music of God. But you were beyond me, I couldn't touch you, because you had your music. You had the divine.

I am trying to rely on my unreliable memory. Your hands brushing my hair, scratching my back, running the bath water, carefully turning pages of a book. I do not believe my memories and dreams. I remember only what I must. I dream what I don't want to remember. And I must tell you, these days I don't dream of drowning, instead I dream of fire.

When I was four I watched our neighbor's house burn from my bedroom window. My own tiny room so safe, yet close enough to smell the smoke. The neighbors, indistinct in the night, huddled, their mouths collectively forming soft Os. I'm sure I saw you mother, in your burgundy choir robe leading them in song. Your arms rose and fell in short staccatos as you pushed yourself up so the music could rise with the heat. Then I heard sounds from the living room piano, the music crescendoing, the tempo increasing. When I looked out the window again, your apparition had vanished with the smoke. The fireman sprayed his hose until all that was left was ash. The neighbors dispersed, trudging home in their slippers and cotton pajamas while you continued playing in the living room.

And then I was in the future, in this very moment, when they told me you were dead, which meant I no longer could tell you everything, and I was floating, watching myself, a solitary stubborn woman who had not come to terms with the small tragedy that was her life, and her mother, Elizabeth, also solitary but not hard, full of forgiveness before the sinner had even sinned, ready to forgive everyone their sins because she had her music, that part of her not caught in time.

∾

Monday Morning with Household Chores

Surprised into tears by an old song.
It's my mother, not a lover, I miss.
How she sang along happily. With abandon.
The words soothed her. Lifted her, too.
I stop in the middle of mopping the kitchen floor.
Nothing to do but sit down on the steps.
Let the tears have their way.

It's my solitude I weep for.
The never-again of it.
Changeable weather. A sweet old song.
Me aging with all these questions.
She not there to ask.

Isn't every motherless girl the same?
Still expecting her phone call.
Even after however-many years.
Mopping's regular rhythm.
Lemon oil on wooden chest.
Honor her with frangipani candles at Christmas.
Sing with abandon. Abandon. Abandon.

Blues Talking

There were trains in my birth,
The hoot of night steam,
Pistons staggering over railbeds
Steely and straight as if only
This steadiness and nothing else
Could contain the sadness,
The force of living beyond
Now, off up North into the night
Where all the black sons
Of switchmen took their strong
Dark music jumping and jiving
Into back-alley dives
All the way from the slow
Mississippi cotton bottoms
Raw with life and music
Falling out of nothing more
Than shacks where hearts
As red as anyone's shook
To beats unknown in origin,
In time, calling up the sweat
From those fields where I began
Halfway between North and South,
White and black, knowing and not knowing,
Heading toward each other
Like two trains in the night
With no lantern hung at the switch
To say this here collision's
Gonna be bad.

Danny Boy vs. Dead End Street

When you turn down Gallant Avenue, you have to remind yourself it's a dead end before your momentum carries you too far. You might think that's not a very courteous arrangement, but there it is. Besides, the first time I visited her there, with the promise of homemade souffle hanging in the air, I was giddy with courage. Virtue, chivalry and such things were very much on my mind because Loretta is an old-fashioned name, a name that had been in the ether since my childhood. I remember staying home from school and watching on television a beautiful woman with raven tresses sweep down a staircase and open palatial front doors into her home. Even in black and white, she was majestic. In fact, she was the only Loretta I had ever met until this one.

I thought I might be swept away by her, my Loretta, that is, because her name suggested exotic places to me. Maybe to Spain, maybe to the foot of the Pyrenees, where water trickles down the side of a craggy black and white mountainside. Gilbert Roland *and* Tyrone Power are there, huddled together, planning their next attack on the stinking Nationalistas. Behind them, lusty Ava Gardner begs Tyrone Power not to go, for he will surely be "keeled," which breaks poor Gilbert Roland's heart because she used to be his girl, the little spitfire.

In the bedroom of Loretta's house, there was a crack up in the ceiling, but I wasn't thinking of London songs then because she was Irish and early into our warm summer evenings together, she showed me home movies of freckle-faced little girls on Christmas mornings, unwrapping presents and modeling their new bathrobes and slippers. She had about a hundred sisters and they all had names that belonged to nuns, and there was a brother, a boy named Terry.

I gathered from Loretta that Terry was a sorry son of a gun who grew up trying to play blues guitar and ride motherhonkin' motorcycles. I never met him, but I have to believe he was trying to make a point.

Anyway, there was a crack up in the ceiling, in the bathroom actually. And there was music behind the home movies. Loretta told me her parents had taken all their ancient super 8s to a guy who could transfer them to video and even lay a soundtrack under it all. Well, the Connellys wanted the music to be Irish and sure enough, the video unwound to the strains of *The Blackbird of Mullamore*, *Carrickfergus*, and under a beautifully held long take of her father, Mr. Dan Connelly, unboxing a pipe, pipe tobacco and slippers, John Gary wailed *Danny Boy*. It was enough to break anybody's heart or drive them to the

229

nearest pub.

It wasn't long before Loretta and I were rolling around and making up our own songs. There was music and wonderful roses, they tell me, in sweet fragrant meadows of dawn and however the hell the rest of that goes.

But as I was saying before, 7 Gallant Avenue is an address that insists on courteous behavior, and the dark-eyed Loretta lived there behind white lace curtains and had kids at elite colleges and what was I thinking? Do you have any idea how hard a man will try to be virtuous when he thinks a woman wants a knight? It's inevitable, a fait accompli, that he's going to come up short. I can't explain what happened, the insides of the thing, how it worked or how it didn't. Sometimes a woman just wants you to be the scoundrel that you are.

Bet on it, as soon as they take care of that Franco business, and if he doesn't get "keeled," Ava Gardner will forget all about valiant Tyrone Power and go running back to Gilbert Roland. How could she not with a moustache like his?

By St. Patrick's Day, I was squeezing tears out of a bar rag while I swear to all the saints of musicians and travelers alike, a spontaneous battle of the bands split my head in opposite directions. On the restaurant jukebox, the Kinks looked in the mirror at their second class lives and asked what in the world they were living for. While under the party tent, where I nursed another pint, a trio of geezers told me that the pipes, the pipes, were calling me, from glen to glen.

I ask you, what could I do but answer the call and go looking for another Loretta? I wiped the beer foam from the ends of my moustache and got to thinking I might take me a little trip to Spain.

∞

A Redheaded Woman

The subway doors opened, and I heard a woman singing. They closed, and she was gone. But I heard the rest of her song as the train lurched on, and all the words sprang up through years.

> *My analyst told me*
> *That I was right out of my head.*
> *The way he described it*
> *he said I'd be better dead than 'live.*
> *I didn't listen to his jive,*
> *I knew all along*
> *that he was all wrong....*

We were all redheads—Annie Ross who wrote and sang these lyrics, Margo who played this album in an apartment where I lived long ago, and me.

I met Margo and her lover, Peter in their railroad apartment on the top floor of a tenement on East Fourth Street. I was with Neil, Peter's best friend. Although I'd known Neil for only three weeks, half-crazed with passion, I had already accepted his invitation to live with him there with these two strangers during our two-month winter break from school. I was 19.

We were a much-photographed generation, a colorful bridge between "beat" and "love." More than one photographer caught Margo and Peter's striking faces. Peter was dark and craggy, wickedly handsome, a Jewish Jean-Paul Belmondo; Margo was pale, with a faint veil of freckles and an amazing mass of curly red hair. In a book of portraits published toward the end of the decade, Margo and Peter are in Tompkins Square Park, cheek to cheek and smiling, each with a cherubic baby propped against a shoulder.

On East Fourth Street, half a dozen years before that photo was shot, we might have looked like a well-matched foursome: two women with long red hair (mine, poker straight, did not approach the effulgence of Margo's), two tall, dark men. Neil, less handsome than Peter, looked enough like him to have been his brother. But we were ill-suited as housemates. Peter and Margo stayed high most of the time and rarely went out. They'd both dropped out of school, and neither talked of any plans. They sold enough of the pot they bought to pay their share of the rent and buy more. Food money wasn't part of the equation. Neil and I both had jobs, though Neil's was only for a few weeks, and we were both trying to write. Actually, I *was* writing. I was also waking early and walking a freezing half mile to the subway to go to my temp job. Peter and Margo didn't much like me, and I didn't like them. I tried, for Neil's sake—I would have walked through fire for him—and at best, a cool truce prevailed.

The living room was Peter and Margo's bedroom, and it was always dark. When they weren't smoking or screwing or sleeping they read sometimes, but mostly they'd play chess or Scrabble, afloat on the horns of Paul Desmond or Miles Davis or Eric Dolphy.

Margo's face was empty and white, and her eyes lay in it like flat green buttons. Peter's was all angles and shadows, his smile arch, his dark eyes shifting and sly.

I can still hear Margo saying, "Man, I'm getting tired of this game."

And Peter: "It'll be over soon."

"It will be over soon," she croons, almost contented. "It will be over soon, over soon...."

They played their games sitting cross-legged on the quilt-covered innerspring that served as their bed. They ate there. They waited there. Music filled all the spaces, and for me it took on shapes and colors, long and narrow in the corridor, spreading as I approached their room, bridging all gaps between sleep and wakefulness and dreams.

We had almost no furniture but we had two phonographs, and piles of LPs that migrated between the one in that living room, and the one in our tiny bedroom at the end of a long hallway. My favorite was Margo's album of jazz solos with names like "Four" and "Twisted," all dressed up with lyrics and sung by two men and a woman who used their voices like bandstand horns and called themselves Lambert, Hendricks and Ross.

The walls had been painted light blue, but most of the paint was covered up with pictures cut from magazines. In between these collages Margo had hung snakes made of straw or plastic or braided rags. She'd covered the windows with old blankets and filled the lamps with red bulbs. A straw rug covered most of the scarred wood floor, and scraps of other rugs were scattered about—all, like the innerspring, remnants of a neighborhood eviction.

Our sustenance was mostly orange juice, chocolate marshmallow cookies, spaghetti and the green magic that filled the rooms with fragrant smoke, sweet and thick, promising laughter.

I lived in two worlds: the outside world where I passed as a diligent working girl; and our apartment with its cracked paint and unwashed pots, my desk a splintery plywood slab balanced on unmatched suitcases, and the mattress on the floor.

232

By day I rolled my long hair into a French twist, put on a sheath dress and heels and typed invoices at an advertising agency on Park Avenue. By night, I sat on the dirty floor in Neil's arms, breathing jazz and marijuana, all the while waiting for the moment when we would finally be alone in the tiny back room with what was for me the most powerful and mind-bending drug of all.

One Saturday night, Neil told me The Man was coming. He asked me if I wanted to see him. I didn't, but I knew I would, if he came. We waited for him. All that night and the next day the four of us waited, and finally, after 11 on Sunday night, there was a knock on the door. The Man was tall, perhaps a few years older than we were, a white man in a plaid flannel shirt, tails out. He sat down on the floor in the snake room, put a brown paper bag on a plywood board, took a sandwich and a bottle of cream soda from the bag, and looked around him at the red mist. He didn't like it. Neil took the red bulb out of the lamp and put in a plain one. Margo paced, watching the man eat, giggling and pushing up her sleeve. When he had finished his sandwich, she became quiet and sat down at the edge of the innerspring. She watched with the eager face of a child as he heated the spoon. There was a spark in her eyes I hadn't seen before. She began to rock back and forth, hugging her legs to her loose brown sweater. One of her knees protruded, impudently white, from a rip in her light cotton pants.

"I don't have any veins," she giggled.

"Sure you have veins," The Man said, not looking at her. "Everybody's got veins."

She pushed her sleeve nearly to her shoulder and examined the inside of her elbow. "Man, *I* don't have any veins," she moaned.

"What happens if you shoot it in the muscle?" Peter asked, smiling his sly half-smile. He was sprawled out behind her, leaning on his elbow, not touching her.

"Nothing," said The Man. "It just takes longer."

"Well, if you can't find the vein, give it to me and I'll stick it in," she said.

The Man didn't speak again until he had found a vein of his own and penetrated it twice. Then he got up and went to the phone.

"Man, we got burned," he shouted into the receiver.

Despite his insistence that the stuff was no good, Margo wanted to try it anyway. They didn't find a vein, but there was muscle in the soft, white flesh. She lay on the floor after The Man had gone, listening to the sharp, narrow blue-white sounds from the phonograph. It was beyond my imagining, what she was looking for. But she'd found it, so she said.

233

Suddenly, after nearly two years, there they were, in the dining room of the barracks-like apartment in married students' housing. We'd all left the East Fourth Street apartment when the spring semester began, and I'd seen Peter and Margo only once after that, on a chilly April Sunday when they dropped in on us at school. In Peter's beat-up car the four of us cruised into Woodstock, where we saw Bob Dylan and Joan Baez walking down an otherwise empty street. Dylan was not yet nearly as famous as he would soon become, and I no longer admitted to the two Baez records I owned. We all considered ourselves too cool to make much of having spotted them.

Now, Neil had graduated and gone to California. Our love affair seemed to be over. I was in my last semester of school. And Peter and Margo were getting married. They were on campus to pick up the couple I'd come to babysit for, art students who would be their witnesses before a justice of the peace.

Peter, in a dark suit, was more wildly handsome than ever, his black hair glistening with rain. Margo looked unchanged. She was sitting at the table, her long red hair streaming around her face, almost hiding it.

Peter was rolling a joint.

"Want some?" he asked me.

"I'd love to, but I have so much work...." Before the words were out of my mouth I felt foolish. He realized, of course, as I had, that my answer had always been the same. Not that I'd *always* refused the joint passed to me in our railroad apartment, but I'd been the only one there who frequently didn't want to be high.

I asked the polite questions and learned that they planned to open an art gallery on East Tenth Street, bought with Margo's trust fund, liberated by their marriage. They'd actually married in Mexico last summer, to hold his draft board at bay, but some questions had come up, and he was to report for a physical next week. The purpose of tonight's ceremony was to settle his draft status.

Dissatisfied with the joint he'd made, Peter undid it and tapped the contents into a pipe. Margo passed it to me. I shook my head.

Sinking deep into an armchair, Peter said lazily, "I guess we'd better go get married. Yes, that's it. I knew there was something we had to do. Or maybe it was something else. I have to go to a public library."

Then they all tried to figure out where the nearest library was.

Peter and the witnesses left the room to find a box for the gold band Margo had just taken off. I was sitting on the sofa and Margo sat down next to me to put on her boots. I'd never known what to say to her. Once more, I relied

234

awkwardly on the obvious.

"So how does it feel to be an expectant mother?"

"Oh, it's great."

"I remember you said once you never wanted to have children...."

"Did I say that? Really? I was joking."

The others came back with the ring in a box and began donning coats.

"Is it still raining?" Margo asked. It was. "Oh, well...." She tried to open her umbrella, but it was broken and half of it folded over itself.

"What do I do if the baby wakes up?" I asked the witnesses.

"She won't. She'd better not...."

"There's food, records, typewriter...you know where everything is."

"Well, we'd better go get married," said Peter.

"Do I look like a bride?"

And then they were out the door.

I went to check the baby, who was asleep in a cold room that smelled of oil paint. Standing by her crib, I looked outside and the unlit window of my empty dorm room glared at me across the wet grass. Neil's absence from my life felt like a gaping hole that went deeper than my insides, opening in me like a cavern that seemed to lead to some hollow center of the earth.

Peter and Margo had two children in as many years. Soon after the second was born, he left her. They reconciled briefly once or twice, then divorced. I'm not sure when Margo became addicted to heroin, but the children were still babies when she became unable to care for them. They grew up calling Margo's aunt and uncle Mom and Dad. Over the years, I'd heard she was living in the West, in the South, was an alcoholic, was in rehab, had become fat, was working with horses.

Peter was the usual conduit for such gossip. With one woman or another, he was a frequent visitor to the beach house where I spent the seventies with Neil, who'd easily charmed me back into his life when he came back east. Eventually, we'd married. Our daughter was born a week before the sixties passed into history. I had no interest in seeing Peter, but he was Neil's friend, and came and went as he pleased. Often, he had some news of Margo from their children. He tried intermittently to maintain contact with them, but he changed careers with dizzying frequency and never sought a job that would have enabled him to participate in their support.

My own marriage almost survived the seventies. Among the numerous reasons for its collapse was that I was convinced that what Neil really wanted was to jog from woman to woman the way Peter did. Neil never denied this. When I left, that's exactly what he did.

In the fall of 1979 I was trying to settle into Manhattan after a decade away, separated not only from Neil, but from our daughter, who remained with Neil while I looked for work. I'd been back in town only a few weeks when Margo surfaced. I was at an art opening with two old college friends, Alice and Judy, who'd been Margo's roommates one summer, when all three had had their eyes on Peter—until Margo won the prize. Suddenly, in the bustling downtown crowd, there was the mass of red hair, unmistakable even pulled back in a clip. Pale as ever, slim, her milky cheeks unlined, Margo seemed utterly untouched by age and yet subdued almost beyond recognition. In the nondescript clothes of charity, a plain white cotton blouse with the kind of collar circle pins were once attached to, and a long gray pleated skirt too heavy for the season, she looked like a nun in street clothes, or someone just released from prison. She was living in a shelter, she told us. But she was getting it together, yes, she was.

About the decade that had passed since any of us had seen her, Margo said nothing. But she spoke bitterly of Peter, how he had left her with her babies. She wore his abandonment as if she still held those babies in her arms. We gave her our phone numbers when she asked. But we were afraid – not for her, but for ourselves. Margo was a wild card. And none of us felt in a position to be magnanimous. Most days, I felt like a ragged wound, bandaging a smile on my face as I arrived at my temp job. Alice, single and long entangled with a very married man, was, like me, just back in town and marginally employed after a decade away. Judy was struggling to support two children and a depressed husband who'd abruptly quit his job. Later that day, as the three of us stood in Judy's kitchen watching coffee drip into a pot through a paper towel, we asked each other what we might have done for Margo under better circumstances. Uncomfortably, we admitted that none of us would have taken her in.

A week or so later, Alice and I saw her again, begging on a street corner. We each gave her five dollars. She phoned Alice, and then Judy, a few times after that. She never got around to me.

My temp job had ended, so I was home the morning Judy called with the news of Margo's suicide. I remember crossing the living room of my furnished sublet to answer the phone, standing by the desk in the stunned sunlight. The world seemed to stop. I stumbled out a few questions, but Judy had been told no details.

A little while later, I got on the subway, going through the motions of what I'd planned for the day. Whatever I'd been feeling before the phone call—had the morning been lit with a faint sheen of hope?—was supplanted by a dark, pervasive ache. How little Margo's death meant to anyone, including myself. Did anyone care? Not enough.

Standing in the subway, my raw face streaming with tears, I thought, each time the door closed, that at the next stop I'd get off, turn around, go back home. Had there been a last straw, I wondered. Had she perhaps encountered Peter on the street? It seemed necessary to conjure reasons. The one I made up had nothing to do with the drugs and alcohol that had plagued her. She had died, I surmised, to escape the pure pain of feeling so alone.

And then the doors of the subway car opened, and the song, Margo's song, entered like another passenger to stand with me.

I recalled seeing her phone number in my address book where she'd written it at the gallery a few months earlier. I'd been paging through the book in search of some friend whose welcome I hadn't worn thin in *my* neediness. Seeing her penciled scrawl, I'd felt a flash of shame, knowing I *never* would call Margo, and hoped I wouldn't hear from her. And it all mixed together there on the subway: Margo's fate, my grief for my own once-promising young life. Abandonment was what *I* felt, when it was I who had done the abandoning. And shame. And terror of my own longing, abruptly undeniable, for such oblivion as was finally hers.

And hadn't I always thought myself better than Margo—at least insofar as I tangled with the world, instead of running away? Now I *had* run, and left my child as well, though it was only meant to be temporary – but surely Margo must have thought that, too, when she brought her babies to her family all those years ago and went off wherever she had gone

My stop came; I left the subway. In the café that was my destination, I ordered coffee, opened a notebook, still pretending I was there to write, still hoping a man would walk in, look my way and be drawn to a thin woman with red hair.

A tune I recognized came through the speakers, a quiet, haunting blues that had—always late, late in the evening—often filled those shabby rooms on East Fourth Street with a poignant depth and light. After a while, I remembered it was called "Stolen Moments." What were we thinking, I wondered, all those years ago? And I recalled some words the young flutist on that tune, Eric Dolphy, had murmured on a later album, his last. "When you hear music, after it's over, it's gone in the air. You can never capture it again."

∞

Heartwood

My heart is the reed
of a bassoon, double-walled
and slick with the saliva of wanting
something it might seize
in the gulf of a low G or early
morning, upright and silver
keys shining, warm wood mirrors
the mystery of flamed Yugoslavian
mountain maple, its sound
profound, round, finding,
as if at the bottom of an unwonted
ocean chamber, one sublime
awful note.

TRITONES

"Why should the devil get all the good tunes?"

– attributed to Martin Luther

Stephen M. Holt

Yea, the Old Devil is Real and, Worse, He's Hereabouts

Lo, here he comes, boys! Red
flannel longjohns soiled and baggy
at the crotch, he rides astraddle

a bargeload of felled virgin timber
groaning out of Tug Fork Valley.
Hooting into buttermilk morning fog

he saws out old-time fiddle tunes,
his bowstring so hot its awful
sulfur stench fouls the river's mouth.

Minor Chords

Early light rolled down the mountain, bounced through the window and fell across my eyes. It propelled me from the bed. Bean Day! It was Bean Day for the Heltons and Clems. I jumped into the shorts and shirt puddled on the floor beside my bed. All the kids were to hit the bean patch and pick each row clean before the heat of the day. Newanna, Dorcas, Thelma and Kaye headed up the line of Clem children. My little sister, and I were the only Heltons. Our family was the smallest in the valley with only two girls and the baby and Daddy a lawyer; we were pitiful. The Clems were miners: six kids strong and one more coming.

After the picking we used the long needles and heavy thread and raced to see who could fill the most strings. The winner might get a nickel for ice cream and a ride in the back of the truck to the store. We might not, too, but you never knew so it was worth the gamble.

Fleetie Clem would hang the long strings of beans on thick nails driven into the edge of the porch stretcher. All summer the beans would swing free to catch the sun and breezes until they dried hard and crisp. Shuck beans, bubbled down with a piece of salt pork, tasted like summer sunshine, and with a pone of cornbread they filled soup bowls and hungry bellies all winter.

Just about the time the last of the dew and morning fog burned off we finished up stripping the thirty rows. We delivered bucket after bushel to the front porch where Fleetie and her sister, Geneva, sat in the swing and broke off the tips and threw them into a large dishpan. From the pan we grabbed a bean, speared it and pulled it along the string until it rested at the end. Bean after bean, we built the long green ropes falling over our knees. After a couple of hours tedium set in, and we begged Fleetie to get out her guitar and sing for us. She could sing bugs off the screen door, but she never picked up the guitar on her own. It was a pure pity because music lived in her fingers. She let the notes flow as free as the stream beside the house. Her voice was deep and throaty, and all of us loved it. After she married Burl, he took hateful pleasure in shaming her about the music. She was careful never to sing or play where he could hear her, and music was never mentioned when he was around.

As Fleetie tuned the guitar we commenced fussing for our favorite. I slipped off the porch and ran up the hill to get Mother, a sure way to stretch the time I could stay. By the time we came back through the yard gate, the whole bunch was harmonizing "Down in the Valley." When Mother stepped through the gate, Fleetie stood up to put the guitar away.

"Oh, Fleetie, you can't stop. Please play some more. The children just love it. It helps the work go quicker. I thought I could help out a little and maybe take a mess of beans home."

We needed more beans like we needed a house fire, but Fleetie always refused to let anyone do a thing for her.

"Just some screechin' going on down here, Kathleen. Come in and set here on the swing. Kids, get Kathleen a pile of beans," said Fleetie.

In a few minutes song after song rolled out and across the yard. Out of the corner of my eye I noticed Johnny Nolan coming down the railroad track. He hunkered down on the tracks listening to the music a minute before he walked through the yard gate.

Fleetie jumped when she saw him and and threw her arms around the guitar and hid her face behind it. "Oh Lordy, Johnny, you about scared me to death."

Johnny grinned, "Say, Fleet, that's some awful sweet music. You oughtn't to stop. The kids will flog me shore if I break up a singing. Have you seen Minty this morning?"

"Mary went up to your house to visit this morning. We haven't seen them since Mary passed by here early."

"I better get on up the creek and see about her. That baby is due any minute. You all go back to singin'. I can enjoy it all the way up the hill," said Johnny.

"Holler down about Minty," said Mother.

"Mommy, sing some more. Sing 'My Own True Love,' said Thelma. Fleetie let her fingers find the tune, and she hummed her way into the song. Before long all of us were either singing or trying to as Fleetie led us with tune after tune. The music streamed from her fingers as if dammed too long against a freshening creek.

None of us spotted the cloud of dust rising down the county road. Fleetie's cheeks were flushed a rosy pink and every foot on the porch was keeping steady time. Mother gathered up an armful of the long strings to drape over the clothesline beside the house.

The cloud of dust moved onto the straight stretch leading to the little cluster of houses at the crossing. Burl's truck slammed to a stop in front of the house catching us by surprise. He was mean drunk. My stomach twisted with dread at the look on his face.

"By God, what do we have here?" Burl roared. Dorcas grabbed the guitar and ran toward the front door, Burl grabbed her arm, snatched the guitar from her hands and flung her off the porch like a rag doll. She rolled into a ball, too scared to cry. He waved the guitar, taunting us, and nearly knocked me off the porch.

"Got us a Opry star, I guess."

Fleetie, trying to distract him, walked to the screen door. "Come in the house, and I'll get your dinner. They's fresh beans and sausage. Save your dinner bucket for tomorrow. The kids can finish this here bean work."

"No, by God. dinner's not going to save you. Next you'll be dancin' and runnin' the hollers like some whore." With every word he swung the guitar closer to the porch post.

Fleetie reached for the guitar, "Burl, give the guitar to Newanna. She can take it up the hill to Mary. It belongs to some of her people."

"You're a lying whore. This was your sorry Daddy's guitar. " He swung one last circle and crushed it against the post. He grabbed Fleetie by the neck and forced her down.

Mother came around the corner of the porch just as Fleetie's knees hit the porch, the pieces of the guitar scattered at Burl's feet.

"You devil!" she screamed. "Take your hands off her. How dare you hurt her, you sorry, good for nothing. Have you lost your mind? Only a yellow coward comes home drunk, beats his wife and scares children. Leave her alone."

Burl had not seen Mother and her attack fanned his fury to a fever pitch. He lunged off the porch, grabbed her and drew back his fist.

"You hit me, Burl, and before the sun sets Ed will have your sorry hide locked up. Do it. Go on! It'll give Fleetie and the kids a break from your fists, you worthless piece of trash."

I was scared he would kill her for standing up to him, but as much as he hated her right then, he must have been more scared of jail. He'd been locked up before after a drunken rampage. He pushed Mother backward, and she stumbled before Geneva caught her. He slammed through the front door and into the house. A loud crash in the kitchen propelled Fleetie through the door behind him.

"Newanna, you run up the hill and get Johnny to come down here," said Mother.

Geneva grabbed her three children, ran out of the yard and down the road. Fleetie pushed open the screen door, a red handprint across her face spreading its angry stain.

"Fleetie, I'm taking the kids up to the house with me for a little while. They've seen too much already, and you better come go with us," said Mother.

"Kathleen, that'd be awful good of you. Burl will be all right after I get him to eat something. He don't usually lay a finger on me unless the kids are around to know it. With them gone he'll ease off," said Fleetie.

"Fleetie, he's dangerous; if you won't come up to the house won't you go to Geneva's? I sent Newanna after Johnny. You can't fight off a strong man half out of his mind with liquor. Let Johnny take Burl off somewhere and sober him up. The children will be fine with me. Are you hearing me?"

Johnny walked up behind Mother. "What's the matter?" said Fleetie, "Is Minty in labor?"

That was Fleetie all over. Burl drinking, the kids scattering, her face swelling from a beating, and she asks after Minty!

"She's fine. She's settin' up there with Mary talking up a storm."

Mother broke in, "Burl's mean drunk. He smashed Fleetie's guitar, and took after her with those fists. Can you get him away from here?"

"I've got a stash of beer and a pint hidden about a half mile down the river. By the time we row there, he'll sober up some. Things was rough at the mine. We had to stand quiet and watch scabs cross the line with the sheriff holding a gun on us miners. It's enough to drive anybody to hard drinkin' and worse," said Johnny.

"I don't care if he drinks the river dry, but he has got to stop using those fists on Fleetie and the children. He's acting like a pure heathen. I will call in the law if I have to and won't that be a pretty sight for these kids to see?"

"Lordy, don't call no law. There's enough trouble already at the mine. I'll get him out of here, I promise. Just don't be calling no law," said Johnny.

I had to hand it to Mother. Fleetie might be all about turning the other cheek, but nobody crossed my mother and came away in a piece. She took no nonsense from fools or drunks. None of this was anything new anyway. Men used fists, straps, belts whatever was handy when they got riled, and you had to learn to duck or be too tough to tackle. Burl was pure spoiled by Fleetie putting up with his mean temper, but those chickens got chased off the roost today.

All us kids ran on ahead of Mother, the Mulberry tree growing by the first curve was full ripe, and we stopped to eat the summer fruit on our way up the narrow lane. I looked back for her as she started out of the gate. She turned around to Fleetie, but there were no words. The smashed guitar had disappeared, and all that lay between the two women right then was the hurt, scraped raw and stinging, the music a memory hanging soft in the hot July air. Bean Day was over.

∞

Stars and Stripes

Ramstein Air Base, Germany, April 2004
The Officers Club Wings Lounge

Nick walks in with his crooked hello, orders
his coffee with a shot. Pulls out a smoke,
remembers, doesn't light it.
In his head—that hopeful movie screen—
the love of his life is about to breeze in,
safe from the Jekyll-and-Hyde of his willingness.
Back in his room his ribboned khakis
sprawl across the bed limp and rumpled as a man
too tired to take off his clothes before sleep.

Nick leans on the bar in his retro
cubist Hawaiian shirt. At the piano Blaise
rolls out one patient glissando after another
but chews a hangnail, maddening, between sets.
The later it gets, the sweeter
her hands slide into syncopation and smoke.
The barkeep grabs a dry towel
and leans on the dimmer, dousing

the spotlight above the keys. Doesn't matter.
For tips Blaise can play with her eyes closed,
and there's the stubborn green glow
of the EXIT signs. In this light Nick's eyes,
muddy even with his cheaters, in this light
even he can see the big black words
topping today's front page: TORTURE
AT ABU GHRAIB. He knocks a few back, neat.
The words are still there.

∞

The Last Noel

A single drop of blood fell black in the moonlight. Blaze watched it land on the asphalt, round as a coin, knowing it came from him. He looked up past frozen crystals of breath to see his index finger caught between the trailer hitch and the ball. The night air pulled heat from his body, but he welcomed the numbing cold. He freed his finger from the rusty tongue of the U-Haul and wondered when the hurt would begin.

"Get her rigged?" Brother Willie asked, excited, when Blaze climbed in and slammed the truck door. The pupils of Brother Willie's eyes jumped and darted, and his head bobbed like a guinea when he spoke. His left arm hung limp out the window, and the heater fan ran full blast. David Allan Coe was singing about cigarettes and Jack Daniels whiskey.

"Yessir," Blaze looked straight ahead at the dashboard, his feet straddling a Homelite chainsaw. He tried not to think about the nausea that pinched his stomach. And he hoped he wouldn't cry in front of Brother Willie. "I got everything hooked up, but I hurt my finger bad. I think I might need to get me some stitches."

"Naw, you don't need no stitches." Brother Willie's voice purred, but his eyes looked white and nervous. "Here, let me see that finger." He cradled Blaze's hand like an autumn leaf. Some of Blaze's blood soaked into the cuff of Brother Willie's coat sleeve. The finger was cut deep between the knuckle and the nail, and it was already beginning to bruise and swell.

Brother Willie let a whistle of breath slide between his teeth. "Boy, that ain't no good at all. You right about that." He fished about the floorboard until he pulled an oily rag from under the seat. "Here," he said. "Wrap your hand in this cloth. I reckon the kerosene might do you some good." Then he nudged his turn signal with a bony knee and eased out of the parking lot, careful not to exceed the speed limit posted at the edge of the highway.

Blaze had some reservations when Brother Willie first approached him about stealing from Toys-for-Tots. It was Christmas-time, so there was Jesus' birthday to think about. Plus the National Guard was in charge of organizing the toy drive, and Blaze wondered if stealing from them might be a federal offense. If nothing else, there were all those other poor children who wouldn't have any presents come Christmas morning. But Brother Willie had thought through all that.

"Christmas," he said, "ain't nothing but a pagan holiday. It's all about trees and lights and Santa Clauses. It don't have a thing in the world to do with Jesus anymore. Besides, why would anyone want to put toys in the hands of a poor child? 'Blessed are the poor,' that's what the Bible says. All this giving just feeds their covetous ways. Way I see it, we'll be doing folks a favor."

Blaze thought about that for a long time. He didn't want to be a stumbling block to the poor. And he knew the church needed money to make the mortgage payment on their new fellowship hall. The Sunday collection had been way down ever since the split. Each week's offering numbers were posted in the vestibule, right next to the hymns. And each week the amount was less and less. Brother Willie kept preaching that they had to stay faithful, that they were the remnant. They were God's chosen people. Of course, Brother Eugene was with the bunch that left. And he was vice president of the bank.

Blaze was still uneasy, especially about the National Guard. But Brother Willie promised him they'd never steal in their own hometown. And they'd only sell their loot at Flea World, which was two counties over. Blaze knew those were small concessions, but at least he could see that Brother Willie was looking out for their well-being.

David Allan Coe was singing about cheap thrills, night after night. Blaze clicked his lap belt and hummed along. The green light of the cassette deck illuminated the truck's cab, and Blaze looked over just in time to see a tear slip down Brother Willie's cheek. His eyes made slits and his nostrils flared in and out.

"Son of a whore!" he hollered, slamming the dash with the flat of his palm. "I wouldn't be sinning like this if it weren't for that radio!"

Blaze's heart hammered against his ribcage. He'd never heard Brother Willie carry on like that. His daddy did, plenty. But not the preacher. He scooted over closer to the passenger door. Then he reached out very slowly and pushed the button on the cassette deck. Nothing happened.

"See there?" Brother Willie said. He was crying harder now. "It's jammed! Dang thing's been in there for three weeks. Won't eject. Won't turn off. Just plays over and over and over."

Blaze considered this. It sounded like it might be an electrical problem. Could be a short. Or maybe a series circuit got wired parallel. Blaze had a vague memory of talking about that in shop class. "Have you tried pulling the fuse?" he asked, wanting to help.

"Tried it!" Brother Willie said. "Don't do a bit of good! When I pull the plug on the radio, my taillights go out. Can't go driving around without any taillights. Somebody'd call the law, sure as the world." He grappled around in the glove box for a Swisher Sweet, then lit it and blew a cone of smoke out the window. He looked like he might be starting to calm down some.

248

The smoke and the heat and the adrenaline swirled through Blaze's brain. He could feel his heartbeat pulsing in his finger, and he was afraid he might throw up. Blaze peeled back the rag and stole a look at his finger. He thought maybe he could see the bone. He didn't want to ask Brother Willie to pull over, but he sure hated to get sick in the truck.

David Allan Coe was singing about a hitchhiker getting picked up by Hank Williams. Or maybe it was Hank Williams's ghost.

"You do know he spent time in prison, don't you?" Brother Willie spoke in a hoarse whisper. Blaze could barely hear him above the sound of the wind and the engine's roar. And the radio.

"What?" Blaze said.

"David Allan Coe," said Brother Willie. "He spent time in prison."

Blaze knew a lot about country music. It was all his grandma ever listened to. Just sat there in her chair and smoked and drank ice water and listened to it. Talked about it in her sleep sometimes. "Yessir," he said. "I believe I did hear that."

"Yeah, he shot a man up there in Ohio," Brother Willie said. "They give him two years in the pen up at Chillicothe. But he always said it was self-defense. I know it was, too. He wouldn't never have killed somebody unless they were provoking him."

Brother Willie was talking crazy, and Blaze wondered what would happen if he just opened the door and jumped. How fast were they going? Forty miles an hour? Forty-five? And Blaze was pretty sure that David Allan Coe never killed anybody. Not that he knew about, anyway. Johnny Paycheck, maybe, back in '85. But he didn't think that man had actually died. And now didn't seem like a very good time to mention it.

Brother Willie was still carrying on, his eyes glazed over, staring at the road. "He seen Johnny Cash three times while he was in San Quentin. Locked up. Incarcerated. Imprisoned. That's what inspired him to become a country music legend, seeing Johnny Cash three times while he was in San Quentin."

"Merle Haggard," Blaze whispered.

"Huh?" said Brother Willie. He turned toward Blaze and tried to refocus his eyes.

"It was Merle Haggard seen Johnny Cash while he was in San Quentin," Blaze said. "It wasn't David Allan Coe. I don't think it was."

Brother Willie looked back at the highway. It had started to snow, and the powder danced on the blacktop like an apparition. "Shot a man in Reno, just to watch him die," he said. "Locked him up in Starkville, Mississippi, for picking some flowers. Who ever heard of such a thing?"

Blaze nodded. "Yessir," he said. "That was Johnny Cash."

"Ah, Lordy, Blaze. I just don't know." Brother Willie's voice sounded paper thin, fragile. Like he might start crying again. "I keep having these bad thoughts. Wanting to sin. Wanting to do wrong. Wanting to take things that ain't even mine. 'The poor you will always have with you.' Jesus said that himself. 'It's easier for a camel to go through the eye of a needle, than for a rich man to enter into the kingdom of God.' I reckon he said that, too."

Blaze closed his eyes and wished he was back at home, sleeping on the couch. He didn't want to be riding in the truck with Brother Willie anymore. He wished he'd never helped steal any U-Haul from Toys-for-Tots. He didn't care about the poor. He didn't care about the National Guard. He didn't care about the new fellowship hall. He didn't care about the baby Jesus.

The sound rang out like gunshot when the front tire blew. Blaze jerked awake to see Brother Willie gripping the steering wheel with both hands, wrestling back and forth, trying to keep the truck on the road. He hunched forward like a fighter pilot, and Blaze studied his movements as the truck flipped across the ditch and crashed into the trees.

The lap belt caught Blaze around the middle, suspending him in midair as the truck slid to a stop. The U-Haul had fishtailed, then jack-knifed, and Blaze could see it clearly through his passenger window. One of the wheels still spun slowly on the axle. Blaze looked left. Some blood trickled out of Brother Willie's ear. The chainsaw lay across his chest, and it looked like the guide bar had cut a deep groove in his head. Everything was still and quiet, except for David Allan Coe. He was still singing that Tanya Tucker song, the one about would you lay with me in a field of stone.

Through the windshield, the world looked tilted at a funny angle. A slender crack in the glass caught the moon's light and splintered its rays like a pale morning star. All around the star, snowflakes were forming an icy halo. Blaze knew about snowflakes from school. Miss Edwards told all about them in science class. She said if you looked at a hundred snowflakes under a microscope, you'd find that every one was different. Unique, she called it. But Blaze knew that wasn't true. If she could just look close enough, Blaze thought, she'd see they were all exactly the same.

∞

Choir Practice

Whatever you do, don't shoot the soprano!
She'll come back to haunt you,
Her high Cs like hypodermic needles
Piercing your brain.

Not the tenor either,
For all of Ireland and a big chunk of Italy
Would slide into the sea
Along with his mutilated vocal cords.

And, oh, spare the bass
Whose rumbling tones
Massage your libido
With orgasmic vibrations.

Go ahead – shoot the alto
Whose sole purpose in life
Is to smooth out the rough spots like
Lubricant on irritated ear drums.

Oh, go ahead – shoot that old alto.
You won't even miss her,
Nor will the soprano or tenor or bass
Who obviously consider her dispensable.

But wait! Don't pull the trigger
Until you ask for a solo
And hear those low notes
Like your mother's lullaby,

Like hot chocolate with smooth-melting marshmallows,
A cloud-garnished sunset in Laramie, Wyoming,
An hour-long, free, full-body massage –

On second thought,
Shoot the soprano.

∞

Ravel Sonata for Violin and Piano
Second Movement

there is a trem-
bling as the strings
are plucked
wood remembers
under layer
upon layer
that first scream

Symphony

The piccolo struts
like a peacock,
a dance of tease and tango.
The trumpet taunts
and flirts, rebuffs
the seduction of the clarinet.
Love glides along
the slide trombone,
tingles the spine
of the tenor sax,
settles in the small hollow
of Yo-Yo Ma's cello,
rises to orgasm
in the kettle drum,
moans in earnest
through the loud mouth
of the French horn.

My Love Affair with Hair Bands

"Why do you know this song?" my husband demanded. I shooed him away with my free hand, as I continued singing the chorus of White Lion's "When the Children Cry" into my large, round hairbrush. *When the children cry, let 'em know we tried...*

He still hasn't gotten used to his wife being a semi-closeted hair band junkie. On our first date, I ate filet mignon and sipped chardonnay. I allegedly impressed him with my knowledge of literature, indie flicks, and international politics. He considered my dark skin and ethnic appearance exotic and alluring. How could he have known that I was raised by a pack of Coors Light-swilling, trailer-dwelling white trash?

When the *Monster Ballads* commercial comes on the TV, I can name the group and title of each song, and sing at least the refrain for everyone. My husband quizzed me one time, and was impressed, yet appalled, by my extensive knowledge.

Personally, I blame my older sister, she of the teased red hair, Guns N' Roses headband wrapped around her petite noggin ala Jon Bon Jovi, army jacket and combat boots, jeans that consisted of more holes than fabric, with band names scrawled over what little material was there. Nine years my senior, my sister was the shit. She changed boyfriends like they were desserts in a rotating diner display case, dipping her finger in one, wrinkling her nose in distaste while tossing it away, then watching, waiting, for the next unsuspecting delicacy to pass by. Not only this, but her friends were cool. They swore, drank, smoked, skinny-dipped, rode four-wheelers without helmets. They were old—seniors in high school—and they were tough.

When we got cable around 1987, my sister and I watched MTV as if it was the moon landing, transfixed, wondering if it was all a hoax. Could that really be the bands we heard on America's Top 40, before our eyes in full spandex and leather regalia? These moving, breathing, living images made the *Tiger Beat* centerfolds we plastered all over our walls pale, obsolete substitutes. And when we got a VCR and could record the videos, we spent hours memorizing the motions of our favorite groups. To this day, I can emulate most of the moves from Bon Jovi's "Livin' on a Prayer" video, and tell you the exact moment the color changes from black-and-white to a Technicolor dream.

In the late 80s and early 90s, MTV was at the height of its music video streaming, and it was all about the look. With hair bands, more specifically, it was all about the hair. Those glowing manes of tousled temptations, fuzzy halos declaring innocence, while beneath sneers and smirks betrayed their inherent bad-boy natures. My sister and I fantasized about becoming groupies, following our heavy-drinking, hard-living men across the globe. We would enamor them; our love would change them. They would write songs named after us, telling the world of their undying love and affection for the one-named wonders of their worlds. We knew it could happen. After all, think of the success of such tunes as "Amanda," "Carrie," and "Oh Sherrie."

And what about those rock-n-roll girlfriends? What woman saw Tawny Kitaen turning cartwheels on the hoods of those cars in Whitesnake's "Here I Go Again" video and didn't want to be her? In that same video, what guy saw David Coverdale's eyes roll into the back of his head when Tawny Kitaen stuck her tongue in his ear—a repulsive yet enticing sight—and didn't want to be him?

They could rock, but they also had a softer side. "Heaven," by Warrant, always brings a nostalgic tear to my eye. The day I moved out of my college apartment to start life as a cube-dwelling serf, I almost cried because I had to relinquish my precious collection of hair band cassettes. Winger, Slaughter, Cinderella—the whole lot. No more strained vocal cords belting out "Headed for a Heartbreak," "Fly to the Angels" (which actually inspired me to give an oral report on Amelia Earhart in seventh grade), or "Nobody's Fool." Fortunately, a friend agreed to adopt the tapes; I was grateful they'd go to a good home. As I took them out of my Caboodles case, I shared the recollections connected to each one, most of them involving statements that began with, "Man, I heard this song the first time..." It was the end of an era, and I have yet to replace most of those cassettes with CDs, as I swore I would.

Part of my reluctance might be due the resistance of the hair bands to stay in their niche of that idyllic time of my life. Come to find out, you could conceal a whole lot of ugly under all that hair. As the new millennium approached, so did the pruning shears. As we got a good look at these ass-kicking, yet sensitive, screamers and crooners, some of us might have cringed at what we saw. Didn't these boys learn anything from KISS? I had a crush on that guy? I must've been inhaling too much Aqua Net.

And it only gets worse as the years progress. How can I happily recall the days of watching Bret Michaels strutting around the stage, singing "I Want Action," when the only image I now have of him is a washed-up, worn-out—and, dare I say, old—man on his VH1 reality show, *Rock of Love with Bret Michaels*? The same applies to Jani Lane, whose blue eyes I worshipped. Now all I can see when I think of him is the bloated, drunken, depressed contestant on *Celebrity Fit Club*.

Indeed, the hair is no longer there, and time hasn't been kind to most of these poster boys for The Hedonism Express. Still, I admit my love affair with their music will last forever.

∾

A Ghost

One morning before the sun got up
and I was walking up the hill

to greet it, I looked down at the pasture
and found the ruined homestead there

and there she was, skipping around the well
behind the house, the pump arm raised

like a boy's strong arm to catch her when
she spun her way to the end of the braid

of other dancers—a shout, a squeal,
and then his arm to steady her

and find its way around her waist.
An old Virginia Reel, or a Skip

to My Lou, My Darlin' square inside
another square? There's no way to know,

but I know from a neighbor woman who'd heard
the story from her granny who'd heard

it first from hers, there was a dance
right here one evening in October

when a band of soldiers stopped for water.
One had a fiddle, another one

could call, and pretty soon all the girls
around the neighborhood showed up,

but the one whose ghost I saw lived here
and she was the one who drew the water,

the one who had a sweetheart before
the night was through and the boys went off

to wager death in the war between
the states, as it was called—a war

between ideas and the means to make
machines. She didn't know that then,

and she didn't live to know one day
there'd be no difference between the two;

and she never knew how, now, the arm
of the pump looks like a young man waving.

In the early morning before he left,
he told her this: If I don't come back

for you, you'll know I'm killed. Then he cut
a U.S. button off his coat

and dropped it in her hand. He stuck
his arm in the air and waved good-bye

as he wandered up the dried-up creek
he never wandered down again.

Legend has it, a few days later
she pitched the button down the well,

then danced around it till she lost
her mind. And then she drowned herself.

I reckon she died of a broken heart,
the woman who told me the story said;

that happened a lot back then, but Lord—
she laughed—who don't die that a-way?

I remembered all of this the morning
I saw the ghost, how my neighbor took

a little pride in telling me
this heartsick story and how I thought

it wasn't right to turn it dark,
but once the sun came up I knew

her story wasn't dark enough,
because as I watched the ghost go round

and round the well I realized, hell,
this poor girl never even died.

∞

Manhattan
for Darnell

City
that never sleeps;
we are somnambulant,
wandering the smoke and stench still
heavy

on us.
There are no more
cellos in the subway;
no balm of Saint-Saens, Debussy.
These are

the days
of Dvorak,
doublebass, low and dark,
dirge for what we cannot bury
or look

away
from. There is no
symphony at all now.
Musicians have closed their windows,
pulled down

the shades,
left us these streets
with no melody but
the flutter and rustle of the
missing

posters,
whipped by the wind,
tape pulling from edges
of lampposts covered in these lost
faces.

∞

CHANTS

∽

"... the mountains and the hills
you shall break forth into singing,
and all the trees of the field shall clap their hands.
Instead of the thorn shall come up the fir tree;
instead of the brier shall come up the myrtle tree ..."

– Isaiah 55:12-13

There Is a Fountain
from Suburban Hymns

Gasoline stink of just-mowed dry grass,
　　　black-bagged trash, mulch,
Station wagon oil driveway stains—out of these

　　　the melody of Southern drought:
The sumac tremolo from a bird I can't name,
　　　this ash-gray lump trilling its fevered hymn

Over the dusty tract house roofs.
　　　Bird of Feathered Putty,
Bird of Oblivion's Blur, Smudge Bird,

　　　unlike you, I am exhausted by the sky's
Indifference. The ground is cracked
　　　and the world ready to blaze,

But I need nothing but this:
　　　your song filling the cul-de-sac,
Your song of fire never to burn out.

∞

After Listening to Norah Jones'
Come Away with Me

I remember your weathered
mouth at daybreak

how it disappeared
over a steaming hill
and my ears filled
with a fierce humming.

Go tend the barbed wire.

I will wait for you
on the shuck mattress
red roof unpinned
and ripening.

I will hold the heavy
bucket, fill it
with golden sagebrush
and puffs of cinnamon smoke.

You be the nightingale
and sing us a song.

Religion

Your mother dances for coffee,
hums lingerie-ordering hymns.
The white Christmas tree's
a center of her universe,

sharp as a pen-point.
She worships index card
catalogs, long handwriting, a's
carved out of diamond,

and running away pain,
the one trait you've taken.
I read, faking asthma.
You leave today

in the rain. Under limbs,
legs blur peachmilk,
lean, sweet. You cross
Bengal's Path, shoes
glugging mud, jog

for that swollen waterfall.
I'll turn a page
when you come back soaked,
prop sneakers on doorstop,
dry meat-raw cheeks,

your eyes the dark
varnish of violins.
And I'll almost sing.

∞

Transported

(after Bach's *The Passion of our Lord According to Saint Matthew*)

Black wings of a tailcoat sleekly folded
    down his spine, the bearded conductor pipes
        the mezzo to her place in midnight silk.

Robed sopranos billow open a high
    white sail of sound—a single flute sparks
        the chancel candle's ruby arc, picking

out the cross that marks the prow. Crowns
    of candles glimmer as the rafter's rigging
        creaks, as the harpsichordist plucks,

the Evangelist's deep pleading tugs,
    unmoors St. Matthew's ship from the cut-
        stone anchors each passenger has sunk

in granite gray with fear. Now, lightened—
    ransomed—we cast off knotted ropes:
        each grudge, betrayal—each cherished

hoard of injury—flame and deception
    of the fugitive romance. Quickened
        by alto and arpeggio, we ride free

before the rudder, the great boat a glow
    above dark ocean—passage underwrit
        by blood-paid debt:
            thirty coins, passion.

∾

For the Percussionists

Today's poem's for percussionists, and it's no joke,
though it's big enough to include some,
a thrum for them despite all the drummer jokes,
like the classic, "What do you call someone who
hangs out with musicians? *The drummer*,"
or the one where God only thinks he is Buddy Rich,

for the ones who, by definition, "strike bodies
together." They don't blow or stroke, but strike,
as flint or a match or up a band. So we're not essaying
just rockers propped up behind Slingerlands, nor only
the marchers who hold it together in eight measures
of flams and flamacues – but all the percussionists,

who have taken on tympani, marimba, xylophone,
glockenspiel, claves, cowbells, and chimes,
the bongo, crotales, vibraphone, whole racks
of Almglocken and triangles, bass or tenor tom-toms,
on floors or straps, with mallets, sticks, brushes, or pedals,
and cymbals: finger, sizzler, the swish of the high hat.

For their patience in the pit, nodding, counting for pages,
their sticks on their thighs, practicing paradiddles
or clicking them out on their teeth, molar-grinding
a roll, syncopating the left and right side of their jaw.
Then they're on: a few bars of rumble, natter, ca-ching,
perfect snatch of underlife in the crescendo and they're off again.

Music schools told me percussion wasn't enough
and though I loved melody, it wasn't my bailiwick,
not in my pad, not what we were deaf to in 1962.
So *this* is for the ones who stuck with striking
and knew that losing one stick never made them maestro,
who make me want to shout, *your solos are life*

without all the boring parts, the quotidian,
syncopated and amplified. Your hands
are our hearts, battered from three extra beats,
a skipped one, a fillip, a thrill before
the snares are flipped off to rattle
in the hush of a French horn's long and sad calling.

I love how Glennie went out beyond Sousa
and Elgar, traveled to the percussionists
of Singapore, Korea, and Indonesia,
the gamelan orchestra of Jakarta,
the indefatigable Lakota powwow players.
I don't mean appropriation but potlatch.

We have to gather the tribes so each can listen
for its arrhythmia and reset our hearts
while we read the lips of the people
around us, our conductor and colleagues
who give us the cues, then bring home the lubdub
that will lift us and move us along.

∾

The Art of Sound

Uncle Jim and Uncle Ronnie sit on the edge of the concrete front porch at Nanny and Pawpaw's house with guitars on their laps. They hold them awkwardly at first, the way you hold something when you're not quite sure what to do with it. They strum a little bit, laugh and joke with each other, act embarrassed about the whole thing. It's been a long time since they played, maybe six months or a year, whenever the family last got together for a holiday or a funeral.

In the 1960s they had a band called The Gators and came this close to making a record. There's a photograph of them dressed in '60s suits with string ties, wearing black Beatles wigs, holding their instruments and grinning like monkeys in Nanny and Pawpaw's living room. Their faces blaze with hope and youth and ignorance of the future. They look like they're about to set the world on fire.

When they start to play, it's like a slow thaw begins. First they sit all hunched over and tense, trying to make chords and strum a little, wringing their hands every little bit to shake off the pain of the strings against their tender fingers. Then they get a little looser and bend closer, looking into the guitars, looking for familiar sounds, for melodies that will lead them to songs.

Uncle Jim finds something first. His head snaps up as he grins and says, "Remember this'n, Ron-Dog?" And like magic they start playing together, just perfect. They play like they never quit, like that music has kept on inside them all these years, even while they were working and getting married and raising kids and forgetting.

As they play, their faces change, they become younger. Something melts and comes loose inside them and the music runs out their fingers into the strings and they're gone, into their own world where none of us can follow, couldn't even begin to try. It's like a wave of electricity between them, the music, and they ride it. Back and forth they trade off taking the lead, each knowing exactly what the other is fixing to do. They're remembering who they are.

But after an hour their fingers get to hurting too bad, they can't remember more than snippets of songs, their wives want to go home. They come back from that distant place where the music carried them. They set aside the guitars, stand, stretch, talk about cars and sports, carry on as if nothing out of the ordinary has happened. They forget.

∞

Mairzy Doats (and Caketoo?)

"Mairzy doats and dozy doats and liddle lamzy divey
A kiddley divey too, wouldn't you?"

The strange little ditty became an earworm in my head as I reached in the cupboard for the oatmeal and other ingredients needed to make Granny's recipe for old-fashioned oatmeal cake.

I suppose it was the oats that stirred the memory of the first time I had heard the song. It was in the early fifties, and I was just a little girl around seven.

I was sitting on the back steps scratching the head of my white cocker spaniel, Skippy. My mama was in the kitchen peeling potatoes to boil for mashed potatoes. She often sang as she cooked or cleaned, but I had never heard the strange song she was singing on this occasion. It sounded like a foreign language. I opened the screen door and peeped inside.

"Mama, are you singing in French?" I asked.

She smiled, "No, it's not French."

"Is it Spanish?" I asked as I came on in and sat at the grey chrome plated table and wrapped my bare toes around the cool chrome legs of the chair.

Mama laughed, "No, it's not a foreign language. Listen as I sing all of it."

Then she sang the song's refrain. As she sang the lyrics of the bridge I began to comprehend the meaning of the crazy sounding words.

If the words sound queer and funny to your ear,
A little bit jumbled and jivey,
Sing "Mares eat oats and does eat oats and little lambs eat ivy,
A kid'll eat ivy too, wouldn't you?"

"Oh, Mama," I begged, "Teach me that song." I was imagining how all my friends at school would wonder what I was singing during recess and only at the end of the day would I tell them what the real words were. It would make a delicious secret to keep to myself all day.

"Did you make the song up, Mama?"

"No, it was popular when I was a senior in high school, and your Daddy and I were dating," she answered.

At seven, I knew what a doe and a lamb was but wasn't sure about what a mare was. I thought the kid in the song meant a kid like me, but Mama explained that it was a baby goat like the babies the nanny goats, which my granny and papa owned, had given birth to last spring. I had always just called them baby goats, but from now on, I would call them kids. I wondered why we children were called kids. We didn't look at all like baby goats!

"You know what made me think of that song from long ago?" Mama asked.

"No. The baby goats. I mean kids," I answered, reaching for a piece of raw potato to eat.

"Your Granny came over when you were still at school today and said she was going to make your favorite cake this evening, and we're going to go over and have some after supper."

"Granny's Oatmeal Cake!" I exclaimed. "Oh, goody! Let's hurry and eat supper and go to Granny's! Do you think mares and does would eat Granny's oatmeal cake, Mama?"

"I'm sure they would love it," she laughed. "Now run back outside and practice your new song with Skippy while I finish cooking supper."

"Mairzy doats and dozey doats and liddle lamzy divey...."

Fifty-five years had passed and here I was singing the song Mama taught me so long ago, but now I was the one cooking, using the same recipe my Granny used to make her delicious oatmeal cake.

Granny and Mama have been gone a long time now, but they left me with a legacy of a love for baking and singing songs, silly or otherwise. I began to laugh and sing aloud, as I put away the stained recipe in Granny's familiar handwriting, imagining how the mares, the does, and even the lambs and kids would surely love this cake.

Granny's Oatmeal Cake

1 c. quick-cooking rolled oatmeal	1 ¼ c. boiling water
½ c. butter	1 c. white sugar
1 c. brown sugar	2 eggs
2 tsp. vanilla	1 ½ c. self-rising flour
1 tsp. cinnamon	½ tsp. nutmeg

Heat oven to 350 degrees. Grease a 9 x 13 inch pan. Combine oatmeal, boiling water and butter in a large bowl. After butter melts, stir in sugars and vanilla. Blend in flour and spices and pour into the pan and bake for 45 minutes. While the cake is baking, prepare the topping:

Heat 1/3 c. butter, 1 c. brown sugar, and ¼ c. evaporated milk until butter melts. Stir in 1 c. coconut and 1 c. chopped pecans and bring to a boil, stirring constantly. Spread over hot cake and put under broiler until it bubbles. Serve warm or cold right from the pan.

∞

The Adoration

A colorless bunch, save one,
hallelujahs and amens from the hard pews
until their time comes
to sing at Big Laurel Church of the Brethren:
an old man, pitted and pocked, ragged-edged,
and two women – one blond-headed,
the other gray, their limp hair pulled straight
back from faces washed-out and worn down
to the grit – follow a teenage girl to the altar;
gather round, look to her. *Honey, where you want us*
to stand? Shoulders back, curly head held high,
the girl draws her family close;
hits a lick on her electric bass and starts them
singing about eyes blinded by sin, opened
to glory. The old song moves through
the congregation with the force of rushing water;
quickens against the white walls of the white
church, bare of Jesus idols except for a crown
of thorns: remnant of an old defiance. The girl's
mother straightens the black-and-white
striped blouse she wears to match her daughter's;
keeps her eyes fastened on her dark child.

The Picture of a Trumpet

The picture of an ancestor's trumpet is on the wall, in front of me.
And its eyes are black dots –
like the center of a dead flower.
The picture of an ancestor's trumpet on the wall, plays to me
the tune I have heard so many times before.
And it does not stop
  because I ask it to continue
  because I need it to fill
the emptiness of my hollow olive tree
the wrappings of presents with nothing inside
the novels I have written of blank pages.

The picture of an ancestor's trumpet on the wall beckons.
And I leave my chair, set my food aside
dance past the cabinets holding the plates and the cups
past the starving table, the wall
the floor
the earth that brings nothing
And I go on and touch it.
Set my lips on its cold brass
And flutter away from homes, and fields, and into whatever lies
between the ocean and the next shore.

∞

The Hayfield

In the sweet, heavy smell of alfalfa,
the clickety-clack of hay-rake joggles
the music of memory: in this same tractor,
he once sat in his Granddaddy's lap,
raking the wind on this same unwinding field.
To the rhythm of rake, he hums the one hymn
his dad always whistled with each squeeze
of udder or bellowed with the thunder's roll.
"Then sings my soul," he boomed
over black and white backs, tails slapping,
milker pulsing, his baritone soothing the herd.
The last swath raked, he turns to watch
barn swallows dart like eighth notes
over the field of windrows strung out
in stanza form, awaiting the next refrain.

Raising a Beam
for L.R.

You could hear their knock-knees
crack: ten men rising

to lift that beam like a litter
hauled to hold the roof – time

to think about gravity, mass,
and, behind me, the composer,

eighty years old and packed right
into his body: light, proportioned,

the whole man unfolding beneath the weight
without complaint. Yesterday he had explained

how the Tibetans built their temple with sound,
monks and musicians formed an orchestra

around an audience of rock, composing a note,
a vibration, in measures rising

until hewn stones leapt the hillside.
Yesterday he said music was made

to shake the world. Yesterday he said
we have fallen so far.

                    Yet we keep on building,
orbiting this general failure

like ants at the scattered mound, nature jubilant
in the rot of a tree, the ever ever wish

to make something better, build time,
build life, build and build up

275

like Babel, now build a hall like an instrument,
the wood on a lift high above the walls, and everyone

watching. Someday, musicians would make this roof
ring. Now I stood atop the rafters, quiet, hot

under sun, under eyes of so many,
and in that light, and guiding that beam,

mass, that most solid idea
with ropes, then shouting

as it stuttered into place,
a staccato to shock the skin

to life, the whole house
heaving beneath me. I shivered,

even in the sun and sweat, and
down below they had driven a piano over

on the back of a pickup and there
he was, in the truck bed, in hard hat

and smiles, hitting each note to be heard
above the machines, constructing harmonies

to hold the frame, to help lift
a beam, amid the falling calls

of carpenters, before
the structural hush of bolts and nuts

and washers and the entire effort
settling into place and becoming still.

2

Ragtime

What I want is "The Maple Leaf Rag,"
feet flashing a euphoric frenzy,
laughter spilling everywhere
the way sunrise fills
the bluest canyon corners,
I want spinning and swirling,
the way the world thumps
end over end as you roll
down a grassy hill,
the itch of green blades
on young skin, red welts
and purple morning glories,
the music soaring through this mania
the way gulls ride on the ocean air,
no dark secrets lurking
at the edge of this desperate happiness.

A Blues Blessing

Let bass drum throbbing
set the cadence of your feet
steady through dark alley midnight.

Let brilliant brass cymbals
crash against your chest
gusting exhilaration on winter cold streets.

Let a muted trumpet
pierce the purple horizon
red-orange-gold promise of skyscraper sunrise.

Let a woman's voice
sing Billie Holiday sad
comfort on streetcorner indigo days.

Let a sax raspy howl
weave through the choruses of your life
a Rollins cadenza tenor deep and whispering
Go.

Let music carry your days
like a wind
moving chrysanthemum clouds
through sapphire
sky
dreaming.

Notes
ON CONTRIBUTORS

B. CHELSEA ADAMS' poems have appeared in *Poet Lore, Lucid Stone, Southwestern Review, Thin Air* and *Albany Review*. Her fiction has appeared in *BlackWater Review, Voices of Appalachia, Potato Eyes* and *Huckleberry Magazine*. A poetry chapbook, *Looking for a Landing,* was published by Sow's Ear Press. She received a master's in Creative Writing from Hollins University.

SYBIL BAKER'S novel *The Life Plan* will be published by Casperian Books in spring 2009. Her fiction and essays have appeared in numerous journals and several anthologies. She lived in Seoul, South Korea, for twelve years, and she now teaches creative writing at the University of Tennessee at Chattanooga.

JANICE WILLIS BARNETT lives in Unicoi, Tennessee where she is hard at work on an Arcadia book featuring her community. Janice's work has appeared in *Southern Arts Journal, Now & Then,* and many other publications. She is a past winner of the Wilma Dykeman Award for best essay, as well as the Harriett Arnow Award for best short story, given by the Appalachian Writer's Association.

DAVID BAXTER has worked as a preacher, a folklorist, a disc jockey, and an elementary school teacher. He has been a regular contributor to *No Depression* magazine since 2001. He lives in Bowling Green, Kentucky, with his wife, Caroline, and their two sons, William and James David.

LAURA TREACY BENTLEY is a poet and fiction writer from Huntington, West Virginia. Her work has been published in the United States and Ireland in literary journals such as *The New York Quarterly, Art Times, Poetry Ireland Review, Antietam Review, Rosebud, The Stinging Fly, Kestrel, ABZ, Crannog, Now & Then,* and in ten anthologies. *Lake Effect,* her first book of poetry, was published in 2006.

CAROLE ANN BORGES, author of *Disciplining the Devil's County* (Alice James Books), was raised aboard a schooner on the Mississippi River in the 1950s. Her poems have appeared in *Poetry, Bardsong, Soundings East, Kalliope* and many others. Her essays and newspaper articles have appeared in *City View, Knox Voice, The Change Agent, Pacific Yachting* and *Rudder Magazine*. She currently lives in Knoxville, Tennessee.

KATHY BRICCETTI earned an MFA in creative writing from Stonecoast. One of her essays was nominated for a Pushcart Prize in 2007 and she was awarded a residency from the Vermont Studio Center in 2008. Her work has appeared in *Dos Passos Review, Under the Sun, San Francisco Chronicle Magazine, Bark, The Writer*, and many anthologies.

BILL BROWN is the author of three chapbooks, four poetry collections and a textbook. His new collection is *Late Winter* (Iris Press). The recipient of many writing fellowships and teaching awards, he lectures part-time at Vanderbilt University. His new work appears in *Prairie Schooner, North American Review, Atlanta Review, Appalachian Journal,* and *Rattle.*

JEANNE BRYNER was born in Appalachia and frequently writes about displacement. A graduate of Kent State University's Honors College, she works as a registered nurse and creative writing teacher. Her books in print are *Breathless, Blind Horse: Poems, Eclipse: Stories,* and *Tenderly Lift Me: Nurses Honored, Celebrated, and Remembered.* She has received fellowships from the Ohio Arts Council and Vermont Studio Center. Her book, *No Matter How Many Windows,* is forthcoming from Wind Publications.

ABRAHAM BURICKSON is a poet, architect, and conceptual artist. His poetry can be found in *Blackbird, Sycamore Review, Marlboro Review, New Orleans Review,* and elsewhere. In 2001 he founded the experimental performance group Odyssey Works, a cross-genre collaborative that created day-long performances for extremely small audiences. He has received fellowships from the Millay Colony for the Arts and the Michener Center for Writers, where he is currently a fellow.

SHANNON BUTLER, a native Texan, is most at home in West Virginia and teaches Spanish at Marshall University. She is currently working on a memoir, *The Reincarnations of a Texan Scorpio.* Her poems have appeared in *Phantasmagoria, The Awakenings Review,* and *Wild Sweet Notes II.* Her book on travel writing to Peru, *Travel Narratives in Dialogue,* was published in 2008 (Peter Lang).

MICHAEL SCOTT CAIN lives in and writes from Frederick, Maryland. His most recent books are *East Point Poems* (Pudding House Press) and a novel, *Midnight Train* (Publish America). Poems have recently appeared in *Amoskeag, Bryant Literary Review, Tar Wolf Review,* and *Tattoo Highway.* He is the blues and jazz editor for rambles.net

LINDA CALDWELL is a poet and playwright. Her poems have appeared in *Prairie Schooner, Appalachian Heritage,* and *Chaffin Journal,* and in the anthologies *New Growth, Poetry as Prayer,* and *Of Woods and Waters.* She lives in Paint Lick, Kentucky.

ANN CEFOLA is the author of *Sugaring* (Dancing Girl Press) and the translation *Hence this cradle* (Seismicity Editions). A 2007 Witter Bynner Poetry Translation Fellow, she also received the 2001 Robert Penn Warren Award judged by John Ashbery. Ann holds an MFA in Poetry Writing from Sarah Lawrence College.

E. GAIL CHANDLER comes from the Appalachian area of Kentucky. After serving in the Marine Corps, she worked for the Kentucky Department of Corrections and later directed a Dismas Charities halfway house for male felons. In 2003, Dismas published Chandler's nonfiction book, *Sunflowers on Market Street*. She now travels and writes.

SUSAN DEER CLOUD is Métis Mohawk/Seneca/Blackfoot whose work has appeared in *Sister Nations: an Anthology of Native Women Writers on Community, Mid-American Review, Ms, Sojourner*, and *North Dakota Quarterly*. Her most recent book is *The Last Ceremony* (Foothills Press). She has edited two anthologies and the 2008 spring issue of *Yellow Medicine Review*. She received a 2007 National Endowment for the Arts Literature Fellowship.

SUZANNE COKER currently lives near Birmingham, Alabama, and works as a pathology lab tech and crisis line counselor. A veteran performance and page poet, she will discuss her scars with even minimal encouragement.

JUDY COOPER has had stories published in *Kudzu* and *Appalachian Heritage* and won the 2008 James Still Prize for Short Fiction sponsored by the Mountain Heritage Literary Festival. She lives in Florence, Kentucky, where she taught at Northern Kentucky University for over twenty years.

WAYNE CRESSER co-founded and co-edits the online magazine, *shaking like a mountain*. He is a teacher of literature and a resident of hopeful Providence, Rhode Island. His fiction has appeared in *Just a Moment, Quix Art Quarterly, Syncopated City, Pigeonfisher*, and other magazines. He was a finalist for the Alex Patterson Cappon Fiction Award at *New Letters*.

BARBARA CROOKER'S poetry collection *Radiance* won the 2005 Word Press First Book Award. Her newest book is *Line Dance*, also from Word Press. Recent work appears in *Apalachee Review, Rattle, Louisiana Literature, Valparaiso Poetry Review, Poetry International*, and elsewhere. Her work has also appeared on *Verse Daily* and been read by Garrison Keillor on *The Writer's Almanac*.

JOHN DAVIS divides his time between parenting, teaching, writing and playing in the band, Never Been To Utah. His work appears recently or is forthcoming in *North American Review, Poetry Northwest*, and *Southeast Review*. He is the author of a chapbook, *The Reservist*.

ALBERT DEGENOVA'S poetry has appeared in numerous anthologies and journals. He is the publisher/editor of *After Hours*, a literary journal of Chicago writing. His first book, *Back Beat* was published in 2001; his second collection, *The Blueing Hours*, will be released in 2008. He holds an MFA in Writing and is a blues saxophonist.

GAIL DIMAGGIO spent her adult life teaching high school English in Waterford, Connecticut. She mitigated this conventional background by marrying Tony DiMaggio, a jazz trombonist, in 1967. In 2004, they became a cliché, retired and moved to Naples, Florida where—Tony having died in 2007—she lives and writes today.

JOANIE DIMARTINO has work published in literary journals and anthologies including *Alimentum, Modern Haiku,* and *New Growth: Recent Kentucky Writings.* She is a past winner of the Betty Gabehart Award for poetry, and was a finalist in the Cultural Center of Cape Cod poetry competition. She is a founding member of Mosaic. Her first chapbook, *Licking the Spoon,* was published in 2007 by Finishing Line Press.

HILDA DOWNER lives in Sugar Grove, North Carolina and is a member of Southern Appalachian Writers Cooperative. Her grandfather led shapenote singing and her mother can play nearly any instrument. Her oldest son, Branch Richter, is an artist and plays banjo. Her youngest son, Meade Richter, at 16, has won first place in fiddling at many old-time music festivals and teaches at the Gathering at Swannanoa.

LAURIE DUESING lives in Louisville, Kentucky. She plays in a flute choir, the Panpipes, with her sister Nancy and studies Latin at the University of Louisville. She has published a chapbook, *Hard Kisses* (Swan Scythe Press).

PAMELA DUNCAN teaches at Western Carolina University and is the author of three novels: *Moon Women* (2001), *Plant Life* (2003), and *The Big Beautiful* (2007). She received the 2007 James Still Award for Writing about the Appalachian South, awarded by the Fellowship of Southern Writers.

K. BRUCE FLORENCE grew up in Rosspoint in Harlan County, Kentucky, and lives in Cynthiana, Kentucky. She has been published in *KY Explorer, Appalachian Heritage,* and online by the Carnegie Center for Literacy and Learning. She was awarded the 2008 Carolyn Pettit Medallion for prose by the Carnegie Center, Lexington, Kentucky.

KATY GIEBENHAIN is on the communications staff at a seminary and is a Master of Philosophy in Writing candidate at University of Glamorgan in Pontypridd, Wales. She has published in *Bordercrossing-Berlin, American Life in Poetry, Prairie Schooner, Die unsterblichen Obelisken Ägyptens,* and *The Belleview Literary Review.*

HARRY GIEG'S work has been published in journals ranging from *Pennsylvania Review* on the East Coast to *Jacaranda* on the West Coast, together with a variety of Appalachian journals and anthologies including *COAL: A Poetry Anthology.* Regarding his poetry, the writer-musician and recipient of an NEA-funded West Virginia Commission for the Arts Fellowship explains, "Mostly I'm just singing."

DIANE GILLIAM has published three books of poems: *Kettle Bottom, One of Everything,* and *Recipe for Blackberry Cake.* She won the 2005 Ohioana Library Association Book of the Year Award in Poetry, for *Kettle Bottom,* which also won a Pushcart Prize. Gilliam was the 2008 winner of the Chaffin Award for Appalachian Literature.

JESSE GRAVES was born and raised in Sharps Chapel, Tennessee, where his family settled in the 1780s. He has a Ph.D. in English from UT Knoxville and an MFA in Poetry from Cornell. His poems have appeared in *Bat City Review, Southern Poetry Review, Potomac Review,* and *CrossRoads: A Southern Culture Annual.* He is co-editor of *Outscape: Writings on Fences and Frontiers,* and is finishing *Field Portrait,* his first manuscript of poems.

CONNIE JORDAN GREEN lives on a farm in Loudon County, Tennessee, where she writes in a small attic study. She is the author of two novels for young people (*The War at Home* and *Emmy*) and a book of poetry, *Slow Children Playing.* Since 1978 she has written a weekly newspaper column for *The Loudon County News Herald.* She and her husband have three grown children and seven grandchildren.

PATTY GRIFFIN is a Maine native who grew up the youngest of seven siblings. She has earned a reputation (and loyal fan base) for exploring varied musical genres. Her songwriting and musical skills have garnered Grammy nominations, covers by other musicians, and features in film and television scores. Her CDs include *Living With Ghosts, Flaming Red, 1000 Kisses, Impossible Dream,* and *Children Running Through.*

RUTH GRUBBS lives in Knoxville, Tennessee. Her writing has appeared in *Birmingham Arts Journal* and in the anthology *A Knoxville Christmas 2007.* She was a finalist in writing contests sponsored by the American Society on Aging and *Writers' Journal.*

GERTRUDE HALSTEAD was born in Germany in 1916. A poet and Holocaust survivor, she is Poet Laureate of Worcester, Massachusetts. Her work has appeared in *Sahara, Diner, VOX, Amoskeag, Surroundings East* and *Columbia Poetry Review.* Her book, *Memories Like Burrs,* published by Adastra Press, is also the title of the documentary film made about her life. She was a 2008 Worcester Cultural Council fellow.

MELANIE HARLESS, a resident of Oak Ridge, Tennessee, is a retired educator who is pursuing a second career in writing. Her first publication was a memoir in the anthology *A Knoxville Christmas 2007.* She now writes a travel column called "Easy Getaways" for the news magazine *Anderson County Visions.*

IRENE D. HAYS, a Washington State native, has lived and worked in Idaho, Hawaii, Colorado, and California. Her first chapbook was *The Measure of Loss* (Pudding House, 2007); her second was *Witness: Landscape to Inscape* (Foot Hills Publishing, 2008). Her poems have appeared in literary journals and other media.

THOMAS ALAN HOLMES lives and writes in Johnson City, Tennessee, where he joined the East Tennessee State University faculty in 1996. His work has appeared in *Black Warrior Review, The Florida Review* and *Appalachian Journal.* He and a colleague are currently editing a collection of essays about iconic country music lyricists.

STEPHEN M. HOLT has three collections of poetry: *Late Mowing* (Jesse Stuart Foundation), *Elegy for September* (March Street Press), and *A Tone Poem of Stones*

(Finishing Line Press). He teaches in the Russell (KY) Independent School System and at Ohio University Southern. His writing and teaching careers were featured in a 2007 segment of Kentucky Educational Television's series *Kentucky Life*.

JENNIFER HORNE is editor of *Working the Dirt: An Anthology of Southern Poets* (NewSouth Books, 2003). She is a poet, editor, teacher and freelance writer who grew up in Arkansas and has lived in Alabama since 1986. She received an MFA in Creative Writing from the University of Alabama. Her work has appeared in many journals, including *Carolina Quarterly* and the *Birmingham Poetry Review*.

RANDALL HORTON is a poet originally from Birmingham, Alabama, now living in Albany, New York. He was runner up in the Main Street Rag Book Award and his manuscript, *The Definition of Place*, was published in their Editor's Select Series in 2006. He has an MFA from Chicago State University and was a 2006 Cave Canem Fellow.

RON HOUCHIN'S work has appeared recently in *Coal: A Poetry Anthology, Kestrel, Now & Then, Redactions, The Cortland Review, Salmon: A Journey in Poetry*, and *Poetry Ireland Review*. His third poetry book, *Among Wordless Things* (Wind Publications, 2004) was the Appalachian Writers' Association 2005 Book of the Year in poetry.

SILAS HOUSE is a Kentuckian and author of *A Parchment of Leaves, Clay's Quilt, The Coal Tattoo, The Hurting Part: Evolution of an American Play, Something's Rising* (co-author), and *Eli the Good*. He is Writer-In-Residence at Lincoln Memorial University and is also a music journalist and press kit writer for numerous Nashville artists. He writes songs and performs with Public Outcry, The Doolittles and Pickled Bologney.

ELIZABETH HOWARD lives in Crossville, Tennessee. She has an M.A. in English from Vanderbilt University. Her work has appeared in *Comstock Review, Big Muddy, Appalachian Heritage, Cold Mountain Review, Poem* and other journals.

JASON HOWARD is a writer and musician from eastern Kentucky. He is co-author of the forthcoming *Something's Rising: Appalachians Fighting Mountaintop Removal* and editor of the upcoming anthology *We All Live Downstream*. His work has appeared in *Paste, Equal Justice Magazine, Kentucky Living* and *The Louisville Review*. He performs with the bands The Doolittles, Pickled Bologney and Public Outcry.

DORY L. HUDSPETH of Alvaton, Kentucky, is an herbalist, historical researcher, freelance writer and poet. Her poems have appeared in *Rattle, Wavelength, Shenandoah, Sow's Ear Review, Buffalo Carp, Slant, Runes, Ninth Letter, Atlanta Review* and other journals. Her first poetry collection is *Enduring Wonders* (Word Tech Press); her chapbook is *I'll Fly Away* (Finishing Line Press).

YAUL PEREZ-STABLE HUSNI was born in 1993, in San Francisco. Yaul is fluent in both English and Spanish and attends the creative writing program at San Francisco's School of the Arts.

ROBIN LESLIE JACOBSON teaches for California Poets in the Schools and privately. She has published in *Atlanta Review, Poetry East, Bellevue Literary Review, Poetry Flash, Natural Bridge, Runes* and elsewhere. She has been honored by, among others, American Pen Women (best poem), *Ruah* (best chapbook), Headlands Center for the Arts (residency).

TRISH LINDSEY JAGGERS has poems in *The Louisville Review, Briar Cliff Review, Round Table, Matter 11: The Woods, Red Rock Review, Clackamas Literary Review; The Heartland Review, Blue Moon Rising: Kentucky Women in Transition, Tobacco, Coming of Age: A Treasury of Poems*, and others. She assists the director of Women's Studies at Western Kentucky University, where she also teaches developmental English.

FRANK JAMISON writes poetry and fiction in Roane County, Tennessee. His first book of poetry, *Marginal Notes*, appeared in 2001. He was nominated in 2006 for a Pushcart Prize. He has work in *Atlanta Review, Carquinez Poetry Review, Chrysalis Reader, Confluence, California Quarterly, Nimrod, Poem, Poet Lore, Red Wheelbarrow, South Carolina Review, Spillway, Tennessee English Journal* and *Xanadu*.

JESSIE JANESHEK is co-editor of the book *Outscape: Writings on Fences and Frontiers*. Her poems appear in *Washington Square, Passages North, Review Americana, Yemassee* and *Caduceus* and have been anthologized in *Low Explosions: Writings on the Body* and *The Movable Nest: a Mother/Daughter Companion*. A doctoral student in the English program at the University of Tennessee, she teaches freshmen writing at UT and holds an MFA in poetry from Emerson College, Boston.

DAVID E. JOYNER is an artist and illustrator and a retired member of the conceptual staff of the Tennessee Valley Authority's Architectural Design Branch. His fiction and poetry have appeared in *New Millennium Writings* and in the anthologies *Literary Lunch, Migrants and Stowaways, Low Explosions* and *Knoxville Bound*.

MARILYN KALLET is the author of 14 books, including *Circe, After Hours* (BkMk Press) and *Last Love Poems of Paul Eluard*, translations (Black Widow Press). With Kathryn Stripling Byer, she co-edited *The Movable Nest: A Mother/Daughter Companion* (Helicon Nine Editions). She was inducted into the East Tennessee Literary Hall of Fame in Poetry in 2005.

ERIN KEANE is the author of the poetry collection *The Gravity Soundtrack*. A recipient of the Al Smith Fellowship from the Kentucky Arts Council, she directs the InKY Reading Series in Louisville, Kentucky, and teaches Pop Music in American Literature at Bellarmine University.

DAISYE KEETON was born in 1918 in Mississippi. She attended All Saint's College in Vicksburg and worked at the University of South Alabama. She moved to Richmond, Kentucky, to be closer to her son and his family. She has upcoming publications in *Appalachian Women's Journal*. She is active in the McCready Writers' Group.

JESSIE LYNNE KELTNER works in social services at Laurel Heights nursing home in London, Kentucky, where she occasionally plays music and sings for the residents. She grew up in Jackson County, Burkesville, and Laurel County, Kentucky. She is active in environmental movements and works with other musicians and writers against mountaintop removal coal mining.

DIANE KENDIG lives in Lynn, Massachusetts. Her most recent chapbook is *Greatest Hits, 1978-2000*. She has work in *Colere, Minnesota Review* and *Slant*, and the anthologies *Broken Land: Poems of Brooklyn* and *Those Winter Sundays: Female Academics and Their Working-Class Parents*. She received the Ohio Arts Council Fellowships in Poetry and a Fulbright in translation.

CATHY KODRA lives in Knoxville, Tennessee, with her husband and two youngest children. Her poetry has appeared in *Tar Wolf Review, Birmingham Arts Journal, New Millennium Writings, Main Channel Voices* and elsewhere. She was the 2008 winner of the Knoxville Writers' Guild's Libba Moore Gray/Terry Semple Poetry Award.

ALISON KOLODINSKY lives on a small island off the coast of Vancouver, British Columbia, and in Florida. Her poems have appeared in *Poetry, Kalliope, Alaska Quarterly Review, The Florida Review* and in many other journals and anthologies. She has had fellowships at the Atlantic Center for the Arts and the Virginia Center for the Creative Arts.

KATE LARKEN is a songwriter and musician, a playwright and essayist, a publisher and producer. She has recorded several collections of original songs; she plays with the musical groups Pickled Bologney, Public Outcry, Sensible Shoes and ALA. Though she has lived far and wide, she spent her formative years growing up on the west coast of Kentucky.

IRENE LATHAM is poetry editor for *Birmingham Arts Journal*. Her book *What Came Before* earned a 2008 IPPY and was named Book of the Year by Alabama State Poetry Society. She lives in Birmingham, Alabama, with her husband Paul and their three sons.

DENTON LOVING lives on a small farm in Speedwell, Tennessee, and works at Lincoln Memorial University, where he co-directs the Mountain Heritage Literary Festival. His story *Authentically Weathered Lumber* was chosen as the 2007 recipient of the Gurney Norman Prize for Short Fiction. Other work has appeared in *Kudzu, Birmingham Arts Journal* and *Outscape: Writings on Fences and Frontiers*.

SYLVIA LYNCH is a high school principal who has published two books of non-fiction. Her short fiction has appeared in *Kudzu* magazine and in *The Louisville Review*. She was winner of the 2008 Gurney Norman Prize for Short Fiction and the 2008 Tennessee Mountain Writers Prize for Non-Fiction.

GEORGE ELLA LYON grew up in Harlan, Kentucky. Her recent books include *Don't You Remember?* (memoir) and *My Friend, the Starfinder* (picture book). She says before she loved writing, she loved singing. Her mother says she could sing from Harlan all the way to Knoxville—two hours—and not repeat a song. She's a member of Public Outcry, an anti-mountaintop removal band.

ZOË MALACHI, writer and teacher, has an MFA in Creative Writing and is currently working on a young adult novel and a memoir. Her work has previously appeared in *The Hiss Quarterly*.

MAURICE MANNING is from Kentucky and teaches creative writing at Indiana University and in the MFA program at Warren Wilson College. He is the author of three books of poems, the latest of which is *Bucolics*.

JEFF DANIEL MARION grew up in Rogersville, Tennessee, and lives in Knoxville. He has published seven poetry collections, four chapbooks and a children's book. His poems have appeared in *The Southern Review, Southern Poetry Review, Shenandoah, Atlanta Review, Epoch* and others. His *Ebbing & Flowing Springs: New and Selected Poems and Prose, 1976-2001* (Celtic Cat Publishing, 2002) won the 2004 Independent Publisher Award in Poetry and the Appalachian Book of the Year Award in Poetry.

LINDA PARSONS MARION is an editor at UT Knoxville and poetry editor for *Now & Then* magazine. Her two poetry collections are *Mother Land* and *Home Fires*. Her work has appeared in *The Georgia Review, Shenandoah, Iowa Review,* and *Prairie Schooner,* among others, and in *The Movable Nest, Listen Here: Women Writing in Appalachia, Her Words: Diverse Voices in Contemporary Appalachian Women's Poetry* and *Sleeping with One Eye Open: Women Writers and the Art of Survival.*

BELINDA ANN MASON (1958-1991) from Whitesburg, Kentucky, was a journalist, fiction writer and playwright. Two of her plays were produced by Appalshop's Roadside Theatre. After contracting the HIV virus in 1987, she became an AIDS educator and activist. She co-founded the Kentuckiana People with AIDS Coalition, was elected president of the National Association of People with AIDS, and was appointed by George H.W. Bush to the National Commission on AIDS, the first person with the disease to occupy a seat on the commission.

TIM MAYO, author of *The Loneliness of Dogs,* has received two Artists and Writers Grants from the Vermont Studio Center and two International Merit Awards from *Atlanta Review*. In 2000 he was a semi-finalist for the prestigious *Discovery/The Nation* Poetry Contest His work has appeared in *Babel Fruit, Poet Lore, Paris/Atlantic, The Chrysalis Reader, Del Sol Review, 5 A.M.* and many other on-line and print journals.

CARIDAD MCCORMICK has work appearing in *Crab Orchard Review, Seattle Review, CALYX, Slipstream, Spillway, MiPoesias, The Pedestal* and others. She received a Florida

Artist Fellowship and was a finalist for the Rita Dove Poetry Award in 2006. She is a Professor of English at Miami Dade College in Miami, Florida, where she resides.

GRETA MCDONOUGH writes the popular weekly column "From This Place to That" for her hometown newspaper in Owensboro, Kentucky. She is working on two books: an early reader about Henderson, Kentucky, native Lucy Furman, and a memoir, *Growing Up Flat: A Western Kentucky Childhood*. She teaches at Owensboro Community and Technical College.

LLEWELLYN MCKERNAN, poet, songwriter, and children's book writer, has lived in West Virginia longer than anywhere else on earth and considers it her home. Her third poetry book, *Llewellyn McKernan's Greatest Hits*, was recently published by Pudding House Press.

BUDDY and JULIE MILLER are Nashville musicians and songwriters by way of Texas (Julie) and Ohio (Buddy). Buddy is one of Music City's most gifted guitar players, producers and recording engineers. His solo work includes the CDs *Cruel Moon, Midnight and Lonesome,* and the Grammy-nominated *Universal United House of Prayer*. Julie is a songwriter without peer; her voice is eccentric, distinctive and deceptive. Julie's solo CDs include *Blue Pony* and *Broken Things*. Together the Millers have staked out unique Americana musical territory. Their CD *Buddy & Julie Miller* was nominated for a Grammy; their third CD together is *Written In Chalk*.

SCOTT MILLER was born and raised in Swoope, Virginia, on a working farm. In 1990, armed with a history degree from The College of William Mary and skills as a self-taught guitarist, he moved to Knoxville, Tennessee, and quickly established himself as a popular solo musician. After a stint as vocalist, guitarist and songwriter with the V-Roys, he began recording his own music as Scott Miller and the Commonwealth, much to the delight of his steadfast fans. His CDs include *Are You With Me?, Thus Always to Tyrants, Upside/Downside, Citation* and *Reconstruction*. His most recent CD is *For Crying Out Loud*.

JIM MINICK has authored two books of poetry, *Her Secret Song* (MotesBooks), and *Burning Heaven* (Wind), along with a collection of essays titled *Finding a Clear Path* (West Virginia UP). His writing has appeared in many places including *Shenandoah, Orion, Rivendell, Encyclopedia of Appalachia, Conversations with Wendell Berry* and *The Sun*. He teaches at Radford University and lives on a farm in Virginia.

SUSAN MITCHELL has published essays, short stories and poems in *Modern Mountain, Outer Darkness, Candlelight Poetry Journal* and *Appalachian Heritage*. She is assistant coordinator of programs for Union College's Bennett Center in London, Kentucky.

JUDITH H. MONTGOMERY'S poems appear in *Bellingham Review, Dogwood, Northwest Review* and elsewhere. Her chapbook, *Passion*, was awarded the 2000 Oregon

Book Award. *Red Jess*, her first full-length collection, appeared in 2006; *Pulse & Constellation*, a finalist for the Finishing Line Press Chapbook Competition, appeared in 2007. She is working on two new manuscripts.

LARRY W. MOORE lives in Frankfort, Kentucky. A published poet, translator, reviewer and photographer, his work has appeared in *Limestone, The Journal of Kentucky Studies* and *Choice*, among other places. He is co-founder of Broadstone Media LLC, a cultural promotion company, publishes books under the Broadstone Books imprint and, with his wife Jane, curates the Broadstone Gallery in Frankfort.

RB MORRIS is a writer and musician from Knoxville, Tennessee. He is a widely published poet and a celebrated recording artist. His CDs include *Local Man, Take That Ride, Knoxville Sessions, Zeke and the Wheel* and *Empire*. Poetry collections include *The Littoral Zone* and *Early Fires*. A former Writer in Residence at the University of Tennessee, he also wrote the one-man play *The Man Who Lives Here Is Loony* (1992), based on the life and work of another Knoxville writer, James Agee.

BETH NEWBERRY earned her MFA in Writing from Spalding University. A native and current resident of Louisville, Kentucky, she has also lived in the mountains of Kentucky as well as the inner city of Washington, D.C. Her creative non-fiction and journalism have appeared in a variety of publications.

JO ANN PANTANIZOPOULOS' ears perk up when a cello is played as she, too, is called to the low human tones of that stringed instrument. She has published Greek lullaby translations in *Two Lines: A Journal of Translations*, as well as essays of creative nonfiction in the anthologies *Breathing the Same Air, Literary Lunch, Migrants & Stowaways* and *Low Explosions*. She lives in Knoxville, Tennessee.

LISA PARKER has an MFA from Penn State. Her work has been published in many literary journals, including *Southern Review, Louisville Review, Parnassus* and *Flint Hills Review*. She received the Randall Jarrell Prize In Poetry and an Academy of American Poets Prize. Her manuscript, *Bloodroot,* is out for publication consideration and she is working on a poetry and photography project with a colleague.

EDDY PENDARVIS was born in Kentucky and lives in Huntington, West Virginia. Her poems, focused on rural Appalachia, appear in journals such as *Appalachian Heritage, Appalachian Journal, Indiana Review, Louisville Review, Now & Then* and *Wind*. Her collection of memoirs of an eastern Kentucky family, *Raft Tide and Railroad: How We Lived and Died* (Blair Mountain Press), was published in 2008.

LARRY PIKE, a Glasgow, Kentucky, poet and playwright, won the 2003 Joy Bale Boone Poetry Award, earned third place in the 2007 contest, and was a finalist in 2008. His work has been published in *The Heartland Review, Wind, Inkwell, Main Channel Voices* and other publications. Kentucky Repertory Theatre produced his play *Beating the Varsity* in 2000.

CANDANCE W. REAVES is a freelance writer and poet who lives on an organic farm in Blount County, Tennessee, with her husband, John. She has published in several anthologies including *New Millennium Writings* and *HomeWorks: A Book of Tennessee Writers*, and has written historic travel articles for *Appalachian Life Magazine*.

EVE RIFKAH is editor of the literary journal *Diner* and co-founder of Poetry Oasis, Inc., a non-profit poetry association dedicated to education, promoting local poets and publishing *Diner*. Her chapbook, *At the Leprosarium*, won the 2003 Revelever Chapbook Contest. She is widely published and currently serves as professor of English at Worcester and Fitchburg State Colleges and as a workshop instructor.

JOSHUA ROBBINS, originally from California, now resides in eastern Tennessee by way of the Pacific Northwest and eastern Kansas. He writes poetry and reviews and teaches writing at the University of Tennessee where he is a Ph.D. student in English and serves as Poetry Editor for *Grist: The Journal for Writers*. His poems have appeared in several national literary journals.

RICHARD ROE, of Middleton, Wisconsin, comes from a family of singers and seeks reincarnation as a bass/baritone. He has published three volumes of poetry, served as co-editor of the 2008 *Wisconsin Poets' Calendar* and has had poems published in *Fox Cry Review, Free Verse, Mobius, Wisconsin Trails* and *Beauty/Truth*

JANE SASSER has had work in *The Atlanta Review, The North American Review, The Lullwater Review, Appalachian Heritage, ByLine* and numerous other publications. She is author of a poetry chapbook, *Recollecting the Snow*. A high school teacher of English and creative writing, she lives in Oak Ridge, Tennessee, with her husband George.

MIKE SCHNEIDER lives in Pittsburgh, where he used to be a lawyer and works as a science writer at Carnegie Mellon University. His poems have appeared in many journals, including *5 AM, Shenandoah, Poet Lore* and *Poetry*. His chapbook, *Rooster*, (Main Street Rag, Editor's Choice), came out in 2004.

GRAHAM THOMAS SHELBY is a writer and storyteller. He lives in Louisville, Kentucky, with his wife and sons.

EVIE SHOCKLEY is the author of *a half-red sea* (2006) and two chapbooks, *31 words* *prose poems and *The Gorgon Goddess* (2001). She currently serves as a guest editor of *jubilat* and has work appearing recently or forthcoming in *The Southern Review, Ecotone, Torch, PMS: poemmemoirstory* and *Achiote Seeds*. A Cave Canem graduate fellow and assistant professor of English at Rutgers University, New Brunswick, she was born and raised in Nashville, Tennessee.

LUCY SIEGER'S essays and articles have been published in *Southern Living, Knoxville News-Sentinel, Metro Pulse, EvaMag* and the literary anthologies *Low Explosions: Writings on the Body, A Knoxville Christmas 2007,* and *Outscape: Writings on Fences and*

Frontiers. She lives in Knoxville, Tennessee, with her husband Mark and their two canine babies, Daisy and Jasper.

JOHN SIMONDS is a retired Honolulu daily newspaper editor and resident of Hawai'i for the past 32 years. A former east coast resident and graduate of Bowdoin, he's been writing poems since the 1970s and in recent years has been published in *The Ledge, Tiger's Eye, Aethlon, Bamboo Ridge, Out of Line* and *The Litchfield Review.*

BARBARA SMITH is the author or editor of several collections, including *Wild Sweet Notes: Fifty Years of West Virginia Poetry.* A self-proclaimed sports nut, she's also a medical ethicist, Emerita Professor of Literature and Writing, and former Chair of the Division of the Humanities at Alderson-Broaddus College, Philippi, West Virginia.

CAROLYN REAMS SMITH is a career consultant and former teacher whose published work includes poems in *Appalachian Heritage, The Midwest Review* and other literary magazines as well as essays about teaching in *English Journal* and other education publications. Born in Laurel County, Kentucky, she lives in Middletown, Ohio.

NOEL SMITH was born and raised in New York City. After graduating from Wellesley College she became a social worker in the Frontier Nursing Service in Leslie County, Kentucky. She lives in New York's Hudson Valley with her husband Peter Fernandez, but spends as much time as she can visiting in eastern Kentucky. *The Well String* (MotesBooks, 2008) is her first poetry collection.

JAN SPARKMAN writes from her home in London, Kentucky. Her published work includes two novels, three nonfiction books, a collection of short stories, a children's story, several magazine articles, a few poems and hundreds of newspaper columns and book reviews. She facilitates the London Writers Group and serves on the board of the Janice Holt Giles Society.

GEORGIA GREEN STAMPER is an NPR local commentator, a columnist, and the author of *You Can Go Anywhere From the Crossroads of the World,* a collection of essays. Her writing has received the Emma Bell Miles Award for Essay, the Carnegie Center Legacies Award, and the Leadingham Prose Award from the Frankfort (KY) Arts Foundation. A graduate of Transylvania University, she lives in Lexington, Kentucky.

A. E. STRINGER is the author of a collection of poems, *Channel Markers* (Wesleyan UP). His work has appeared in such journals as *The Nation, The Ohio Review, Denver Quarterly, Shenandoah,* and in the anthologies *Wild Sweet Notes* and *Backcountry.* He selected the poems and wrote the introduction for *Paradox Hill* by poet Louise McNeill, forthcoming from West Virginia UP. He directs the Marshall Visiting Writers Series.

NEELA VASWANI, Ph.D., is the author of *Where the Long Grass Bends.* Her fiction and nonfiction have appeared in numerous journals and have been widely anthologized.

She is the recipient of an O.Henry Prize and an Italo Calvino Prize. She teaches at Spalding University in Louisville, Kentucky, and the Center for Reading and Writing in New York City.

DAVI WALDERS' third collection of poetry, *Gifts,* was commissioned by the Milton Murray Foundation for Philanthropy. She has over 200 publications in journals and anthologies and is the recipient of several grants, including the National Endowment for the Humanities. Her work has been choreographed and performed in New York City and elsewhere, read by Garrison Keillor on *The Writer's Almanac,* and nominated for a Pushcart Prize.

FRANK X WALKER is a graduate of University of Kentucky and Spalding University and founding member of the Affrilachian Poets. He is a Cave Canem Fellow and a Lannan Literary Fellowship for Poetry recipient. The author of four poetry collections, he is also the editor of *PLUCK! The Journal of Affrilachian Arts & Culture* and serves as Artist-In-Residence at Northern Kentucky University.

SUE WALKER is the Poet Laureate of Alabama 2003-2008, Stokes Distinguished Professor of Creative Writing at the University of South Alabama, and the publisher of Negative Capability Press. She has published poetry, fiction, creative non-fiction, critical essays, and recently co-edited *Whatever Remembers Us: An Anthology of Alabama Poetry,* a 2008 finalist in the SIBA book awards.

BIBI WEIN'S memoir, *The Way Home: A Wilderness Odyssey,* won the Tupelo Press Award for Prose. Her essays and short stories have appeared in magazines including *Iris, Mademoiselle, American Letters & Commentary, Other Voices* and *Kalliope.* Twice a Pushcart nominee, she has been a fellow of The New York Foundation for the Arts, Virginia Center for the Creative Arts, and Yaddo.

ROBERT WEST is the author of two chapbooks of little poems: *Best Company* (2005) and *Out of Hand* (2007). He is associate editor of the scholarly journal *Mississippi Quarterly: The Journal of Southern Cultures* and teaches in the Department of English at Mississippi State University.

KAYLA RAE WHITAKER is a graduate of the University of Kentucky. After a period spent being rootless, she returned to live in Lexington. She is currently at work on a novel.

BRENDA K. WHITE lives in Somerset, Kentucky with her husband and their seven dogs. She is employed by University of Kentucky's Center on Drug & Alcohol Research. She has published in the *Seattle Journal for Social Justice* and in all three volumes of Western Kentucky University's Feminist Writer Series.

KATHY WHITLEY is a native of eastern Kentucky. She has worked in the music industry for over 20 years and currently resides near Nashville, Tennessee.

DANA WILDSMITH is the author of four collections of poetry, the most recent of which, *One Good Hand* (Iris Press, 2005), was a SEBA Poetry Book of the Year nominee. She lives in Bethlehem, Georgia, where she teaches English as a Second Language at Lanier Technical College.

TIFFANY WILLIAMS received her BA in English from Pikeville College. Before obtaining her MAT from East Tennessee State University, she worked at the Tennessee School for the Deaf in Knoxville. She is the recipient of the 2008 Jesse Stuart Prize for Young Adult Fiction. Currently, she resides in her hometown of McRoberts, Kentucky.

MATTHEW "WA-YA" WOLFE is a writer and musician living in Huntington, West Virginia. His written work has appeared in *Animus, The Teacher's Voice* and *Newsweek*. He received the 2005 Artist Fellowship from the West Virginia Commission on the Arts. Wa-ya plays "Jessica," his guitar, as often as he can.

SYLVIA WOODS is a high school English teacher in Oak Ridge, Tennessee. An award-winning poet, her work has appeared in *Appalachian Heritage* and *Now & Then*, as well as in several anthologies. She has work forthcoming in *Binnacle* and is a founding member of Gap House Writers.

JEFF WORLEY is editor of *Odyssey*, the University of Kentucky magazine for research and scholarship. His latest book of poetry, *Happy Hour at the Two Keys Tavern*, was co-winner of the Society of Midland Authors Literary Competition and named Kentucky Book of the Year in Poetry by the Southern Kentucky Book Fest. The recipient of an NEA fellowship and three Al Smith Fellowships from the Kentucky Arts Council, his work is widely published.

About
THE EDITOR

MARIANNE WORTHINGTON, a native of Knoxville, Tennessee, is a poet and educator living in Williamsburg, Kentucky, since 1990. Her poetry chapbook, *Larger Bodies Than Mine* (Finishing Line Press, 2006), was included in Finishing Line's New Women's Voices series and chosen as the 2007 Appalachian Book of the Year in poetry by the Appalachian Writers Association. She is book reviews editor for *Now & Then: The Appalachian Magazine*, associate professor of Communication Arts at University of the Cumberlands, and a creative writing instructor for the Kentucky Governor's School for the Arts. Her poems, essays, reviews and feature articles have appeared in over sixty publications and in several anthologies, including *Knoxville Bound, Tobacco, A Kentucky Christmas, Outscape: Writings on Fences and Frontiers* and *Women.Period.* She received a Berea College Appalachian Music Fellowship in 2009, the Al Smith Fellowship from the Kentucky Arts Council in 2008, an Individual Artist Grant from the Kentucky Foundation for Women in 2007, and the Denny C. Plattner Award for Creative Nonfiction in 2007. She often teaches writing workshops in various venues throughout Kentucky and the Southeast.

∾

Printed in the United States
212442BV00001B/7/P

9 781934 894088